6/04

Indian Country

Indian Country

▼ **TRAVELS IN THE AMERICAN SOUTHWEST** ▼

▲ **1840–1935** ▲

Martin Padget

UNIVERSITY OF NEW MEXICO PRESS
▲ ALBUQUERQUE ▼

Published in cooperation with the William P. Clements Center
for Southwest Studies, Southern Methodist University

Library of Congress Cataloging-in-Publication Data

Padget, Martin, 1964–

   Indian country : representations of travel in the American Southwest, 1840–1935 /
Martin Padget.— 1st ed.

        p. cm.

Includes index.

   ISBN 0-8263-3028-2 (alk. paper)

   1. Southwest, New—Description and travel.   2. Southwest, New—Social life
and customs.   3. Southwest, New—Historiography.   4. Indians of North America—
Southwest, New—History—19th century.   5. Indians of North America—Southwest,
New—History—20th century.   6. Authors, American—Travel—Southwest, New.
7. Artists—Travel—Southwest, New.   8. Travelers' writings.   9. Southwest,
New—In literature.   10. Indians in literature.   I. Title.

F786.P16 2003

917.9'0204—dc22

                              2003027035

For my grandmother, Mary,

my parents, Bob and Ann,

and sisters, Sally, Susan and Maria

Contents

List of Illustrations

Acknowledgments

I have accumulated many debts in the course of researching and writing this book, and I anticipate a collective sigh of relief from mentors, colleagues and friends at its completion. At the University of California, San Diego, where I first embarked on the project, I thank Michael Davidson, Bill Deverell (now at the California Institute of Technology), Wai-chee Dimock (now at Yale University), Ross Frank, Ramón Gutiérrez, Fred Lonidier, Lisa Lowe, Roy Harvey Pearce, Nicole Tonkovich, and Don Wayne for encouraging and critiquing my work at an earlier stage. Stephen Hartnett, Caroline Senter, Perry Vasquez, and Wendy Walters proved firm friends as well as incisive critics.

The research for the book was facilitated by the award of several library fellowships. I thank the Huntington Library for supporting two stints of research, the second co-funded by the late Wilbur Jacobs, to whom I am especially grateful. The library staff, particularly Peter Blodgett, Alan Jutzi and Jennifer Watts, provided many helpful suggestions for texts, manuscripts and photographs to consult. The award of the Archibald Hanna, Jr., Fellowship at the Beinecke Rare Book and Manuscript Library and a British Academy-Newberry Library Fellowship to visit the Newberry Library helped considerably to round out the study. I thank the staff of both libraries, particularly George Miles and Patricia Willis of the Beinecke Library and Frederick Hoxie and John Auberry of the Newberry Library. Further thanks are due to Erin Chase of the Huntington Library, John Powell of the Newberry Library, Rebecca Davis of the Butler Institute of American Art, Paula Fleming of the Smithsonian Institution, and Curtis Hinsley for helping to secure the book's illustrations. I am also indebted to staff of the Southwest Museum in Los Angeles for helping with my research on Charles Fletcher Lummis, Theodore Jojola for providing me with a copy of his unpublished paper on Lummis and Isleta Pueblo, and Alan Jutzi for sharing his unpublished manuscript on photographers of the Southwest. My research into the life and art of Elbridge Ayer Burbank was aided by Susan Kaiser Scarff's kind provision of a copy of the unpublished biography of Burbank written by her late father John Kaiser, while Melissa Wolfe generously shared her own extensive research on Burbank.

Southern Methodist University's Clements Center for Southwest Studies provided a stimulating and collegial environment in which to revise the manuscript and participate in all manner of activities southwestern through the award of the Clements Fellowship in Southwest Studies. I thank the Center's director David Weber and Sherry Smith, Acting Director for 2000-2001, for their support of the project and their guidance through the year. Above all, I must thank the Center for organising a seminar at the outset of my time in Dallas which provided a remarkable opportunity to critique the manuscript and re-think the project. I am indebted to Curtis Hinsley and Steve Tatum, who led discussion of the manuscript, and to Edward Countryman, Richard Francaviglia, Raúl Ramos, Sherry Smith, and Marsha Weisiger for participating in the seminar. I also thank Jane Elder and Andrea Boardman of the Clements Center for their day-to-day help in Dallas, and John Ubelaker and Paula Martin of the SMU-in-Taos summer lecture program for providing the opportunity to give a talk in the Fort Burgwin lecture series and spend a night in Tony Lujan's bedroom at the Mabel Dodge Luhan House. Dennis Foster, Nina Schwartz, and Rajani Sudan from the SMU English Department made the year all the more rewarding through their generous friendship.

I am grateful to the University of Wales, Aberystwyth for granting a research semester and a period of unpaid leave, taken at SMU, to complete the project. In addition the University provided funds to cover the cost of securing illustrations for the book. My colleagues in the Department of English have created a supportive environment in which to conduct research and writing. In Aberystwyth, I am particularly grateful to Tim Woods for keeping the faith, Clive Meachen for sharing his enthusiasm for literature and film of the American West, and Richard Marggraf-Turley for his camaraderie at work and next door in Llanddeiniol, our home village. Away from Wales, Kevin Sharpe provided equal measures of firm advice and irreverent observations concerning the world of academe. In England John Beck, Neil Campbell, Mick Gidley, Maria Lauret, Mike McDonnell, and Shamoon Zamir have kindly shared their interest in the Southwest, Native Americans, and American literature and photography. I remain grateful to Peter Nicholls, Cora Kaplan, and Stephen Fender of Sussex University, and David Robertson of the University of California, Davis, for showing the way to further academic study. The annual meetings of the British Association for American Studies, the Western History Association, and the Western Literature Association have provided much-appreciated opportunities to present work-in-progress and learn from my peers. I am grateful to the British Academy and the University of Wales Learned Societies Fund for funding travel to these conferences.

Editor Joe Wilder has kindly given permission to publish revised versions of two articles that appeared in *Journal of the Southwest*: "Travel, Exoticism, and the Writing of Region: Charles Fletcher Lummis and the 'Creation' of the Southwest" (37, no. 3, Autumn 1995: 421-49), and "Travel Writing, Sentimental Romance, and Indian Rights Advocacy: The Politics of Helen Hunt Jackson's *Ramona*" (42, no. 4, Winter 2000: 833-76). At University of New Mexico Press, David Holtby has been unwavering in his support of the project, while Sonia Dickey and Evelyn Schlatter have generously fielded many queries, Jill Root has proved an admirable copy editor, and Melissa Tandysh has created a fine design. The anonymous reviewer of the manuscript made many helpful suggestions for revision to which I hope to have responded adequately.

One of the great pleasures of researching this book has been the opportunity it has provided to travel through the Southwest and interact with all manner of people in locations as varied as the trails of the Grand Canyon, the canyonlands of the Yampa and Green rivers, Old Oraibi in the Hopi Reservation, and El Santuario de Chimayo, not to mention the Wigwam Motel in Holbrook, Arizona, and other spots along Old Route 66 and the backroads of Arizona and New Mexico. For their hospitality on the southwestern road and while visiting libraries throughout the United States, I thank Sarah and Andy Ingersoll of Pasadena, California; Doug Sortino, Anne Lauter, and Martin Pierce of Los Angeles, California; Ruth and John Wood, formerly of New Haven, Connecticut; Penny and Phil Kirk of Arroyo Seco, New Mexico; and friends at Taos Pueblo who wish to remain anonymous. Thanks also to Jeff Stone for visiting San Diego and coming along for the ride on several occasions, and to Steve Buckmaster who never made it to the States but always provided an interested welcome back in Britain on visits home. My parents Bob and Ann Padget, sisters Sally and Maria Padget, and grandmother Mary Padget and late grandfather Tom Padget have shared the road on various journeys through the Southwest. I thank them all, along with my sister Susan Padget Dunthorne, for being such a supportive family. And to Sara Penrhyn Jones, who by now must realise that our life together will call for rather more travel along the roads, paths, and rivers of the Southwest, I say *diolch yn fawr, cariad* for her intelligence, enthusiasm and love.

Martin Padget
Aberystwyth, Wales
October 2003

Introduction

EARLY ONE SUMMER'S morning in 1990, I first visited Santa Fe, New Mexico. It was hard not to share in a collective sense of anticipation as a crowd of people clustered about the plaza. Before long a ragged chorus of whoops and hollers, together with the clattering of horses' hooves on asphalt, announced the arrival of a host of cowboys, who proceeded to ride about the plaza with their rifles and six-shooters held aloft, firing blanks and rearing their steeds' heads. Greeted with cheers by a predominantly white and casually attired crowd of tourists, the riders made their way twice about the plaza before slowing down to distribute fliers advertising the "Mountain Man Hash," a barbecue that was to be held a couple of days later. At the time I was unsure whether I was more captivated by the spectacle of the horses and riders or more bemused at the near frenzied reaction of onlookers. My first thought was not that the "real" Wild West had come to life, but that the actors within a Western had broken out of the screen and boisterously taken to the streets of Santa Fe. I felt that as an onlooker I was embracing a myth of the past even as the "myth" was being sold for commercial purposes.

Several days later I made my first visit to Taos Pueblo, which was a starred attraction in the American Automobile Association's guidebook to Arizona and New Mexico. Visiting the pueblo cost money: a $5 charge per visitor and an additional $5 fee for permission to take photographs. I recall chafing a little at this requirement to pay an entry fee. Only later did I realize that the issue at stake was not a reluctance on my part to provide Taos Indians with much-needed revenue but that the grounds of exchange between myself, a tourist, and the place and the people I was visiting had been predetermined. Walking around the pueblo that day, I grew fascinated by the actions of fellow tourists. On arrival, all visitors had been given instructions not to take photographs of Taos Indians, except by consent. And yet I witnessed visitors photographing pueblo residents, particularly children, without asking for permission to do so. Why was there such a desire on the part of many outsiders to photograph the adobe buildings and local people? After all, I had bought a camera permit too and was by no means immune from the desire to photograph the pueblo. As I reflected on the experience of visiting the pueblo, more questions came to mind. To what extent did tourists' photography crystallize an urge to consume and appropriate the culture of Taos Pueblo and to what extent did it express an earnest wish to learn more about Native American cultures? How did Taos residents view their visitors, and did they differentiate between the ranks of tourists?

Pondering such questions soon leads one to consider the ways in which the Southwest emerged as a distinctive region of the United States between the 1840s—the decade of the U.S.-Mexican War—and the 1930s. I had set out to discover a Southwest glimpsed in guidebooks, magazines, photographic books, and television programs. To a large extent these contemporary sources echo texts and images from a century before, including the travel writing of key figures such as Charles Fletcher Lummis and the iconography created by corporate advertisers, most notably the Atchison, Topeka, and Santa Fe Railway, to sell the Southwest as a romantic destination to consumers. In the 1890s, Lummis proclaimed that in California, New Mexico, Arizona, "and whatever further patches constitute the Southwest," the traveler would encounter "the most romantic part of the country." There could be found "the tallest and noblest peaks in the United States, the deepest and noblest chasms in the world, our finest (and our only) ruins, the strangest and grandest scenery, the most remarkable geographic contrasts."[1] Thirty years later, the Santa Fe Railway initiated a new service of rail and road tours of the Southwest. The Indian Detour was designed to appeal to wealthy customers taking the transcontinental route to or from Los Angeles. Between Albuquerque and Las Vegas, New Mexico, the brochure promised, "lie unforgettable days in a new-old land far from the beaten path—days of leisurely comfort spent in visiting the ancient Indian pueblos and prehistoric cliff-dwellings of the New Mexico Rockies, the old Spanish capital of Santa Fe, the inhabited Indian pueblos of Tesuque, Santa Clara, Santo Domingo, and other places in the great valley of the Rio Grande, as well as the huge ceremonial ruins of Puye—a cliff pueblo twenty centuries old."[2] Significantly Lummis's Southwest included southern California. When photographer Adam Clark Vroman and his companions boarded a train in Pasadena for Holbrook, Arizona, from where they journeyed by horse and wagon to the Hopi mesas in order to view the Snake Dance ceremony at Walpi, there was a clear sense of a shared identity for southern California, northern Arizona, and the Four Corners region more generally. But with the advent of mass travel by automobile and the corresponding weakening of the Santa Fe Railway's influence on public consciousness, together with the consolidation of southern California's social and economic development after the 1920s, that older sense of regional identity was greatly weakened.

In 1990, while traveling through the Four Corners region, I looked at the "Indian Country" map produced by the Automobile Club of Southern California, for guidance on where to go. This map provides a detailed overview of the Four Corners region, where the borders of Arizona, New Mexico, Colorado, and Utah converge. Significantly, places highlighted on the "Indian Country" map, such as the Grand Canyon, the Petrified Forest, Zuni Pueblo, Inscription Rock, and Acoma Pueblo, are all subjects of individual chapters in Lummis's travelogue *Some Strange Corners of Our Country,* published in 1892. Indeed, when the text for the map states that "the southwestern United States offers a seemingly endless array of majestic geological and archaeological wonders" and "is steeped in the history, arts and crafts of past and present American Indian cultures," the words could have come from the pages of one of Lummis's myriad essays and books on the Southwest.[3] Why had I come to associate a sense of discovery and liberation with the prospect of traveling in this area? How, indeed, had the Southwest become available to commercial tourism and imaginative engagement in the nineteenth and twentieth centuries? And what did it mean to become uneasily aware, through those initial visits to Santa Fe and Taos Pueblo, that the rhetoric and iconography of tourism help to structure and even determine the experiences of the individual tourist today.[4]

Indian Country is an attempt to answer these questions. It examines the writing, art, and photography of a number of Euro-Americans who visited, and sojourned in, the Southwest between the 1840s and 1930s. Focusing on representations of travel enables us to see how written and visual representations played a crucial role in constructing the cultural geography of the Southwest during the nineteenth and early twentieth centuries. To this end, the book discusses a cross-section of representations that not only helped clarify for readers the geographical and cultural boundaries of the region, and the nation of which it was a part, but also called such boundaries into question. These representations include military reconnaissance reports, exploration narratives, travelogues, private letters, and novels, as well as paintings, drawings, and photography. In common, they demonstrate a preoccupation with describing Native Americans and Mexican Americans encountered in the southwestern "field."

Why is the book titled *Indian Country*? It has been done so with the words' multiple connotations in mind: as land claimed by Native Americans in the face of European, Mexican, and American territorial expansion; as land construed in a more general sense by official representatives of the United States to be enemy territory (a practice also associated with the Vietnam War); and as a resource, particularly in the Four Corners area of the Southwest, that became identified with recreational and cultural tourism during the twentieth century. As early as 1929, Rand McNally produced a map of the Colorado Plateau region that had this title. This map was created during a period in which great numbers of tourists were drawn to Arizona and New Mexico, many of them driving cars. Today's "Indian Country" map follows in the century-old tradition of highlighting spectacular natural landscapes and the ancient ruins of Native American cultures.

Even a cursory glance at today's "Indian Country" map suggests that the Four Corners region is not merely associated with the archaeological antiquities of Native American cultures, such as the ruined pueblos of Chaco Canyon and the cliff-dweller sites of Canyon de Chelly and Mesa Verde, or the homelands of contemporary Pueblo Indians, Navajos, Apaches, and Utes, but also with Spanish colonial settlements, such as Taos and Truchas. In 1830, Americans were already in the process of laying claim to Mexican land in Texas, and during the 1840s the charged rhetoric of Manifest Destiny played a crucial role in promoting the God-given "right" of Americans to conquer New Mexico and California. The book's first chapter begins by analyzing the role Anglo texts played in "opening up" the Southwest to American trade and territorial expansion in the years before and immediately after the U.S.-Mexican War. Examining texts by Richard Henry Dana, Josiah Gregg, Lieutenant James Simpson, and W. W. H. Davis enables us to explore the ways in which the Southwest was mapped along cartographic, geological, ethnological, and aesthetic lines between the 1830s and 1850s. The term "mapping" connotes the process by which landscapes and the people who inhabited them were possessed by the colonizing eyes of Anglo writers and artists. Notably there are significant ideological differences among these texts as their treatment of territorial expansion in the decade of the U.S.-Mexican War varies. The chapter then goes on to discuss the ways in which crucial aspects of the earlier narratives, such as ethnological concerns and often highly judgmental attitudes toward Mexican Americans, changed in both subtle and distinctive ways in travelogues of the late nineteenth century. When Susan Wallace wrote the travel essays collected in her book *The Land of the Pueblos,* published in 1888, she paved the way for the celebration of the "romance" of New Mexico and the Southwest even as her writing maintained a rather straight-laced Protestant orthodoxy in the face of what she regarded as the corrupt customs of Catholic Hispanos and "pagan" Indians.

Subsequent chapters examine a range of texts through which the Southwest was "produced" for Euro-American readerships. The second chapter examines Major John Wesley Powell's navigation of the Colorado River through the Grand Canyon in 1869 and his mapping of the Colorado Plateau region in three texts: an official report on the exploration of the Colorado River and its tributaries (1875), a travel essay about Hopi Indians (1875), and an official report made on the Numic-speaking peoples of the Great Basin region (1874). After completing his run down the Colorado River, Powell was appointed head of the newly instituted Geographical and Geological Survey of the Rocky Mountain Region, thus joining survey teams led by Ferdinand Hayden, Clarence King, and Lieutenant George Wheeler in the western field. In time Powell became one of the most influential scientists of his generation as head of both the Bureau of American Ethnology and the U.S. Geological Survey. Powell's report of exploration is both one of the key texts of nineteenth-century American nature writing and a literary romance that dramatizes the partial domestication of the very landscapes it represents. Filled with wonder at landscapes passed through, Powell nevertheless imaginatively transformed those lands into new aesthetic and scientific visions of incorporation. Through making regional Indians the objects of ethnological inquiry, he added to the raw data from which he made overarching syntheses about the nature of human evolution. Powell viewed reservations as "schools of industry" through which Native Americans would take up "white" ways and eventually become assimilated into mainstream culture. This view shared a logic similar to Powell's belief that the careful utilization of natural resources and the responsible provision of welfare were essential for the exercise of social justice and the future prosperity of all Americans. Despite Powell's conviction that his work at the BAE and the USGS was his most important contribution to public life, it is as the explorer of the Colorado River that he is principally remembered. The chapter concludes by explaining why this has become the case.

The third chapter moves from the Colorado Plateau to southern California in order to focus on the cultural work of a traveler and writer who also became deeply interested in the lifeways of Native Americans. Helen Hunt Jackson's polemic *A Century of Dishonor*, published in 1881 at the beginning of Powell's tenure at the BAE, was a severe indictment of federal Indian policy. On the strength of her knowledge of Indian affairs, Jackson was appointed Commissioner of Inquiry into the condition of the Mission Indians of California. Much of what she witnessed as a commissioner was used in her novel *Ramona* (1884), which unleashed a withering assault on the expropriation of Indian lands in southern California. Both an attack on the injustices of Indian displacement and a romanticized lament for the passing of "Spanish" Mexico, the book aimed to put into fictional, and thus more popular, form the critique of federal Indian policy that had begun with *A Century of Dishonor*. The chapter looks closely at the hierarchies of ethnicity, gender, class, and nationhood that Jackson establishes in the novel. Additionally, it examines the popularity of visits to sites associated with *Ramona,* visits that began in the late 1880s and lasted well into the twentieth century. San Diego underwent a real estate boom in the late 1880s, and promoters at this point first used the locations of the novel to attract tourists and potential residents to the area. Despite the dismissive interpretations of *Ramona* by the historians Carey McWilliams and Mike Davis, arguably what makes the novel so interesting today is its very failure to reconcile the complex issues that it raises.

The fourth chapter examines how Charles Fletcher Lummis, through his myriad articles and books of travel, history, and fiction about the Southwest, sought to create the Southwest as an area in which ethnic and cultural differences, archaeological and anthropological antiquity, and spectacular natural landscapes were made the cornerstones of a new regionalism that became centered in Los Angeles. From the moment he walked into the old Mexican settlements of southern Colorado and New Mexico in 1884, Lummis was actively engaged in mapping a new cultural geography of the Southwest. Through descriptions of natural landscapes and the traits of Native Americans and Hispanos, Lummis literally transcribed selected parts of the region into the bodies of written texts. Although Lummis exoticized the Southwest and saw the region as a proving ground for a reinvigorated "Anglo-Saxon" identity, he was also sympathetic to

Native American cultures and was one of the first well-known figures to take the Spanish colonial history of North American seriously.

The fifth chapter examines the career of Elbridge Ayer Burbank, an artist who traveled extensively among Native Americans throughout the West between the 1890s and around 1915. Although Burbank roamed all over the West, the majority of his art depicted Indians of Arizona, California, and New Mexico. First commissioned by his uncle, Edward E. Ayer, to paint Geronimo at Fort Sill, Oklahoma Territory, Burbank's stated mission in life was to paint every Indian tribe in the United States. One of a generation of Euro-Americans who thought American Indian cultures were dying out, he sought to salvage their identities in thousands of paintings and drawings. I investigate the extended network of patronage that sustained his work, a network that included private collectors, art museums, libraries, and anthropological archives. Burbank's painting and extended travel away from his home in metropolitan Chicago offered a release from the pressures of urban life and the manic depression from which he suffered throughout his adult life. For the Indians he represented, his art marks a particularly difficult part of their history and—despite the premises on which it was based—a remarkable record of cultural survival.

The sixth and final chapter examines the development of cultural tourism in the Southwest between the 1890s and 1930s. It begins by discussing photographic representations of the Hopi Snake Dance, a ceremony that formed an integral part of the Hopi ceremonial calendar at the beginning of the last century and to which Euro-Americans were drawn in their many hundreds by the 1920s. Whereas Euro-American viewing of the Snake Dance had begun as a small-scale endeavor as news of the ceremony spread first by word of mouth and then in travel and ethnological writings, the Indian Detours conducted by the Santa Fe Railway in tandem with the Fred Harvey Company were organized by corporate sponsors from the outset. Introduced in 1926, the detours were specialized rail and automobile tours of the Southwest that invited wealthy tourists to go off the beaten track and explore the distinctive landscapes and Native American communities of the region. Putting a premium on the accessibility and availability of Indian communities to welcome tourists, the detours consolidated a long process of social, economic, and political incorporation through which the rich natural resources and ethnically diverse human population of the Southwest were colonized by the United States and drawn into the Union. The work of writers who became sojourners in the Southwest in the first two decades of the twentieth century stands in an ambivalent relation to the rhetoric of the Indian Detours brochures. Mary Austin, John Collier, and Mabel Dodge Luhan each wrote articles and books that played upon the motif of travel within the Southwest, and particularly among Pueblo Indians, as a means for Euro-Americans to enter into a new consciousness of place and community. The chapter ends by considering the degree to which the views espoused in the work of intellectual exiles in the Southwest existed in counterdistinction to the language and iconography of popular tourism during the 1920s and 1930s.

The book concludes with a discussion of representations of travel in the work of two contemporary southwestern writers.

If we are to discuss the evolution of representations of travel and tourism in the Southwest, we must establish an approach to the analysis of such documents. Over the past two decades, critics such as Barbara Babcock, Leah Dilworth, Curtis M. Hinsley Jr., Sylvia Rodríguez, and Marta Weigle have paid particular attention to the ways in which the Southwest was constructed as America's "Orient" during the late nineteenth and early twentieth centuries.[5] Babcock contends that European and Euro-American literary and visual representations of the region have played a key role in exoticizing and policing southwestern Indians. According to Babcock, not only has the Southwest "been subjected to unlimited visibility for several centuries now," but Native American women in particular have suffered from the "representational violence" that keeps them "imprisoned in 'timeless indigeny.'"[6] Dilworth begins her study *Imagining Indians in the Southwest* by stating that the Southwest is not only a place, but also a region of the imagination "on which Americans have long focused their fantasies of renewal and authenticity." She argues that representations of southwestern Indians by ethnographers, promoters, arts-and-crafts reformers, and modernists writers and artists not only "imagined a primitive that was a locus for idealized versions of history, spirituality, and unalienated labor" but also "doomed [Indians] to vanish or live as living relics of the past."[7]

I argue that to claim that Euro-American representations of Native American cultures have subjected the Southwest to "*unlimited* visibility" underestimates the degree to which Indian communities responded in both creative and conflicted ways to their colonization and incorporation into the United States during the nineteenth and early twentieth centuries. The claim also fails to account sufficiently for the ways in which

Euro-American authors and artists, through their representations of Native Americans, could themselves reflect on issues of selfhood and collective identity in their own culture and through this reflection call into question what it meant to be "American." Mary Austin, for instance, wrote in 1930: "For those who have been admitted, ever so slightly, to the reality of Indian life, there is a profound and humble thankfulness."[8] In addition to these qualifications of Babcock's statement, one might add that critiques which stress the capacity of Euro-American representations to objectify, consume, and appropriate southwestern Indians risk overemphasizing the degree to which Euro-Americans could contain the ethnic and cultural differences of Native Americans from the mid-nineteenth to the early twentieth century.

Through analyzing what Babcock and Dilworth may consider retrograde texts, this study strives to delineate a potentially liberating space in which the tensions, ambiguities, and silences of Anglo discourses on the Southwest are brought into play. Such an endeavor can be hazardous. One risks valorizing the colonizing imagination of writers from the dominant Anglo culture by focusing on their texts and by not condemning out of hand certain of their ideological biases. Furthermore, it might be argued that it is inappropriate to give too much intellectual weight to some of the texts considered in this study because they were written hurriedly and without a great deal of forethought for a middlebrow audience of readers. I counter such objections by stressing the close attention paid throughout this study to the dialectic between incorporation and resistance.

In his study *Social Change in the Southwest, 1350–1880,* sociologist Thomas Hall outlines a sociological understanding of how territorial expansion, modernization, and nation-building are linked:

> According to modernization theory, nation-building involves a process of integration of formerly diverse social groups into one political-economic order with a shared sense of identity. The modern nation-state, according to this theory, was to become the organizing unit of the modern world as various non-nation-states became nation-states, either through conquest or absorption, through colonization, or through diffusion.[9]

As the title of Hall's study suggests, by the 1880s both national and regional conditions had changed sufficiently to mark the end of a long process of social change in the Southwest. With the most rapid and

far-reaching changes in a five-hundred-year time span taking place between
the decade of the U.S.-Mexican War of 1846–48 and the arrival of the future
Atchison, Topeka, and Santa Fe Railway in New Mexico in 1879, it would
appear that toward the end of the nineteenth century the Southwest had
been absorbed into the national economy and its ethnically diverse population was gradually becoming "Americanized." In actuality New Mexico's
Anglo population was for many years far outnumbered by Native
Americans and Hispanos and this is one reason why its territorial status
lasted so long. Indeed, during the early 1900s, both President Theodore
Roosevelt and Senator Albert J. Beveridge of Indiana spoke out against
statehood. Following the Spanish American War and the annexation of
Puerto Rico and the Philippines, on coming into office in 1901 Roosevelt
wished to pursue an imperial approach toward the administration of New
Mexico and the exploitation of its natural resources. Meanwhile Beveridge
did not consider New Mexico's Spanish speakers sufficiently acculturated to
the American legal system, its educational institutions, or the English language to warrant the conferral of statehood. This lack of acculturation
confirms Hall's claim that "[t]he nationhood of nation-states is more frequently a political aspiration than a social reality. Instead there has been a
constant re-emergence of separate local identities."[10]

Significantly Roosevelt's and Beveridge's fears—that in holding onto
distinct cultural practices that marked them as "different" from Anglos,
Native Americans and Hispanos could not be assimilated into American
culture—were articulated in the midst of contentious debates over the
impact of "new" immigration on the American population, the legacy of
the Spanish American War, and the place of African Americans in the
United States. At the heart of such debates lay crucial questions about
American national character, the ways in which the United States should
come to terms with its history of slavery and westward expansion, and the
degree to which people of diverse ethnic origins could form a common
citizenry. Roosevelt and Beveridge thought that New Mexico should
become more "Americanized" in order to gain statehood, suggesting that
in maintaining certain cultural traditions Indians and Hispanos compromised their suitability for full inclusion in the Union. And yet at the same
time their fears were expressed, a huge amount of travel and promotional
literature trumpeted the romance of the Southwest to audiences throughout the United States by stressing the region's rich archaeological history,
the romantic traditions of Native American and Hispano society, and the
unique beauty of natural landmarks such as the Grand Canyon. These

texts leave an ambiguous legacy of patronage and paternalism toward Native Americans and Hispanos. For New Mexico's "native" peoples came to be valued for residual cultural practices that appeared to predate the alienating effects of modern American life even as they were exposed to greater numbers of tourists whose travel to New Mexico had been facilitated by the spectacular growth of railroads in the 1870s and 1880s and encouraged through new forms of corporate advertising.

In recent years, literary critics have paid great attention to the poetics and politics of representation in colonial situations.[11] At the heart of *Indian Country* lies the argument that Euro-American representations of the Southwest became a fundamental means of narrating, accounting for, and even criticizing the imposition of American institutions on lands and peoples that had been incorporated into the United States through westward expansion. Representations of travel had a profound influence on how landscapes and indigenous and residual populations were understood in the face of American colonization of the Southwest. Similar to Mary Louise Pratt and other critics, I strive to "decolonize knowledge" by paying close attention to the ways in which Euro-American writers constructed the "native" Southwest for domestic readers.[12] Through mapping the terrain of Euro-American representations of the region between the 1840s and 1930s, I argue that in the process of American annexation and incorporation of the lands and peoples of the Southwest there was necessarily a dialogue between cultures.

Whereas this study draws from influential debates in contemporary literary and cultural studies, it also derives inspiration from ongoing debates in Western American history and ethnic studies. In recent years historians have been at pains to reinvigorate the study of the American West by paying increased attention to issues of race, class, gender, sexuality, and nationality. At the heart of revisionist Western history lies a far-reaching argument over national meaning and racial, cultural, and gendered belonging. As Patricia Nelson Limerick points out, key words of the New Western History have included "invasion, conquest, colonization, exploitation, development, expansion of the world market."[13] The use of such language to narrate stories about (to paraphrase Elliot West) continued cultural dislocation, environmental calamity, economic exploitation, and individual failure and madness is at odds with earlier paradigms of westward expansion that provided a more straightforward story of triumphant nationalism and nation-building.[14] Today's historians strive to create a more complete understanding of the multicultural

Southwest by focusing more closely on the stories and experiences of groups previously excluded or marginalized from historical narratives. Certainly a more complicated picture of the experiences of Native Americans and Mexican Americans in the Southwest has emerged in recent decades as historians have detailed the processes by which people within these communities were incorporated into the United States and the ways in which they resisted such incorporation, both historically and through to the present day.[15] This study contributes to the ongoing efforts of scholars to make sense of the cultural geography of the Southwest, both past and present. Focusing on representations of travel enables us to understand not only how Euro-American writers and artists made sense of their interactions with the Southwest between 1840 and 1935, but also how their texts and images helped determine and call into question the grounds on which the region became part of the United States in the decades after the war with Mexico.

CHAPTER ONE

From Manifest Destiny to Historical Romance: The Southwest in Narratives of Exploration and Travel between the 1840s and 1880s

ON AUGUST 15, 1842, Lieutenant John C. Fremont stood on top of what he thought was the highest peak of the Rocky Mountains. The ascent of Fremont Peak culminated the westward drive of Fremont's first major exploring expedition, for which he had been charged with the responsibility of reporting on "the country lying between the Missouri river and the Rocky Mountains on the line of the Kansas and Great Platte rivers."[1] The summit—a "precarious slab, which it seemed a breath would hurl into the abyss below"—proved too dangerous for any but one individual at a time to ascend. But a little below it the team set about establishing their presence in a place where "we thought ourselves beyond the region of animated life." Fremont planted a barometer in the snow and a pole in a crevice at the summit of the Wind River Range. Then he "unfurled the national flag to wave in the breeze where never flag waved before."[2]

The top of the Wind River Range afforded Fremont a panorama of land he had explored and was yet to explore in succeeding expeditions. His commanding view took in the headwaters of the Yellowstone, Missouri, and Columbia Rivers. The springs that fed the Platte River could be found among the peaks at the southern end of the range, while to the west lay the lakes and streams that served as the source of the Colorado River. Fremont surveyed the gathering waters of a river that exited the continental land mass into the Gulf of California, making its way through largely uncharted territory into Mexico and the landscapes of what would later become the states of Utah and Arizona. From his vantage point atop the Rocky Mountains, Fremont anticipated the conquest and settlement of land yet to be incorporated into the American republic.

Fremont had been sent west by the Army Corps of Topographical Engineers to describe, map, and measure the country lying between the Missouri River and the Rocky Mountains. He paid particular attention to charting the course of the emigrant trail to Oregon. To this end he was accompanied by a cartographer, Charles Preuss; a crew of Creole and Canadian voyageurs; and a guide, Kit Carson. Resulting from the expedition were not only a report on lands surveyed and peoples encountered but also a rhetorical gesture calling for the incorporation of those lands into the United States.

Fremont's *Report of an Exploration of the Country Lying between the Missouri River and the Rocky Mountains on the Line of the Kansas and Great Platte Rivers* was presented to Congress in 1843. The report consisted of a narrative presented in the form of a day-to-day journal; a catalogue of plants collected on the expedition with an accompanying description of the soil in which they were found; a table of latitudes and longitudes; and a list of comparative meteorological observations made simultaneously en route and in St. Louis, from where the expedition had departed. Following a pattern of military exploration that had begun with the Lewis and Clark expedition of 1804–6, Fremont was charged with the responsibility of assessing existing and potential routes of communication, particularly rivers and mountain passes; accurately describing the lay of the land and the flora and fauna it sustained; measuring distances, elevation, and climatic conditions; and reporting on the condition of Native Americans dwelling in the region.[3]

Cartography was crucial to the success of the expedition. The reproduction of the geographical lay of the land on the flat surface of a map was contingent on the capacity of the cartographer to gain an omniscient perspective on land surveyed. The physical acts of astronomical observation and ground-level measurement were complemented by the projective imagination of the mapmaker. At the heart of the expedition lay the disciplined mind of the cartographer, representing three-dimensional space and freezing time within the two-dimensional confines of the printed sheet. Cartography was an act of translation through which foreign terrain was made familiar through the expressive form of the map. Fremont's maps embodied the urge to possess the terrain his team surveyed.[4]

Fremont followed his first major reconnaissance of the West with a second expedition to the West Coast. The account of this journey, *A Report of the Exploring Expedition to Oregon and North California in the Years 1843–44,* was published in 1845 and read enthusiastically by thousands of expansion-minded Americans. The broadsheet map accompanying the report charted land west of the confluence of the Kansas and Missouri Rivers to the far Pacific Ocean. While the courses of the north and south forks of the Platte River, the Kansas River, and a small section of the Missouri River were rendered in detail, the cartography was highly selective. The Rocky Mountain, Cascade, and Sierra Nevada ranges were drawn with varying degrees of accuracy, but the bulk of the map was blank. Across a great swath of unmarked paper, in a section that ran from the Blue Mountains in the then disputed territory of Oregon to the southern extreme of the Sierra Nevada in northern Mexico, the following words were printed:

THE GREAT BASIN: diameter 11 degrees of latitude, 10 degrees of longitude: elevation above the sea between 4 and 5000 feet: surrounded by lofty mountains: contents almost unknown, but believed to be filled with rivers and lakes which have no communication with the sea, deserts and oases which have never been explored, and savage tribes, which no traveler has seen or described.[5]

Today the statement reads as a peculiar hybrid of rationalization and hearsay, equating the unknown with grotesque natural features and human savagism. Building on the earlier reconnaissance of Captains Lewis and Clark, Lieutenant Zebulon Pike, who explored the Southwest in 1805–7, and Major Stephen Long, who in 1821 described the arid terrain of the far West as a "Great American Desert," Fremont strove to create an accurate measure of land beyond the Mississippi River and along the line of the Oregon Trail. Geared toward the complete bodying of information about the West, Fremont's explorations were characterized by fervent patriotism and a willed possession of landscape.

To many Euro-Americans of the mid nineteenth century, Fremont's reports of exploration greatly influenced their own sense of selfhood and of national purpose. The emblematic gestures of conquering mountain summits where it was thought no person had climbed before and from on high surveying land that through its integration into the United States would help realize Thomas Jefferson's vision of an empire for liberty that would stretch from sea to shining sea proved highly inspirational to them. Subsequent events appeared to confirm that sense of heroic endeavor. Through the Oregon Boundary Settlement of 1845, new lands were made available for agrarian settlement. The conquest of New Mexico and California during the U.S.-Mexican War of 1846–48 seemed to confirm the superiority of American republicanism to the perceived shortcomings of Mexico's government and largely mestizo population. And while the conflict over the extension of slavery into the western territories and states and the subsequent Civil War fragmented the Union and deeply divided the population, the completion of the first transcontinental railroad in 1869 appeared to provide a renewed sense of national identity.

Scholars have long called such a vision of the glory and honor achieved through westward expansion into question.[6] But what of Euro-American travelers to the Southwest in the antebellum period? How did their writings levy a cultural claim on lands that were first imaginatively and then physically incorporated into the United States during the 1840s? What sense of mission accompanied their journeys into California and New Mexico in the decades immediately before and after the U.S.-Mexican War? How did their writings uphold and sometimes call into question commonly held prejudices about the superiority of American society to Mexican and Native American cultures? And how is it, given the frequently judgmental and hostile tone of these narratives when representing the Southwest's "native" cultures, that they also created the space for an imaginative engagement with the region's past?

To answer these questions it is necessary to look at several texts that played a key role in introducing California and New Mexico to American readers. My reading of these texts is guided in part by the historian Patricia Nelson Limerick's argument that the American West should be regarded as conquered territory and as a meeting ground of diverse cultures. Limerick explains: "Conquest basically involved the drawing of lines on a map, the definition of lines on a map, the definition and allocation of ownership (personal, tribal, corporate, state, federal, and international), and the evolution of land from matter to property." She continues by stating that this "evolution" took two stages: first, the frontier stage when lines were first drawn, and second, the stage that is still underway when meaning and power were given to those lines.[7]

Richard Henry Dana's *Two Years Before the Mast* (1840), Josiah Gregg's *Commerce of the Prairies* (1844), Lieutenant James Simpson's *Journal of a Military Reconnaissance from Santa Fe, New Mexico, to the Navajo Country* (1852), and William W. H. Davis's *El Gringo; Or, New Mexico and Her People* (1857) all belong to the frontier stage that Limerick discusses. Although each writer was concerned with explaining and justifying the American presence in the Southwest in the decades on either side of the U.S.-Mexican War, there were notable differences as well as similarities to their experiences and the texts they wrote. Whereas Dana and Gregg participated in trade between the United States and Mexico during the 1830s and 1840s, before the outbreak of war, the army officer Simpson and the judicial official Davis were representatives of the U.S. government in New Mexico (which at this time included the land that later became Arizona) in the years immediately after the war's conclusion. Despite his privileged background Dana shipped from New England as an ordinary sailor in order to take part in the California hide trade, while Gregg, who was brought up in a backwoods family on the Missouri frontier, pursued a career as a businessman during the decade he was a Santa Fe trader. Just as Dana described the long voyage from the Northeast to the Pacific Coast via Cape Horn, so Gregg detailed the eight-hundred-mile journey between Independence, Missouri, and Santa Fe. Similar to Fremont in 1842, Simpson was a lieutenant in the Army Corps of Topographical Engineers and part of a military force making a reconnaissance in "foreign" country. But while Fremont made a symbolic gesture of possession on top of the Wind River Range, Simpson helped establish hegemony over land and people newly incorporated into the United States by taking part in negotiations with Navajo leaders. Davis was also part of the new American administration of New Mexico's affairs, working in the territory as district attorney for U.S. district courts. By virtue of long-distance travels through the territory, Davis became familiar with many aspects of Hispano life. Back in Santa Fe he spent much of his spare time perusing Spanish language sources in the Palace of the Governors to satisfy his curiosity about the territory's past. He drew on this combination of personal observation and scholarly research to write *El Gringo,* one of the first Anglo-authored books to take a serious view of Spanish colonial history in New Mexico.

Whereas texts from the 1840s and 1850s belong to the era of conquest and annexation, Susan Wallace's travelogue *The Land of the Pueblos,* published in 1888, belongs to the stage when, to echo Limerick, meaning and definition were given to the American conquest of the Southwest. Wallace wrote with great ambivalence about New Mexico, praising its romantic and picturesque qualities while condemning many of the practices of Hispanos and Pueblo Indians. Analyzing her writing, together with representations of southern California from the same period, helps us build a bridge between representations of the Southwest in the antebellum period and in the late nineteenth century, when the region came into the popular consciousness as an exotic location within the United States.

Richard Henry Dana's Melancholy

In 1840 *Two Years Before the Mast,* Richard Henry Dana's narrative of his sea-faring adventures along the coast of California, was published and soon became one of the most popular books in the antebellum period. Dana, a young Boston Brahmin, had gone before the mast as a common sailor in an effort to regain his health, particularly his failing eyesight, after an attack of measles. Not yet graduated from Harvard, he embarked on a voyage around Cape Horn to California on August 14, 1834, and did not return to Boston until September 22, 1836. Dana fascinated readers with his descriptions of California culture and the hide trade, through which Anglo merchants traded for the hides of cattle raised on the ranchos of wealthy Californios. Published eight years before the signing of the Treaty of Guadalupe Hidalgo in 1848, whereby Mexico relinquished its northern territories to the United States, *Two Years Before the Mast* nevertheless prefigured the American annexation of Alta California. Although Dana did not make an overt call for warfare against Mexico, his description of the California hide trade created a space in which the possibilities of American social and economic development could be postulated, if not openly proposed. Famously he proclaimed of California: "In the hands of an enterprising people, what a country this might be!"[8]

Dana's authority for writing about the West Coast and the hide trade was derived form his intense personal participation in the scenes described—he worked and socialized with Californios, local Indians, and the crews of other ships while collecting, curing, and loading hides. Although Dana wrote neither a polemical nor a promotional book, nevertheless he separated out what he saw as the developmental potential of California from the prevailing patterns of resource usage in the region. He mapped the physical and cultural attributes of the landscapes and people he viewed, and through his observations formed a hierarchy of racial and class differences in the region. Not surprisingly, given his own elite standing within New England society, Dana could be favorably inclined toward socially privileged Californios while casting a more critical eye on the disposition of American traders in the region. However, all compliments were subject to qualification. On the one hand Dana praised Californios—"next to the love of dress, I was most struck with the fineness of their voices"— and on the other hand he made sweeping generalizations about their character: "They are an idle, thriftless people, and can make nothing for themselves."[9] Between the two poles of attraction and repulsion in Dana's narrative lay the concessionary logic of a third position, namely the myth of the Californios' fated demise: "they sometimes seemed to me a people on whom a curse had fallen, and stripped them of everything but their pride, their manners, and their voices."[10]

A decade after Dana returned to Boston, "enterprising" Americans did indeed claim California as part of the United States. When Dana returned as a tourist to visit the West Coast in 1859, he found it hard to find traces of the places and people he had known in his youth because of the effects of rapid urbanization in San Francisco in the aftermath of the Gold Rush. He traveled south to San Diego to discover locations that appeared the same way that he remembered them. Dana enjoyed his hours of solitude in San Diego precisely because the town and coast appeared so little changed from two and a half decades before—unchanged except for the absence of old faces. "Twenty-Four Years After," his account of this return visit, was originally written as a journal and, from 1869, added to later editions of *Two Years Before the Mast*. Dana described the conclusion of his visit to San Diego:

> I must complete my acts of pious remembrance, so I take a horse and make a run out to the old Mission, where Ben Stimson and I went the first liberty day we had after we left Boston. All has gone to decay. The buildings are unused and ruinous, and the large gardens show now only wild cactuses, willows, and a few olive-trees. A fast run brings me back in time to take leave of the few I knew and who knew me, and to reach the steamer before she sails. A last look—yes, last for life—to the beach, the hills, the low point, the distant town, as we round Point Loma and the first beams of the light-house strike out towards the setting sun.[11]

Dana's image of pronounced melancholy for the departed past is affecting because it captures not only the personal disappointment of a middle-aged man looking back on his youth but also the sense of promise and potentiality that became associated with California in the mid nineteenth century. Whereas in *Two Years Before the Mast* Dana captured the spirit of what historian Kevin Starr calls "the elusive possibility of a new American alternative," in "Twenty-Four Years After" the tone is more muted, partly because Dana perceived that the utopian qualities of life in California had already been thrown into doubt.[12] Visiting California a quarter of a century after his time there as a youth, Dana would have been forced to recognize the profound social and economic changes wrought on the region by American conquest and the Gold Rush. He had returned to California in middle age as a means of combating depression. Walking and riding through San Francisco, though, must have been a disconcerting experience. For there, in a place so transformed as a consequence of the Gold Rush, Dana would have found it difficult to match memory to place, even though he was well received by many Californians who granted him some celebrity for having written *Two Years Before the Mast*. And so, as we have seen, Dana made his way to San Diego.

If Dana had made that last visit to southern California at the conclusion of his life in 1882, he might have experienced greater difficulty in locating his old haunts. To be sure, traces of the old Franciscan missions and their abandoned gardens could still be found in southern California, but by 1876 the Southern Pacific Railroad had reached Los Angeles while the first train running along the Atchison, Topeka, and Santa Fe Railroad's tracks through northern New Mexico and northern Arizona would arrive in 1887. (After bankruptcy, the latter railroad was reorganized as the Atchison, Topeka, and Santa Fe Railway in 1895.) The completion of the two transcontinental railroads, together with a spur line to San Diego, was central to the social and economic development of southern California in the late nineteenth century. In the 1880s there was an economic boom in Los Angeles whereby the city's population increased fivefold and the region become more "Americanized." Historian Leonard Pitt points out that the new Anglo dominance created profound changes in everyday life as well as in political affairs: "The type of consumer goods advertised for sale, the tastes in food and dress, the prevalence of English over Spanish in daily and official conversation, the Gilded Age recreations, and the style of commerce—all changed rapidly and irreversibly."[13]

Concomitant with the "Americanization" of southern California, socially elite Anglos took an interest in the culture of Californios, the Spanish-speaking landowners they had helped displace. Helen Hunt Jackson, as we shall see in chapter 3, played a central role in romanticizing the livelihoods of wealthy Californios in both her travel writing and her novel *Ramona*. Writing several years before the great boom, she nevertheless described the city in the midst of transformation:

> The City of the Angels is a prosperous city now. It has business thoroughfares, blocks of fine stone buildings, hotels, shops, banks, and is growing daily. Its outlying regions are a great circuit of gardens, orchards, vineyards, and corn-fields, and its suburbs are fast filling

up with houses of a showy though cheap architecture. But it has not yet shaken off its past. A certain indefinable, delicious aroma from the old, ignorant, picturesque times lingers still, not only in by-ways and corners, but in the very centers of its newest activities.[14]

By the 1880s, over thirty years after the signing of the Treaty of Guadalupe Hidalgo and the incorporation of former Mexican territories into the United States, the sorrowful plight of dispossessed Californios could be safely mourned in the pages of travelogues. Helen Hunt Jackson characterized Californios as both "children" and "poets," indolent and charming, culturally backward and of the Old rather than the New World.[15] She looked with ambivalence and even horror at the impact of American expansion on Californios and Native American populations. While she praised the development of agricultural industry in southern California—the state was ready to be "Garden of the world"—she grimaced outwardly at what she saw as the exploitative and often immoral culture of white settlers. Such ambivalence was further dramatized in her novel *Ramona*, which was designed to awaken the nation to the plight of displaced California Indians. In actual fact, Jackson's highly romanticized image of California's ranchos and missions was seized upon by promoters who wished to boost the state's image to potential investors, settlers, and tourists, by appealing to its "Spanish" (and not Mexican) past.

In the early 1890s, the newspaper editor and travel writer Charles Augustus Stoddard made a long journey from New York to Los Angeles on the Southern Pacific Railroad, returning to Chicago and the East Coast from San Francisco on the Union Pacific and Central Pacific line. Visiting San Diego, he noted that scenes in *Ramona* took place in Old Town, the heart of the settlement during the Spanish and Mexican eras. Now the place had been abandoned. For Stoddard the abandonment of Old Town and the ruined state of many mission buildings in southern California were sure signs that the day of the Spaniard and the Mexican had long gone. Traveling through southern California, there was no doubt in Stoddard's mind that the future had already arrived in southern California. His narrative glows with approval for the rapid growth of Pasadena, then a city of some 10,000–12,000 inhabitants, which had been founded just twenty years before by settlers from Indiana: "[T]here are few places in Southern California where better climate, and water, and soil, and society, and civil and religious privileges are combined." Stoddard praised the city's broad avenues, spacious lots, elegant homes, abundant palms and eucalyptus trees, and its fine orchards and gardens. Here, he observed, was a town that had "not grown up hap-hazard, made up of drift-wood and débris" and was "absolutely destitute of a saloon or grog-shop." Instead the town was architecturally beautiful and populated by middle-class Anglo Protestants who attended church regularly and provided for the welfare of future generations by establishing a fine public library and public schools. He recalled one trip in the vicinity of modern-day Los Angeles and Pasadena: "One of our drives took in the San Gabriel Mission, with its ancient chime of bells, wonderful grapevine, and Mexican inhabitants. The contrast between this sleepy village, with its rows of wine-shops, adobe houses, and ancient air, with brisk and thrifty Pasadena—prohibition, enterprising, Protestant—was amazing."[16] Significantly, the tone of Stoddard's writing is similar to that of Susan Wallace and Charles Fletcher Lummis when, in their descriptions of New Mexico, they too stressed the antiquity, sleepiness, and adobe architecture of the "Spanish" past.

For all that Stoddard praised Pasadena as an idyllic modern city, the "picturesque" qualities of life in the pastoral period of southern California's history proved as irresistibly romantic to him as they did to Jackson and so many Anglo settlers and tourists at the beginning of the last century. Visiting Santa Barbara, he found the "quiet beauty of the place" a welcome respite from time spent in Los Angeles, then a city of sixty thousand inhabitants. He commented on a trip to the mission using familiar language. The church and surrounding buildings were in ruins, the courtyards were choked with weeds, and the orchards and vineyards had grown wild and no longer bore fruit. He noted too that such a state of decay had a particular appeal for one member of his party: "To the artist who was our companion in travel, this outward ruin only made the missions more picturesque, and his paintings more valuable, and the younger members of our party found the moonlight more attractive in a dilapidated mission, than upon a hotel piazza."[17]

The link between this image of Santa Barbara and representations of New Mexico and Arizona becomes clearer when we consider the career of Charles Fletcher Lummis and the role of the Atchison, Topeka, and Santa Fe Railway in capitalizing on the "exotic" qualities of the Southwest in its advertising for passenger service. In subsequent chapters I will have much more to say about both Lummis and the Santa Fe Railway. For now it is sufficient to know that from the 1890s until the 1920s, Lummis wrote enthusiastically from his home in Arroyo Seco, midway between Los

Angeles and Pasadena, about the efforts of Franciscan friars to convert Native Americans to Catholicism, and he campaigned to restore southern California's mission churches to what he considered their former glory. And while Mission San Diego de Alcala, whose dilapidated state Dana remarked upon, was not restored by Lummis and his fellow members of the Landmarks Club, which campaigned for the restoration of southern California's missions at the turn of the last century, it was eventually rebuilt during the 1930s. By this time so much of southern California's landscape had been changed from its appearance in Jackson's travel articles and *Ramona* that the connection between the Spanish and Mexican eras and modern, urban life in metropolitan Los Angeles seemed most palpable in nostalgic theater, pageant, and film productions rather than in "real" life. As we shall see, a different fate was in store for Santa Fe and northern New Mexico. But before considering the condition of New Mexico at the beginning of the last century, we should turn the clock back to the 1830s and 1840s.

Commerce of the Prairies

In May 1831 Josiah Gregg set out on the Santa Fe Trail from Independence, Missouri. Gregg was, by his own admission, in a "morbid condition," and he had taken to the prairies on the advice of his doctor to recover his health. A week after starting out, however, he swapped a place in a carriage for riding on horseback and eagerly participated in a buffalo hunt. Thus began, as Gregg put it, "a passion for Prairie life which I never expect to outlive."[18] Gregg joined one of the great caravans of traders that traveled the eight hundred miles between Missouri and Santa Fe, New Mexico, hiring on as a bookkeeper for the trader Jesse Sutton. When Gregg embarked on a second trip to Santa Fe in spring 1834, he and Sutton were business partners, trading American goods for silver and mules from Mexico. This time Gregg pushed well into the heart of Mexico, traveling to the cities of Chihuahua and Durango, and did not return to the United States until fall 1836. Two further trips rounded out his travel on the Santa Fe Trail.[19]

When Gregg narrated his life as a trader on the Santa Fe Trail, the differences between his adventures and Dana's experience of the hide trade were significant but hardly extreme. Like Dana, he wrote about Americans trading with Mexicans in the period between Mexico's independence from Spain and the outbreak of war with the United States. Similarly, he wrote about a social milieu in which Anglos and Mexicans cooperated with one another and built strong personal friendships as well as commercial ties. In addition, by virtue of their travels away from the United States, both men felt liberated from the social constraints they experienced while in their home country. And they each anticipated the conquest of Mexico by making derogatory remarks about the supposed indolence of Mexicans and by imagining California and New Mexico in the hands of "enterprising" Americans.

By the time Gregg made his first journey to New Mexico, the Santa Fe trade had become well established. William Becknell was the first American to take advantage of new opportunities for trade between the United States and New Mexico after Mexico gained its independence from Spain in 1821. That year Becknell traveled to Santa Fe with pack mules, but the following year he returned from the United States with wagons. Over the following two decades the number of traders involved and the quantity of merchandise transported soared, to the point where in the 1840s the value of the Santa Fe Trail trade may have been as much as $1.5 million per year.[20] Gregg participated in the process whereby the northern frontier of New Mexico was brought into much greater proximity to Missouri, the hub of commercial activity for the West as a whole during the 1830s and 1840s. For the historian Howard R. Lamar, the conquest of New Mexico by Americans was motivated neither by the land hunger of settlers nor the call for the extension of slavery, but rather by merchants who wanted to consolidate and safeguard their commercial arrangements.[21] Gregg's attitude was typical of many traders when he complained of a "strong prejudice" against Americans in New Mexico. This prejudice, he claimed, was "an inevitable result of that sinister feeling with which the 'rival republic' views the advancement and superiority of her more industrious neighbors."[22] Gregg was further vexed by what he regarded as excessive taxation on the goods he traded and the acts of corrupt officials. In addition, he chafed against the requirement to carry a passport: this "to free-born Americans, is a truly insupportable nuisance."[23] This motif of unconstrained freedom runs throughout the trader's life.

Gregg appears to have been a fastidious and at times prickly character who was inclined to be self-righteous and judgmental of others—traits that are on occasion conveyed through his writing. Ill at ease in cities and in social gatherings, Gregg valued the "the wild, unsettled and independent life of the Prairie trader," which, he claimed, "makes perfect freedom from nearly every kind of social dependence an absolute necessity of his being."[24] Gregg neither married nor, it seems, experienced a longing for home while away from the United States; indeed, he remarked that married men "are peculiarly unfitted for the chequered life of a Santa Fe trader." He then added: "The domestic hearth, with all its sacred and most endearing recollections, is sure to haunt them in the hour of trial, and almost every step of their journey is apt to be attended by melancholy reflections of home and domestic dependencies."[25] In addition to not missing the domestic hearth, Gregg displayed an ambivalent attitude toward his own country. After his final trading journey across the Southern Plains, he struggled to adjust to "civilized life" in the United States. While writing *Commerce of the Prairies,* he longed to be out on the plains again, roving at will and in command of his own situation. According to Gregg, the trader's self-reliance put him somewhat at odds with society on his return to American soil. Before, he had carried a gun for his own protection and could not rely on a court or jury to exercise justice if he were wronged. Indeed, noted Gregg, "He knows no government—no laws, save those of his own creation and adoption." Next to this, the return home could be a sore disappointment:

> The exchange of this untrammelled condition—this sovereign independence, for a life in civilization, where both his physical and moral freedom are invaded at every turn, by the complicated machinery of social institutions, is certainly likely to commend itself to but few—but even to all those who have been educated to find their enjoyments in the arts and elegancies peculiar to civilized society;—as is evidenced by the frequent instances of men of letters, of refinement and of wealth, voluntarily abandoning society for a life upon the Prairies, or in the still more savage mountain wilds.[26]

Having kept detailed journals during the eight times he traveled between Independence and Santa Fe, Gregg decided to write a book in the early 1840s. *Commerce of the Prairies,* his account of his decade-long participation in the trade between Missouri and New Mexico, was published in 1844. It is a fascinating account of travel that provides many details about life in New Mexico in the period immediately before the U.S.-Mexican War. The book consists of two volumes and thirty-one chapters in which Gregg narrates his journey across the Southern Plains, introduces readers to Santa Fe, comments on the "manners and customs" of Hispanos, describes a further trip to Chihuahua, and outlines the livelihoods of Indians living on the plains and in New Mexico. In the preface, Gregg referred to Washington Irving's *Tour of the Prairies* as a key influence on the text. He considered his own book an invaluable source of reliable information on the lands and peoples of the Southern Plains and northern Mexico. Gregg excused himself for "trespassing" on the territory of "the regular historian" and interjecting many observations about New Mexico's history and the manners and customs of its people on the basis that there was a "dearth of information" about New Mexico at this time.[27]

Within two years of the book's publication, the United States had annexed Texas and declared war on Mexico for disputing the new border between the two countries. For Mexico, this war of aggression concluded the loss of around half of its territory to the United States. Gregg was very much of his time insofar as he doubted the capacity of Mexicans to rule themselves. According to his viewpoint, next to the democratic institutions of the United States, Mexico appeared to be sorely lacking in honest government and a reliable legal system. Both the Spanish government and the Catholic Church had ensured that the great majority of New Mexicans were kept ignorant of the development of American society "lest the lights of civil and religious liberty should reach them from their neighbors of the North." Furthermore, despite Mexico's having gained independence from Spain, the North remained an underdeveloped and benighted region: "There is no part of the civilized globe, perhaps, where the Arts have been so much neglected, and the progress of Science so successfully impeded as in New Mexico."[28]

When Gregg embarked on his first journey to Santa Fe in 1831, the Southern Plains constituted an extended borderlands between two nation states: the United States, still a young republic, and Mexico, which was only a decade into its independence from Spain. Equally important, the plains were home to many Native American tribes, some of whom had been displaced from lands claimed by the United States. One hundred and fifty miles into the journey from Independence, Gregg surveyed the plains environment at Council Grove and imagined American ownership of the land:

> All who have traversed these delightful regions, look forward with anxiety on the day when the Indian title to the land shall be extinguished, and flourishing 'white' settlements dispel the gloom which at present prevails over this uninhabited region. Much of

this prolific country now belongs to the Shawnees and other Indians of the border, though some portion of it has never been allotted to any tribe.[29]

Arguably Gregg anticipated Americans' gaining title not only to the Southern Plains but also to New Mexico. This is not to claim that Gregg made an overt call for the colonization of northern Mexico by Americans. Notably his book lacks the outright patriotism of writers and politicians in the mid-1840s who claimed that the Manifest Destiny of the United States would be fulfilled by waging war on Mexico. Nevertheless, expansion-minded readers during this period would have found in the book evidence to justify the conflict they postulated.

At a time when much American travel and exploration writing on the southwestern borderlands represented Mexicans as being, in the words of the literary critic Raymund Paredes, "cruel, cowardly, treacherous, immoral, indolent, and backward," *Commerce of the Prairies* shared those prejudices and to a limited extent called them into question.[30] Gregg highlighted the supposed failings of Mexican society throughout the book. Its citizens lacked the intelligence, independence, and freedom of Americans, he claimed. The paucity of public schools combined with the lack of a free public press, the poor standard of medicine, and the primitive state of industry to create a backward and downtrodden population. "No wonder," he continued, "that the people of Northern Mexico are so much behind their neighbors of the United States in intelligence, and that the pulse of national industry and liberty beats so low!" He also commented negatively on the "intolerance," "bigotry," and "fanaticism" of the New Mexicans, reserving particular opprobrium for what as he saw as the capacity of men to be deceitful and arrogant. And yet despite the supposed tendency of New Mexicans to present "a false glare of talent, eminently calculated to mislead and impose," Gregg found some virtue: "I am fain to believe and acknowledge, that there are to be found among them numerous instances of uncompromising virtue, good faith and religious forebearance."[31] It would be disingenuous to suggest that Gregg was open-minded when representing the "manners and customs" of New Mexicans. After all, his zeal for mercantilism contributed to the momentum for American conquest and expansion. But we have also seen that Gregg could be critical of American institutions and his fellow Americans, and it is not altogether clear where his social and political allegiances lay. We should also not forget that in common with other traders Gregg became oriented toward life on the plains and in New Mexico in his years as a trader. Hence, in the completed book, Gregg expressed the wish to travel on the Southern Plains again, to spread his bed with the mustang and the buffalo, and to mingle "with the little prairie dogs and wild colts, and the still wilder Indians—the unconquered *Sabaeans* of the Great American Deserts."[32] The sense of kinship with nature and Indians that is expressed here lies at the heart of frontier mythology and expresses a profound ambivalence toward the development of American society in the mid nineteenth century.[33] Viewed from "the broad, unembarrassed freedom of the Great Western Prairies," the lives of people living in large American cities appeared "pent up" and uninviting.[34]

Whereas Gregg distanced himself from city dwellers in the United States and from the Mexican and Indian inhabitants of the Southwest, he also remarked on the differences between himself and other Anglo travelers along the Santa Fe Trail. He noted that on his first trip his fellow travelers included tourists and invalids, like himself, as well as traders. Gregg differentiated between "the amateur tourist and the listless loafer," disdaining the latter—to whom he also referred, in the plural, as "lounging *attachés*"—for what he saw as a refusal to muck in with day-to-day tasks, including guard duty. He wrote:

> There is always a set of genteel idlers attached to every caravan, whose wits are forever at work in devising schemes for whiling away their irksome hours at the expense of others. By embarking on these 'trips for pleasure,' they are enabled to live without expense; for the hospitable traders seldom refuse to accommodate even a loafing companion with a berth at their mess without charge.[35]

By virtue of this passage Gregg contrasted his own industry compared with the perceived idleness of other people. He also claimed authority for his observations of the Santa Fe Trail trade by stressing that from the outset of his travels he participated directly in the scenes he described. There is an earnest quality to Gregg's writing. Even if he had managed to become a great success as a businessman, it is hard to imagine him using his wealth to travel in leisure and style in, for example, Italy or France. Gregg was a restless individualist, practical-minded and on the lookout for commercial opportunities, and certainly not a cosmopolitan figure interested in rounding out his aesthetic sensibility by making a grand tour of Europe.

It is not surprising to learn that after publishing *Commerce of the Prairies* and pursuing various ventures, including a medical practice in

Mexico, Gregg became restless again and returned to the "untrammelled condition" of his former life by traveling with a botanical expedition to Mexico City, the west coast of Mexico, and northern California in 1848–50. While in California, he was asked to lead an expedition from a mining encampment along the Trinity River to the Pacific Coast. The object was to map a new road to the coast and to establish the whereabouts of a harbor from where goods could be transported by sea to San Francisco. Gregg set out in the late fall of 1849. Instead of taking just over a week, as it should have, the journey lasted a month due to the tough terrain, poor weather, and Gregg's nearly insatiable desire to identify and measure flora and fauna along the way. After reaching the coast and traveling south, the party finally viewed a large bay. However the glory and the name—Trinity Bay—attached to this discovery were lost to another, seafaring, expedition, which named the location Humboldt Bay. The party set out for San Francisco, but encountered more problems as they lost their way, grew hungry and exhausted, and argued. In the vicinity of Clear Lake, in today's Sonoma County, Gregg died at the age of forty-four after falling from his horse.[36]

A Military Reconnaissance to the Navajo Country

In mid-August 1849 Lieutenant James Simpson set out with a military expedition through territory newly claimed by the United States in the aftermath of its war with Mexico. The force, led by Colonel John M. Washington, was charged with the responsibility of pacifying Navajo Indians who had taken advantage of unrest in New Mexico to raid Pueblo Indians and "Mexican" settlements. Ten days after departure eighty Mexican mounted militia joined the force, making a total of four hundred men, which included fifty-five Pueblo Indian mounted militia. At the end of the month Washington met with three Navajo chiefs—Narbona, José Largo, and Archulette—to inform them that their people were now under the jurisdiction of the United States and that they must return all Mexican captives, give up the "murderers" of Mexicans, and return all stock stolen from Mexicans since Americans had assumed control of New Mexico. Furthermore, Navajos should grant American citizens free access to their territory. In return the U.S. government would "from time to time, make them presents, such as axes, hoes, and other farming utensils, etc." As the council concluded, a Mexican man accused a Navajo man of owning a horse that had been stolen from him. The Navajo refused to part with the horse, claiming that the man to whom it belonged had run away and that he did not have the authority to give it up. American troops then tried to take a horse from a group of Navajos, who were fired upon when they ran away. Narbona and six other Navajo men were killed in the ensuing melee. Simpson commented, with emphasis, that Navajos would continue to be "tricky" and "unreliable" so long as "*troops are stationed immediately among them.*"[37]

The following year, when four years of military rule of New Mexico gave way to a new territorial government, around 1,000 Anglos controlled a "Spanish-Mexican" population of 50,000 while 40,000–58,000 Navajos, Utes, Apaches, Comanches, and Kiowas lived autonomous lives and effectively controlled 80 percent of the territory's land. The population of 7,000–10,000 Zuni, Hopi, and Pueblo Indians further marginalized the Anglo population.[38] Until the 1880s, when Chiricahua Apaches were infamously transported away from their southern Arizona homelands to Fort Marion, Florida, armed conflict between Americans and certain sections of the Indian population broke out recurrently. The fact that many Anglos in the mid-nineteenth-century Southwest felt embattled helps explain, if not justify, their aggressive rhetorical stance toward "hostile" Indians, who were frequently viewed with condescension and fear. While Simpson concluded that through the expedition the United States had "assumed the paternal control it has been in the habit of exercising over the tribes of Indians within or bordering upon its domain," his report nevertheless witnessed the continuing political independence and cultural autonomy of Navajos.[39] In fact it was not until the next decade that the Navajo resistance was curbed through the pursuit of a far more aggressive, and controversial, military strategy under the guidance of Kit Carson, which culminated in the forced march of Navajos from their homelands to a military reservation at Bosque Redondo in southeastern New Mexico in 1864.

Simpson's report on the expedition into Navajo country was published by a popular press in 1852. It espoused the right of the United States to take control of territory won through the U.S.-Mexican War and justified overt acts of violence as necessary to the establishment of American hegemony in the Southwest. The report's impetus was clearly militaristic, it appealed to prevailing attitudes about Manifest Destiny and westward expansion, and it supplied readers with a variety of geographical, geological, archaeological, and ethnological information.

In the course of the military reconnaissance Simpson passed through Chaco Canyon and Canyon de Chelly, where some of the most significant ancient Puebloan, or Anasazi, ruins are located. Simpson contemplated the history of these places and the fate of the people who had once populated them. From a contemporary perspective, Simpson's observations provide a fascinating mixture of informed opinion and wild speculation on the human history of the Southwest. Based on information provided by Pueblo Indian and Navajo informants and his reading of Gregg's *Commerce of the Prairies* and William H. Prescott's *The Conquest of Mexico* (1843), Simpson debated whether the ruins of Chaco Canyon could have been built by the Aztecs prior to their migration to Mexico City and concluded that the canyon probably "constituted the last resting-place of [the Aztecs] before entering upon the conquest of Anahuac."[40] In Simpson's view this made sense because in the three hundred years between the abandonment of Chaco Canyon and the Spanish conquest of Mexico the Aztecs might well have gained the knowledge to build the temple of Xochicalco, the palaces of Tezcotzino, and the great stone calendar in Mexico City. Simpson combined such insights with his view that the aridity of the Southwest was effectively a form of punishment by God on the people who had thrived at Chaco Canyon to round out his view of both ancient Native American cultures and contemporary Indians in the Southwest. Thus "high" Indian civilization was consigned to pre-Columbian history and, three hundred years after the Spanish conquest, New Mexico was represented as a degraded environment where the land was infertile and the people lacked vitality.

Simpson was not wholly dismissive of Pueblo Indians, who in his eyes were the descendants of the absent Aztecs. He characterized Hosta, the governor of Jemez Pueblo who helped guide Washington's force and provided much historical information about the country passed through, as "handsome" and "magnanimous."[41] Simpson also praised the Pueblo men who accompanied the American force: "in their calm, reflective countenances, I think I can perceive a latent energy and power, which it requires only a proper political and social condition to develop and make useful." Clearly the precondition of such praise was the perceived orderliness and industry of Pueblo Indians and, of course, their "useful" role as helpmates in the expedition into Navajo country. Alongside such comments Simpson provided observations of Pueblo Indians' ongoing lives. Visiting Santo Domingo Pueblo, he estimated eight hundred inhabitants and described their housing, dress, and diet. After eating a thin bread named "*guayave,*" which he compared to the Mexican tortilla, he complained of feeling slightly nauseous despite his excessive hunger. At Jemez Pueblo he witnessed a Corn Dance and commented dismissively: "The movements in the dance differed but slightly from those of Indians generally." But on being shown a painting of San Diego bearing a cross in the pueblo's mission church, he was moved to write: "None but a true son of the muse could have thrown into the countenance the expression of beautiful sadness with which it is radiant." These details help us to appreciate the degree to which Simpson based his observations of Pueblo culture on hasty viewing and scant information, in the process making value judgments about the significance of ceremonies that within a half-century would become the subject of detailed research by ethnologists.[42]

Although Simpson loyally reported on the Pueblo Indians and Navajos he encountered, he was most enthusiastic when narrating his brief explorations of ancient Indian ruins in Chaco Canyon and Canyon de Chelly. Traveling into the latter, he commented on "stupendous" walls that had been created by the "hand of art." Here, once again, Simpson responded with imagination as he tried to link present-day Navajos to the ruins found in the canyon. He conjectured that the Navajos were a remnant of "Aztec stock" from before the period in which Chaco Canyon was created. Alternatively, aridity had caused the once unified ancient people to become more dispersed and mobile, and so they had come to live in hogans rather than pueblos. This sort of imaginative engagement with the ancient history of the Southwest helped shape an aesthetic through which the region's past was romanticized in many later travelogues. In this regard Simpson's narrative points the way ahead to travelogues published in the 1880s and 1890s by civilian writers such as Susan Wallace, Charles Fletcher Lummis, and George Wharton James. Before moving on to assess a further travel account from the 1850s, we do well to remind ourselves that as Simpson exercised his romantic interest by marveling at the sheer rock walls of Canyon de Chelly, so he took part in the pacification of Navajo people. As he traveled through the canyon, Simpson congratulated himself on exploding the myth that the Navajo possessed an impregnable fort near the mouth of the canyon. Overall the geographical knowledge assembled by the expedition would be "of the highest value in any future military demonstration it may be necessary to make."[43]

El Gringo

William Watts Hart Davis began his journey from Independence to Santa Fe in November 1853. Together with eleven fellow passengers, he traveled with one of the mule teams that carried the mail back and forth between New Mexico and the "States." There was a wagon each to carry mail and baggage, and another two wagons for passengers. A couple of outriders rode with each wagon, armed for defense against Indians and to hunt game. Davis was traveling to Santa Fe in order to take up a political appointment. Having seen active service in the U.S.-Mexican War and having demonstrated loyalty to the Democratic Party, Davis had petitioned prominent politicians in President Franklin Pierce's new administration for a consulate or port position. This effort proved unsuccessful, but in September 1853 Davis was offered the position of District Attorney for the Territory of New Mexico. The thirty-three-year-old lawyer arrived in Santa Fe on November 24, having left his home in Doylestown, Pennsylvania, ten weeks earlier. He lived in New Mexico until 1857, when he returned to Pennsylvania and became the owner and editor of the *Doylestown Democrat* newspaper.[44]

Similar to Simpson, Davis was a representative of the U.S. government, albeit a civilian official who played a key role in consolidating the new system of territorial government that superceded the military administration of New Mexico. Davis arrived in Santa Fe a politically ambitious man with aspirations for higher office. Later in life he would stand unsuccessfully for election to Congress. In New Mexico his sights were set lower. After serving as district attorney, he was appointed Secretary of the Territory in May 1854. In the latter position he was responsible for recording and publicizing the territorial government's legislation and other affairs. He also deputized for the governor, David Meriwether, when he was called away from Santa Fe. Davis provided the public with notice of the territory's proceedings through the pages of the *Santa Fe Gazette,* a bilingual newspaper that he also edited. He was fluent in Spanish, having learned the language while serving in the U.S.-Mexican War. While living in Santa Fe, Davis earned a contract with the publishers Harpers & Brothers to publish a book based on his experiences of travel in New Mexico. That book, *El Gringo; or New Mexico and Her People,* was published in 1857. A decade later Davis followed up his interest in the history and cultures of New Mexico by publishing *The Spanish Conquest of New Mexico* (1869). This history drew on his copious reading of Spanish colonial documents and books held in the Palace of the Governors, the seat of government in New Mexico since the 1600s. Its publication also suggests the seriousness with which he took the responsibility of chronicling the pre-1846 past of New Mexico. Later in the nineteenth century popularizers of the Southwest, such as Lummis, would build on such work when celebrating the "Spanish American" history of New Mexico and California.

In his capacity as district attorney, Davis was required to make a circuit of the U.S. district courts throughout the territory in the spring and fall. Each circuit was a thousand miles in length and took three months to complete. For the most part Davis traveled on horseback because "the roads in many places are quite impassable for carriages."[45] *El Gringo* was in large part based on these experiences of travel, which provided many opportunities to report on the character of life in New Mexico. Davis also proved to be a keen-eyed and partisan observer of the attempts of American officials to create a new legislative and judicial system for the territory. Unlike Gregg, Davis had a very firm sense of the inherent virtue of American government and justice that was confirmed rather than called into question by his experience of living in New Mexico. Gregg, in contrast, was not as tightly bound to American institutions as Davis and was also, of course, not part of American efforts to impose on New Mexico's Hispano and Native American population a new regime.

El Gringo is of significance precisely because of its author's politically and culturally biased representations of New Mexico's Hispanos and Native Americans. The book consists of an account of the author's passage across the Southern Plains, a historical sketch of New Mexico and the territory's Pueblo Indians, observations of the "manners and customs" of Santa Fe's population, an extended account of riding the territory's legal circuit, and a narrative of a trip to the Navajo country in 1855. As the title *El Gringo* suggests, Davis not only felt himself an outsider within New Mexico but also considered the territory to be profoundly different from the rest of the United States.[46] He traveled throughout a region where social, economic, and cultural differences between Hispanos, Native Americans, and Anglos prevailed in the aftermath of the U.S.-Mexican War, mutual wariness and hostility at times escalating into outright conflict. Davis envisaged the railroad's aiding the development of New Mexico by bringing an "enterprising population" of Anglos that would exploit the region's mineral wealth and more limited opportunities for commercial agriculture. He little realized that the railroad he recommended constructing would later bring to New Mexico tourists who marveled at the undeveloped desert, the Southwest's archaeological "wonders," and the "unchanged" lives of Hispanos and Pueblo Indians.

Davis considered it necessary to write *El Gringo* because "[t]here is no country protected by our flag and subject to our laws so little known to the people of the United States as the territory of New Mexico." He continued:

> Its very position precludes an intimate discourse with other sections of the Union, and serves to lock up a knowledge of the country within its own limits. The natural features differ widely from the rest of the Union; and the inhabitants, with the manners and customs of their Moorish and Castilian ancestors, are both new and strange to our people. For these reasons, reliable information of this hitherto almost unknown region can not fail to be interesting to the public.[47]

There is a tension at the heart of these words. Davis wrote about New Mexico in order to make Americans more familiar with lands and peoples they had colonized a decade before. He assumed the superiority of American institutions to those employed by the previous Spanish colonial and Mexican administrations, while hardly crediting Indians with being capable of possessing any substantial form of government. He also argued that it was the duty of Americans to use their free institutions to achieve "the regeneration of the people of New Mexico, morally, socially, and religiously."[48] And yet by stressing the geographical remoteness of New Mexico and the largely unknown characteristics of its people, Davis also acknowledged that it was a place apart from the rest of the Union with a significantly different human history and range of cultural traditions. There is, then, an equivocal quality to Davis's writing. He praised the conduct of New Mexicans in his account of riding the circuit of district courts: "Every thing convinced me that they are orderly and respectful people, and I have observed better decorum among them in the court-house than I ever noticed in the States in the most intelligent community." But he concluded the book on a different note: "The minds of the people are as barren as the land, with as little hope of being better cultivated."[49]

To a certain extent this equivocal attitude toward New Mexicans can easily be explained. Davis praised Hispanos when he saw them successfully adapting to the American judicial system and he censured them, among other things, for resisting efforts to reform education and the Catholic Church. From his perspective the livelihoods of New Mexicans would be transformed through exposure to "a purer code of morals and a wiser system of laws" that would lead them "to the standard of enlightenment."

Their "regeneration" as citizens of the United States rather than Mexico would be accomplished through their participation in the new colonial order.[50] But things grow more complicated when we consider Davis's attitude toward issues of race. In common with many Americans at this time, Davis believed that Hispanos in the mid nineteenth century had inherited their progenitors' racial characteristics. Mexicans, he claimed, "possess the cunning and deceit of the Indian, the politeness and spirit of revenge of the Spaniard, and the imaginative temperament and fiery impulses of the Moor." Thus they had "inherited a portion of the cruelty, bigotry, and superstition that have marked the character of the Spaniards from the earliest times"—traits that appeared "constitutional and innate in the race."[51] The tension within Davis's argument lay in accounting for differences between Hispanos and Anglos that would not be easily reconciled as American control over the territory was consolidated. By stressing a history of inherited racial characteristics that explained Hispano culture, Davis suggested that Anglos would have to struggle hard to remove the veil that kept so many Hispanos in a benighted condition. Such remarks provided a tacit acknowledgment that Hispanos' sense of cultural identity was rooted in values that had sustained their community for many decades—values that, from the perspective of Hispanos themselves, were not only different from but even antithetical to American society.

The tensions revealed in Davis's way of seeing Santa Fe and New Mexico as a whole were compounded in the scene of arrival in the city. Significantly Davis narrated this scene over halfway through the book, so that the reader's view of Santa Fe is prefaced by 234 pages of text and mediated by judgmental remarks about the need for New Mexicans to be regenerated. Davis wrote:

> The first sight of Santa Fe is by no means prepossessing. Viewed from the adjacent hills as you descend into the valley, whence it falls the first time under your glance, it has more the appearance of a colony of brick-kilns than a collection of human habitations. You see stretching before you, on both sides of the little river of the same name, a cluster of flat-roofed mud houses, which, in the distance, you can hardly distinguish from the earth itself.[52]

Davis stressed the foreignness and strangeness of Santa Fe. Viewed from a distance away, the combination of the remote geographical setting and adobe architecture made the city appear unreal. Riding through the city's

streets only enhanced this sentiment. Davis was disconcerted by the realization that the city's inhabitants regarded him as a foreigner even though
he was moving through American territory. Writing about the commonplace experience of homesickness among Anglo travelers, Davis explained:

> To a greater or less degree, this feeling will seize upon all comers
> from the United States when they place foot in Santa Fe for the
> first time. The whole aspect of things is so entirely different from
> what they have been accustomed to: a foreign language salutes
> their ears; a strange race of men gape at them without a particle
> of sympathy, and the mud city with its dirty streets and no less
> dirty population—all presents such an uninviting picture to the
> stranger, that, in spite of all he can do, he will feel a little 'down
> in the mouth.'[53]

The sense of alienation conveyed through these sentences recurs throughout *El Gringo*. Describing a Catholic procession through the city's streets
on Good Friday, Davis labeled the parade "disgusting to the sight." He
took exception at the display of images of saints, which encouraged in him
"pity for the worshipers of these unmeaning bits of ill-carved wood," and
the appearance of local women with allegedly questionable morals as *vir-
gines* in the procession. Through such practices, Davis reckoned, the common people of New Mexico were kept in thrall to idol worship while the
Church itself sanctioned sexual immorality in women. This is clearly a
culturally biased perspective and yet within four decades of the publication of *El Gringo* religious ceremonies and Hispano arts and crafts, including the carving of religious figures known as *santos* and *bultos,* would be
highly praised by a new generation of Anglo writers. The same can be said
for Davis's perspective on Spanish colonial and Mexican-era adobe
churches. In Las Vegas, New Mexico, Davis walked into a small church
that was in a very poor state of repair. The bell was old and cracked, the
floor was the damp earth, the nave lacked seats, and behind the altar were
"three daubs of paintings, one of which is intended to represent Christ
nailed to the cross."[54] By the end of the nineteenth century concerned
Anglos would campaign to preserve adobe churches like this and prize
retablos, painted altar boards, as authentic expressions of religious piety.

Unlike subsequent Anglo writers in New Mexico, Davis did not
emphasize the romance of Spanish colonial history, which accounts for
his failure to embellish his portrait of the "antiquated mud church" with

picturesque flourishes. When Davis turned his eye to the circumstances in which poor Hispanos lived, he was struck by great inequalities in wealth. He described an almost destitute family living in Socorro in a room that was "cheerless to the extreme," continuing: "They were surrounded with filth, with hardly enough clothing to cover them, and yet in this condition live the great mass of the people of the country." It would have been difficult for Davis to conjure romance from such a situation, assuming that his representation of the family's poverty is accurate. By stressing the poverty of the majority of Hispanos he provided a clear rationale for "reclaiming" their lives through access to American institutions and embracing liberal ideology.[55]

Casting his eye on Pueblo Indians, Davis employed a far more romantic perspective than when viewing Hispanos. Like Simpson, Davis was fascinated by the origins of Pueblo Indian society. He stated that all intelligent Americans would desire to know more about their history on learning of the ancient Indian ruins that abounded in the Southwest. He continued: "Who they are and whence they came must always remain shrouded in mystery, unless a modern Oedipus should spring up to unravel their romantic history." Davis contributed to the Anglo viewpoint that prevailed through the remainder of the nineteenth century and into the twentieth, that those abandoned dwellings were "the mute memorial of a once powerful race of people now almost extinct." On a similar note, he stated that contemporary Pueblo Indians were "degenerating as a race" because of intermarriage within the same pueblo. "In this respect," he concluded, "they seem to follow the example of the royal families of Europe, and their blood is losing strength about as rapidly."[56]

As we have seen with Simpson, and as we shall also see with Wallace, this theme of the degeneration of Pueblo Indians was commonplace in writing about the Southwest during the nineteenth century. It was also common among writers to speculate about the "mystery" of the Pueblo Indians' origins and the precise link between their nineteenth-century villages and ancient Puebloan cultures. For example, Simpson interpreted the history of Chaco Canyon at least partly through the perspectives of the German geographer Alexander Von Humboldt and the American historian William H. Prescott. Simpson argued that the location of Chaco Canyon matched Humboldt's claim that before the Aztecs migrated south and founded Tenochtitlán, the seat of their empire, they had resided between the 36th and 37th parallel of northern latitude and between 109 and 112 meridians of west longitude.[57]

After the publication of Prescott's *History of the Conquest of Mexico* in 1843, it would appear that all southwestern travelogues included imaginative interpretations of the link between contemporary Pueblo Indians and the figure of Montezuma, legendary leader of the Aztecs in their confrontation with the Spanish conquistadors led by Hernando Cortes. Both Gregg and Davis related details of a myth that would be increasingly familiar to American readers over the ensuing decades. According to this myth, Montezuma had set a holy fire at Pecos Pueblo, to the east of Santa Fe, which was not to be put out until he returned. Gregg claimed that he had seen the smoldering fire in a kiva. Alas, the fire had gone out, and this catastrophe had caused the final inhabitants of Pecos Pueblo to abandon their home in the early nineteenth century. Gregg added that according to some sources, men had died of exhaustion and from the fumes of the fire as they attended it and that their bodies, along with live children, had been fed to a huge snake that the people idolized.[58] Davis quoted Gregg's account of the snake but was on the whole skeptical about the Montezuma myth. Rather than lend credence to it, he was dismissive of the ability of the Pueblo people to know their own history: "Among these people there exists neither semblance of music or poetry never so rude, and it is at least questionable whether correct tradition can be preserved among those who have no knowledge of these two arts."[59]

The refusal of Davis and other commentators of the mid nineteenth century to acknowledge the capacity of Pueblo Indians to govern themselves effectively, create accounts of their own history, and forge religious practices that were equally as profound as Christianity's would give way over the ensuing decades to a more appreciative understanding of their culture among certain Anglos. The journalist E. Conklin anticipated this change in attitude after touring Arizona in the fall and winter of 1877, just after the completion of the Southern Pacific Railroad. Soon, he forecast, the railroad would take travelers into the Southwest and "a tide of pre-historic study" would take place. Not forgetting that his book *Picturesque Arizona* was sponsored by mining interests, Conklin noted that in addition to mining's constituting "the chief value and support of Arizona, if not the nation so to speak," it would be the Southwest's ancient Indian landmarks *and* "the actual existence of the pre-historic people (in their descendants) that yet remain in a goodly number" that would excite the interest of "an additional class of people, in our scientists, archaeologists, travelers and tourists."[60] Two years after Conklin toured Arizona, the writer Susan Wallace moved to Santa Fe from Crawfordsville, Indiana.

She echoed Conklin when praising the "extremely gentle and friendly" manner of Pueblo Indians. She explained: "Their quaint primitive customs, curious myths, and legends afford rich material for the poet, and their antiquities open an endless field to the delving archaeologist."[61] Similar to Gregg and Simpson, she would write about the Montezuma myth, lending an air of romance to her account of Pueblo Indian history. In addition to writing lyrically about Indians, she would criticize them for holding onto their cultural traditions. Simultaneously her writing would contain a tacit acknowledgment of the Pueblos Indians' fierce desire to be true to themselves: "a rigid unbending adherence to old time observances sets their faces against everything new and foreign, and our mission-work seems dashing against a dead wall."[62] In time Anglos would value Pueblo Indians precisely because they had resisted absorption into modern American society.

The Land of the Pueblos

Susan Wallace arrived in Santa Fe just over twenty years after Davis's departure from New Mexico. She traveled there in the company of her husband, Lew Wallace, governor of New Mexico between 1879 and 1881 and author of the best-selling novel *Ben-Hur* (1880), written while he resided in the territory.[63] Noting the "tender light of the evening," Wallace wrote: "As we approach, [Santa Fe] is invested with indescribable romance, the poetic glamor which hovers about all places to us foreign, new, and strange." Hearing Spanish being spoken, she rhapsodized: "At last, at last, I am not of this time nor of this continent; but away, away across the sea, in the land of dreams and visions, 'renowned, romantic Spain.'"[64]

The Land of the Pueblos appeared in 1888 after individual chapters had been published in eastern journals through the previous decade. Wallace exclaimed in the opening pages: "I am 6,000 feet nearer the sky than you are. Come to the sweet and lonely valley in the West where, free from care and toil, the weary soul may rest; where there are neither railroads, manufactures, nor common schools; and so little is expected of us in the way of public spirit, we almost venture to do as we please, and forget we should vote."[65] Directing her comments at a readership she assumed to be unfamiliar with the Southwest, Wallace stressed the value of New Mexico's high altitude, aridity, and spectacular scenery for health seekers and tourists. Crucially, through pointing out New Mexico's *lack* of communications and industrial development Wallace suggested that a primary aspect of the territory's appeal was its geographical and cultural isolation from the United States. The Southwest appeared unpressed by the forces of incorporation that were in the midst of transforming the American economy in the late nineteenth century. While Wallace's comments on the lack of both common schools and the expectation of public duty in New Mexico suggest her unease with Catholicism and the continuing strength of Indian and Hispano cultural traditions, she also discovered in the Southwest a place where romance and imagination thrived:

> Hawthorne, in a tender gayety, laments the lack of the poetic element in our dear native land, where there is no shadow, no mystery, no antiquity, no picturesque and gloomy wrong, nor anything but commonplace prosperity in broad and simple daylight. Here is every requisite of romance—the enchantment of distance, the charm of the unknown—and, in shadowy mists of more than three hundred years, imagination may flower out in fancies rich and strange.[66]

These complimentary remarks stand alongside statements that are far less kind in their characterization of New Mexico's distinctive qualities. Wallace followed both Simpson and Davis in characterizing widespread cultural decline within the region's Native American population. The nineteen pueblo communities of New Mexico were in the process of "slowly decreasing in numbers" and in time due to their "lack of self-assertion" would disappear as the nomadic and warlike tribes already had. Meanwhile the Hopis in Northern Arizona were "sluggish and dead." Abundant ancient Indian ruins indicated that "in long forgotten days the Pueblos were numerous and powerful; a nation and a company of nations," but in the present there appeared little prospect of cultural revival. Mexican Americans fared even worse in Wallace's hierarchy of racial types because as a mestizo population the particular attributes of white, black, and red blood were undermined: "The restless energy of the Spaniard, the quick perception of the Moor, even the cunning of the roving Apache, appear to be lost in the sluggish current which lazily beats in the pulses of the modern Mexican."[67]

Wallace also had harsh words for Pueblo Indians. She expressed frustration at the Indians' resistance to acculturation efforts. Unable to grasp the fact that their renowned secrecy may have been developed as a strategy of resistance in the face of Spanish and more recently American colonization, Wallace characterized it as an inherent characteristic. She took it for granted that Pueblo Indians lacked a system of religious belief equal in profundity to Christianity. Indeed, Wallace undermined those commentators who thought there was a fundamental difference between Pueblo and nomadic Indians. Although the "noblest Roman wore his imperial mantle with no better grace" than one Pueblo man she saw, she reckoned that "[t]he attribute of civilization fails to make our aborigines at all like 'the white brother.'" She continued: "These peace-loving Pueblos, a pastoral people pursuing their simple industries and trudging to market with their poor products, are as thoroughly Indian as the wildest Apache, with brandished knife and dripping scalp in hand, dancing on the battle field and whooping in triumph over the banquet of blood."[68]

Wallace kept up a negative commentary on the attributes of not only southwestern Indians but also all Native Americans. In a typical gesture, she made an unfavorable comparison between Native American history and, in this case, the ancient Greeks when she commented on the mystery surrounding the mound-building Indians of the Midwest: "Let us believe we have lost no grand epic in the Iliad of the lost race."[69] When Wallace wrote that Pueblo Indians were "degraded descendants of haughty princes," she was at pains to undermine what she considered the more outlandish claims that fellow Anglos had made about the long-deserted cliff dwellings of the Four Corners area: "These edifices are not mysterious except to fevered fancies, and their tenants were not diverse nations, but clans, tribes of one blood, and civilized only as compared with the savages surrounding them—the tameless Apache, the brutish Ute, the degraded Navajo."[70] And yet, as her reference to Hawthorne and the romance of New Mexico suggests, Wallace also contributed to the mythologizing of the Southwest. Although she almost always qualified her comments on the similarities between New Mexico and the Holy Land— to the detriment, as she saw it, of the former—later writers would reproduce her comments largely without the qualifications. Reflecting on a trip from Santa Fe to Santo Domingo Pueblo to see a Corn Dance, she wrote: "There was much . . . to remind us of Bible pictures; the low adobe houses, the flocks with the herdsmen coming to drink at the shallow stream, the clambering goats in scanty pastures high up on the rocks . . . the Mexican women, straight as a rule, carrying water-jars on head or shoulder, like maidens of Palestine." Alas, she intimated, this was not really the Holy Land and it contained Indians rather than Jews: "The lofty presence, the high eagle features of the Jewish race, the lustrous eyes of the Orient are not here, nor is the barren magnificence of New Mexico more than a suggestion of the land once the glory of all lands, with its verdure of plumy palms, beauty of olive orchards, the dark foliage of cypress trees, and white and scarlet blooms of orange pomegranate."[71]

Wallace contributed to the mythologizing of the Southwest not least in stressing its underdevelopment. But she was of the opinion that the supposed backwardness of the region would soon become a thing of the past. Watching a crew working on the future Santa Fe Railway, she forecast the railroad would break the "poetic glamour" of New Mexico:

> If you would dream dreams and see visions, now is the time to come. If you would taste the wild charm, hasten to catch it before the wear of every-day travel tramples out the primitive customs. It is still to a good degree a country apart from the rest of the United States; mountain-locked and little known, severed, as it has been, from the great highways of commerce. Its history is a romance and a tragedy, and, as in every country imperfectly explored, it holds more or less of the mysterious. Here are extensive ruins; unparalleled natural phenomena; mountains, "flaunting their crowns of snow everlastingly in the face of the sun," that bear in their bosom undeveloped mines, dazzling the imagination; cañons with perpendicular sides a mile in height; savages merciless and bloodthirsty, who in undying hate still dispute the progress of foreign civilization. But the civilizer is coming; is here. The waste lands of the wandering tribes will be divided and sold by the acre, instead of the league. The dozing Mexican will be jostled on the elbow, and will wake from his long trance to find himself in the way.[72]

To a large extent Wallace here articulated the founding language of tourism in the Southwest. Through stirring images and lyrical prose, she compelled the reader's attention by pointing out the residual qualities of Native American and Hispano livelihoods in New Mexico and forecasting their demise.

In the face of what she saw as inevitable modernization and Americanization, Wallace urged readers to take account of New Mexico's geographical and cultural isolation before the process of social and economic incorporation was complete. For Wallace the most obvious sign that the "civilizer" was not only present in New Mexico but also making wholesale changes to the territory's older patterns of life was the railroad.

In a powerful passage, she wrote: "[t]he epic of history cannot abide the screech of the locomotive nor its penetrating headlight. It requires broken, disconnected threads, doubtful testimony, dim lights—above all, the mist lines of distance. The locomotive brings the ends of the earth together, and dashes into nothingness delicate tissues woven in darkness, like certain delicate laces, whose threads break in the weaving by day."[73]

Wallace included this passage in her account of a visit to the turquoise mines near Cerillos. On returning to Santa Fe, Wallace would have seen signs of the state capital's being transformed into an "American" city under the influence of Anglo merchants and officials. But, as the architectural historian Chris Wilson demonstrates, beginning a decade or so after Wallace left Santa Fe, calls came from concerned Anglos and local Hispano leaders for the preservation of Santa Fe's buildings and a return to its pre-1846 appearance. Significantly, adobe architecture, which had been disparaged by Davis, came back into style. Adobe buildings that had been disguised through the application of stucco and brick "tattooing" were returned to their natural appearance. During the 1920s and 1930s, the buildings, most notably La Fonda hotel, were made out of steel and concrete and then plastered with an adobe exterior in order to look more authentic.[74]

Returning Santa Fe to its former appearance was neither possible nor what even the most ardent advocates of Santa Fe Style architecture really wanted. So, to a degree, Wallace was correct to emphasize the irrevocable changes that were taking place in Santa Fe during the late 1870s and early 1880s, even though she might have been surprised to see the appearance of restored buildings fronting the plaza in the early twentieth century had she lived that long. In *The Land of the Pueblos* she envisaged social and economic change as inevitable even as she appeared to lament the intrusion of the steam locomotive into New Mexico. Unlike Davis, who considered American industry the means to New Mexico's economic and moral salvation, Wallace appears to have been more wary about what the region might become after the arrival of the railroad. She displayed an uneasy recognition of the capacity of the railroad to destroy "delicate tissues woven in darkness" as well as to connect places and people in a way that could only have been imagined by her forebears. For all that Wallace condescendingly viewed the Mexican as "dozing" and the Pueblo Indian as "degraded," she also recognized that there was a dimension to their lives all too often lacking in American society. First asking how humble Hispano women kept soul and body together and then entering a small cottage to find out, Wallace determined:

These are the people happy people sighed for by weary poets in all the ages. Simple souls who love the sun, live close to Nature, and in the dirt house, to which nothing is added, where nothing is repaired except by additional dirt, are serene as summer, filled with a measureless content. Can we say so much for the eager, ambitious conqueror in a struggle, a battle, and a race; always getting ready to live, looking to the future when he may have time to rest and enjoy?[75]

Clearly this commentary displays stereotypical assumptions about Hispano culture and more particularly the experiences of poor women, but it also manifests a critique of American aggression and materialism that soon became amplified in writing about New Mexico.

After the publication of *The Land of the Pueblos,* the Southwest became a region of refuge to increasing numbers of literary writers and artists who trekked and sojourned in the region precisely because they wanted to experience its "foreign" qualities. They were joined by tourists on the Santa Fe Railway and later by people who traveled extensively by car. Gregg and Davis might well have been surprised to learn that it was the very "primitive" qualities of life in New Mexico that visitors came to value. In the coming chapters I will account for the varied responses of many travelers to the experience of visiting not only New Mexico but also southern California, Arizona, and the Four Corners region. Not only were visitors' responses varied, so were their motives for travel and the ways in which they traveled.

CHAPTER TWO

John Wesley Powell's Mapping
of the Colorado Plateau Region

ON MAY 24, 1869, a party of ten amateur enthusiasts and hired hands set out from the town of Green River, Wyoming Territory, to explore the largely unknown lands of the Green and upper Colorado River valleys. Conducted under the auspices of the Illinois Natural History Society, of which Major John Wesley Powell was secretary at the time, the expedition culminated three previous seasons of exploration in the Rocky Mountain region. From May 24 until August 30, Powell's team voyaged down the Green and Colorado Rivers to the mouth of the Rio Virgen, a small distance beyond the Grand Canyon. In ninety-nine days the team travelled 1,037 miles by boat through some of the roughest water and terrain in the western United States.

Powell gained a high public profile through completing the first Colorado River expedition, and his travel articles describing the voyage made for popular reading in the magazine *Scribner's Monthly*. The public at large initially learned of the journey through newspaper reports. Later, when Powell lectured and wrote popular travel articles about the voyage, revenue gained through these outlets was plowed back into further seasons of travel and survey in the Colorado Plateau region, which covers a large part of northern New Mexico, northern Arizona, southern and eastern Utah, and southwestern Colorado. In the aftermath of the voyage he was appointed head of the Geographical and Geological Survey of the Rocky Mountain Region, or the Powell Survey, to give its more popular name. Powell was highly active in the western field and as a scientific bureaucrat in Washington, D.C. As head of both the Bureau of American Ethnology, between 1879 and 1902, and the U.S. Geological Survey, from 1881 to 1895, Powell became one of the most influential scientists in the nation.[1] He was part of a new generation of professional scientists who produced and disseminated knowledge through government channels, encouraging extensive research in the field to provide the data for analyses of the earth's history and humankind's social evolution. Powell combined wide-ranging interests in the natural sciences and ethnology with his influential position in government circles to give him considerable influence in public policy decisions, but not without controversy and challenges from his political rivals. Chronologically his survey of the Colorado Plateau region stood toward the end of exploration in the continental United States and was representative of a historical period in which civilian agency largely took over from military authority in both mapping the country's natural resources and conducting Indian affairs. Powell sought to consolidate knowledge derived from the field by influencing suitable federal policy decisions and sensitizing the public at large to the problem of how to develop the arid and semiarid regions of the far West.[2]

This chapter examines a number of texts through which Powell represented the Colorado River, the surrounding lands and natural resources of the Colorado Plateau, and Native Americans of the Great Basin and Southwest in order to create a comprehensive description of the last unmapped territory in the United States in the aftermath of the Civil War. These texts were written while Powell surveyed the Colorado Plateau during the 1870s and amounted to a thorough attempt to represent this great land mass. When Powell's men first ran the rapids of the Colorado River through the Grand Canyon in 1869, they discovered a region "both sublime and wonderful." The account Powell submitted to Congress is entitled *Report of the Exploration of the Colorado River of the West and its Tributaries: Explored in 1869, 1870, 1871, and 1872, under the direction of the Secretary of the Smithsonian Institution* (henceforth *Report of Exploration*), and it remains one of the classic texts of nineteenth-century exploration. I shall examine this narrative alongside other texts Powell wrote during the 1870s. These texts include newspaper letters; travel articles; a report to the Commissioner of Indian Affairs on the condition of the Numic-speaking Indians of the Great Basin, undertaken in 1874; Powell's landmark *Report on the Lands of the Arid Region of the United States* (1878); and scientific papers on the evolution of humankind. Confronted with the vast and wondrous landscape of the region, Powell, with the assistance of his team, used a personal journal, geological notes, cartography, photography, line-drawing, sketching, and painting in subsequent survey work to produce a multifarious image of the Colorado Plateau. On the one hand Powell's work contributed vital data and a moral perspective to crucial debates within the nation over the most appropriate ways in which to develop the region's natural resources and create a just and efficient federal Indian policy. But on the other hand these representations expanded the process of expropriating territory claimed by Native Americans.

For much of the nineteenth century the United States expanded at an unprecedented rate. Through the Louisiana Purchase of 1803, the Transcontinental Treaty of 1819, the Texas War of 1836 and the subsequent annexation of Texas in 1845, the Oregon Boundary Settlement of 1845, the U.S.-Mexican War of 1846–48, the Gadsden Purchase of 1853, and myriad conflicts with Native Americans, it became relatively easy for many Americans in the aftermath of the Civil War to believe that they had created the empire for liberty that Thomas Jefferson had envisaged stretching from the Atlantic to the Pacific. Although Euro-Americans and Indians continued to fight on the plains and in the southwestern borderlands, gradually the charged rhetoric of Manifest Destiny gave way to debate in policy-making circles over how to settle and develop western lands. It is to this era that Powell's survey work belongs, an era in which the push for national expansion gave way to conflict over what forms of settlement and development should have precedence in the West. Until their consolidation in 1879 under the newly instituted U.S. Geological Survey (henceforth USGS), teams led by Clarence King (Geological Survey of the Fortieth Parallel), Ferdinand V. Hayden (Geological and Geographical Survey of the Territories), Lieutenant George Wheeler (Geographical Surveys West of the Hundredth Meridian), and Powell conducted a variety of topographical, geological, and natural science studies, transforming the western environment and indigenous peoples through visions of utility and assimilation. With a certain amount of overlap in the field and in reports, an annual scramble for congressional appropriations, and a large degree of personal rivalry between team leaders, the surveys competed with one another for funding and institutional support. The USGS was instituted to make survey work more efficient in the field and more tightly regulated in Washington, D.C. Its founding was part of an era in which the motif of exploration and discovery gave way to the survey and quantification of natural resources.[3]

Powell's survey functioned in the larger context of expanding networks of communication and control established through the western territories and states after the Civil War. Classifying geographical terrain and explaining geological history prefaced the planned exploitation of natural resources in the West. This taxonomy of place extended to local Indian tribes. In 1873, when Powell wrote a report on the Numic-speaking Indians of the Great Basin, he stated that the implementation of a more effective reservation system was contingent upon review of ethnological data collected in the field. The appropriation of landscape and Native peoples continued when Powell used his own ethnological studies of southwestern Indians as material for universalizing statements about the development of humankind when he was head of the Bureau of American Ethnology.[4]

But this is not the whole story. Powell recognized that he was not only an observer of lands and people that would change irrevocably over the ensuing decades, but also an agent of social, economic, and environmental change in the Southwest. This self-consciousness adds an ethical dimension that is apparent in much of his writing on the region. Powell commanded Americans to think about the consequences of their actions as they took possession of the West as a whole. In his view they had a responsibility to use natural resources wisely, to show respect to Native Americans and to deal with them fairly (albeit firmly), and to work cooperatively to build communities and share resources rather than to look out only for their own selfish interests. Doubtless Powell's moral vision was paternalist and even elitist, but it was also based, as we shall see, on a commanding knowledge of the region.

"The Book Is Open and I Can Read as I Run": The Exploration of the Colorado River

When Powell embarked on his journey on May 24, 1869, his immediate goal was to voyage down the Green River to its confluence with the Grand River, and from there travel along the Colorado River into the 238-mile-long Grand Canyon. Whatever his greater hopes at this time, Powell did not gain authorization by Congress to create an official survey team until after the completion of the Colorado River journey. That happened on July 12, 1870, when the Geographical and Geological Survey of the Rocky Mountain Region was instituted and Congress voted an appropriation of $10,000 for continued exploration and survey work in the Rocky Mountain region. In the meantime, Powell's exploration and research were supported through an assortment of funds from the Illinois State Natural History Society, the trustees of both Illinois State Normal University (where Powell was a professor of geology at the time) and Illinois Industrial University, the Chicago Academy of Sciences, personal friends, and Powell's own savings. Railroads supplied free travel for the team members and equipment, while Congress permitted the drawing of rations and some supplies from army posts. Lastly, the Smithsonian Institution provided the team with a number of scientific instruments.[5] These details not only tell us that the party was funded in a somewhat piecemeal fashion, but also that to a large degree Powell needed to make the expedition in order to legitimize his claim for future scientific funding. Successful passage through the Grand Canyon, then, was potentially Powell's ticket to greater respect as a scientist, and publicity garnered through the intrepid river journey could only help Powell's wider reputation, as long as he avoided disaster and even death in the process.

His team in 1869 was made up of Jack C. Sumner, a Civil War veteran and Rocky Mountain hunter and guide; William H. Dunn, "a hunter, trapper, and mule-packer in Colorado for many years"; Captain Walter H. Powell, Powell's cousin, a "silent, moody, and sarcastic" man in the aftermath of his imprisonment by the Confederacy during the Civil War, but also one "whose coolness never deserts him"; George Y. Bradley, an army officer who had been discharged at short notice in order to join the exploration team; O. G. Howland, "a printer by trade, an editor by profession, and a hunter by choice," and his brother Seneca Howland, "a quiet, pensive young man, and a great favorite with all"; Frank Goodman, an English adventurer; Billy Hawkins, employed as cook, another Civil War veteran who had gone west to be a teamster and hunter; and Andrew Hall, a nineteen-year-old Scot who already had "experience in hunting, trapping and fighting Indians."[6] Their journey was adventurous and arduous. Often they had the laborious task of negotiating rapids by portaging boats (carrying empty boats and supplies around rapids), lining them (carrying supplies around rapids and letting the lightened boats down the rapids using ropes), or actually running rapids (a passage through rough waters that risked losing control of boats and causing destruction of equipment and supplies). A large amount of food supplies and some clothing and equipment were periodically lost overboard through rough passages, while at worst boats risked being wrecked. Late in the journey morale lowered and dissension grew to the point where three members of the team left the expedition in order to try climbing out of the canyon and heading overland toward white settlements. They were killed by a band of Southern Paiutes, apparently mistaken for some Euro-American miners who had recently abused and killed a Hualapai woman.[7]

In the first of five letters sent to the *Chicago Tribune* newspaper, Powell clarified the purpose of the expedition. With a bow to his institutional sponsors, Powell announced that he would be collecting geological, archaeological, and other specimens for the study of natural history. His language turned more grandiose when he stated:

> Not the least of the objects in view is to add a mite to the great sum of human knowledge. Science has its devotees in the laboratory; peering into the infinitesimal; on the observatory, keeping an outlook into the universe, and it has its laborers searching and exploring all over the earth for more facts, these characters in which the truth is written. Now if we can record a few more facts, and from them learn a lesson, we shall feel repaid for toil, privations and peril.

But Powell returned to a more familiar understated tone when describing that summer's work. During several months of geographical and geological study of the Colorado River valley, the team would navigate "the 'Grand Canyon' yet unexplored.[8]

While the resources of the team were relatively meager, Powell's aspirations were grand. Rhetorically the emphasis was on the greatness of science and the truths it afforded humanity, and the moral credit of Powell and his cohorts could only be boosted by their association with such a high ideal of public service. Even as Powell led his team down the river, the region that was home to numerous bands of Indians and in recent decades had been tracked by traders and mountain men was increasingly being encroached upon by cattle ranchers, miners, Mormon settlers, and other homesteaders. The question of how best to utilize natural resources, develop irrigation, and aid agriculture and industry in the West became a lifelong preoccupation for Powell. The exploration also provided opportunities to meet and study Native Americans. Just as Powell read the geological past through the naked rock forms of the canyonlands, so he sought to interpret the process of human evolution by examining the ruins of old cliff dwellings along the Colorado River and collecting linguistic data from local bands of Indians.

Powell gained a high public profile through completing the first Colorado River expedition. Published letters and news reports at the time of the journey, combined with lecturing and the publication of travel articles describing the team's activities, contributed greatly to Powell's popular appeal as an explorer-scientist. Each year he went before the House of Representatives Committee on Appropriations to bid for his survey's continued funding. In 1872 Joseph Henry, the secretary of the Smithsonian Institution, supported Powell's bid for congressional funding for his continued survey work by writing: "The importance of the exploration . . . is not confined to the advance of science, but is also associated with practical results of value, such as the discovery of coal, salt, the metals, and other resources of the country." He then noted: "From the specimens deposited in the Institution by Professor Powell, which include, besides those of mineralogy and geology, illustrations of the manners and customs of the people, as well as from maps and drawings which have been exhibited to us, it appears that the work has been well and economically done, and that it forms an important addition to our knowledge of the physical geography of our continent, yet so imperfectly known."[9] Powell found that for his scientific activity to be legitimized in the eyes of the government he had to prove himself as both a scientific expert and a popular communicator. While congressmen desired hard evidence that Powell's survey would yield valuable information about the potential for economic development in the lands he surveyed, they also responded favorably to the leitmotiv of exploration and discovery in his work. Powell explained that when he met the appropriations committee in 1874, its chair, James Garfield, "in a pleasant manner, insisted that the history of the exploration should be published by the government, and that I must understand that my scientific work would be continued by additional appropriations only upon my promise that I would publish an account of the exploration."[10] Thus the Powell Survey's survival was contingent on the publication of a narrative of the trip down the Colorado River. Powell had justified the lack of such a narrative of exploration by explaining that the scientific results of his expedition work in 1869 and a second trip in 1871–72 already had been published, or were being prepared for publication, and that "[t]he exploration was not made for adventure, but purely for scientific purposes, geographic and geologic, and I had no intention of writing an account of it, but only of recording the scientific results."[11] In actual fact Powell did write a narrative of the Colorado River journey for the popular magazine *Scribner's Monthly* that was published in several installments in 1874, and it was these articles he drew on to complete the *Report of Exploration*. Powell was well aware, both in the mid-1870s and twenty years later when he revised his popular account of exploration in his book *Canyons of the Colorado* (1895), that his more serious "scientific" work in geology and ethnology was in large part underpinned by the popular appeal of his early exploration and travel writing.

Powell's *Report of Exploration* consisted of a journal account of the 1869 trip down the Colorado River together with one section entitled "On the Physical Features of the Valley of the Colorado" and another section on zoology. While the report only recorded the first season of exploration, it actually drew heavily on information gathered from a second, fully accredited survey of the river in 1871–72—an expedition that was better planned and equipped, and consequently not as adventurous as the first pathfinding expedition. It was not until after the second voyage that Powell's more accurate measurements of the region were recorded. By that time he had also gathered together a more scientifically capable team of volunteers and paid employees. However, when Powell came to write up his experiences of travel, he combined the first and second river journeys for dramatic effect. This way he yoked together the motifs of conquest and scientific inquiry: the first voyage fulfilled an expansionist agenda of exploration of the continental interior, while the second voyage provided a more detailed scientific understanding of the region's topography, geology, and human history.

After completion of the first and second expeditions, Powell's thinking and writing were in a state of flux. What are we to make of the fact that the personal journal he wrote on the first Colorado River trip in 1869 served as the basis for not only the series of popular magazine articles published in *Scribner's Monthly* but also the report to Congress? Written several years prior to Powell's fully accredited status as head of both the USGS and BAE, these were hybrid texts, striving to be scientific while maintaining their capacity to entertain a general readership. For instance, the *Report of Exploration* employed vivid aesthetic imagery while also using the "concrete" language of scientific rationalism to describe the dynamic processes that had produced these landscapes.

Powell began the expedition knowing that many Americans were eager to learn the potential for development in the canyonlands. Could the Colorado River serve as a water route from the Rocky Mountain region to the Gulf of California? If so, should a railroad be built in close proximity to the river or even through its canyons? What mineral resources existed in the river's locale, how easily could they be developed, and what riches might they yield? Could the land the river ran through be used for farming? How might the river's waters transform the arid and semiarid regions of the West through irrigation? Although Powell did become very interested in how the arid lands might be developed for agriculture and ranching, he tended to be far more interested in studying the geography, geology, and climate of the Colorado Plateau than in searching for potential mineral riches. He had no personal interest in profiting financially from his travels, but he did sustain a sincere and rather grand vision of how the nation as a whole would benefit through exploration and survey.

Arguably just as exciting as the adventure story told in the report was the drama of articulating a language commensurate with the sheer vastness and plenitude of wonder within the land itself. Adventure, storytelling, and romance each had their place here. Powell's language in the report was largely constituted through the constant tension between awestruck wonder at the landscape passed through and the desire to rationalize and make sense of that landscape. The present tense of the day-by-day account brought immediacy to the narrative. The voyage down the Colorado involved not only the negotiation of rapids, submerged rocks, and treacherous currents, but also the mediating of expectation and outcome. Put another way, out of the dialectic of reading and running the river emerged an invigorated prose style that responded to the textures and contours of a land Powell considered "so strange." Thus Powell drew on a number of textual forms to bring the landscapes of the Colorado River and the surrounding plateau region into the national consciousness. While Powell's journal of the expedition, written in his own form of shorthand, was not particularly expressive, letters sent from the earlier stages of the voyage to the *Chicago Tribune* were rich in detail and written in the present tense continuous to lend an ongoing account of the journey.

To illustrate how Powell's writing in the field found its way into the 1875 report, I shall quote a journal entry and geological notes for the same day, comparing each with the enlarged account published in the *Report of*

Exploration. By juxtaposing these separate accounts it becomes apparent how Powell drew from his earlier writing and then embellished original observations in composing the later "official" record of the expedition. In his journal entry for August 25, 1869, Powell made unusually lengthy comments when describing a long, thirty-five-mile stretch of river, which was completed only days before the party concluded its journey through the Grand Canyon. Powell was particularly impressed by a lava monument and lava falls, both signs of volcanic upheaval and subsequent erosion by the river. For several miles along the canyon there were many signs of the lava, above and below the water level. He wrote: "Great patches of rock [lava] were seen on both sides along the walls, sometimes as a thin lining, sometimes filling up old amphitheaters and alcoves . . . Much of it was columnar in structure which was best seen looking at a mass. These columns were seen to start from concentric points and shoot out until they met."[12] Powell used such language as a base point from which to start describing the evolution of the landscape he had just passed through. Compared to the bulk of other entries in his journal, which often amounted to only a couple of lines, this was a lengthy report on the day. The entry was characterized by the use of foreshortened prose and the abbreviated record of thoughts that Powell enlarged upon later. Notable is the relatively small amount of interpretation in the journal entry, which was mostly given over to description.

Turning to Powell's geological notes, which were kept separately from the journal, we find only a rough preparatory sketch for the more fulsome account that was to come later:

> At noon Camp on the 25th we came to a bed of igneous rock that had at some time dammed the river. I estimated that it was 1500 ft. high. Could not see back. Might be higher. Have some specs.
>
> Lower members of carboniferous up to this point along the water slowly coming up today as they went down yesterday. Still through lower members of carboniferous granite. Reappeared about 5 miles above Camp on the 25th. See journal for description of lava.[13]

In this instance we see through the description of the lava how the journal entries and geological notes criss-cross, so that information from the latter is found in the former. This traversing of "personal" and "scientific" observations was essential to the recording of progress down the Colorado. When Powell drew on these two texts in his articles for *Scribner's Monthly* and his report to Congress, his subsequent writing was far more expansive. Of course he was now writing for an audience and not merely for himself. He combined detailed landscape description with a rich geological imagination and interpretive history to provide an educational account of how a particular part of the canyonlands had been created while also conveying the excitement of a day spent successfully running challenging rapids.

Powell began the entry by describing the lava encountered twelve miles into the day's journey. He envisaged a great volcano from which had run vast floods of lava that had filled the canyon to a height of twelve hundred or fifteen hundred feet. The river, held back by the great lava dam, had subsequently cut new channels, leaving much of the hard lava in place at the sides of the canyon. Powell did not make a final interpretation as to this part of the canyon's precise geological history; instead he allowed conjecture to be part of his narrative. This way the reader could be drawn into imagining the dynamic process of forming a striking natural landscape. Powell ended the entry with some flair by describing the point when volcanic lava and river met: "What a conflict of water and fire there must have been here! Just imagine a river of molten rock running down into a river of melted snow. What a seething and boiling of the waters; what clouds of steam rolled into the heavens!" And then he added: "Thirty-five miles to-day. Hurrah!"[14]

In characterizing the imagery Powell used to put the landscape of the Colorado River into play, the literary critic David Wyatt's notion of spectatorship and abandonment is useful for understanding a tension found throughout the *Report of Exploration,* namely the tension between disengaged observation of place and process and engaged participation in the scene viewed. In a discussion of the expedition reports John C. Fremont made for the Army Corps of Topographical Engineers in the 1840s, Wyatt claims that Fremont fell into a self-consciousness that confused the lines between spectatorship and abandonment: "The figure they render up is a man looking at himself at the center of a map of his own making." For Wyatt such self-consciousness marks the end of a "liberating dialectic between spectatorship and abandonment." The imposition of an "imperial self" onto landscape meant that Fremont "fell out of an imaginative and into a political relationship with landscape."[15]

Whether an imaginative relationship to landscape was ever dissoci-
ated from a political relationship in Fremont's travels and writings is
perhaps questionable, but Wyatt's ideas are useful for understanding
Powell's *Report of Exploration* as a document that itself explored the space
between first contact and imperial design. As an example of how the narrative of exploration constantly moved between spectatorship and abandonment, one has only to think of Powell's almost daily attempts to reach
a height sufficient for an overview of territory ahead. On a practical level
such climbs were made in order to take barometric measurements and to
anticipate the lay of the land ahead. However the prose used to describe
these ascents invariably lightened with the journey upward. At such
moments a greater perspective was afforded through overview, and often
the bigness of the sky, instead of the narrowed view from the river, was
emphasized in descriptive passages.

Powell's entry for June 24, 1869, recorded a climb made by team member Bradley and himself to the summit of a mountain ridge some three
thousand feet above camp. The view from Mount Hawkins to the gorge
below, which the two men named Split Mountain Canyon, was described
in the *Report of Exploration* through detailed prose that displays a variety
of aesthetic touches. He wrote:

> We are standing 3,000 feet above the waters, which are troubled
> with billows and are white with foam. The walls are set with
> crags and peaks and buttressed towers and overhanging domes.
> Turning to the right, the park is below us, its island groves
> reflected by the deep, quiet waters. Rich meadows stretch out
> on either hand to the verge of a sloping plain that comes down
> from the distant mountains. These plains are of almost naked
> rock, in strange contrast to the meadows,—blue and lilac col-
> ored rocks, buff and pink, vermilion and brown, and all these
> colors clear and bright. A dozen little creeks, dry the greater
> part of the year, run down through the half circle of exposed
> formations, radiating from the island center to the rim of the
> basin. Each creek has its system of laterals, and again these are
> divided; so that this outstretched slope of rock is elaborately
> embossed. Beds of different-colored formations run in parallel
> bands on either side. The perspective, modified by the undula-
> tions, gives the bands a waved appearance, and the high colors

gleam in the midday sun with the luster of satin. We are tempted to call this Rainbow Park. Away beyond these beds are the Uinta and Wasatch mountains with their pine forests and snow fields and naked peaks. Now we turn to the right and look up Whirlpool Canyon, a deep gorge with a river at the bottom—a gloomy chasm, where mad waves roar; but at this distance and altitude the river is but a rippling brook, and the chasm a narrow cleft. The top of the mountain on which we stand is a broad, grassy table, and a herd of deer are feeding in the distance. Walking over to southeast, we look down into the valley of White River, and beyond that see the far-distant Rocky Mountains, in mellow, perspective haze, through which snow fields shine.[16]

This is measured writing with a premium put on detailed observation. Quick-witted but not hurried, the panoramic eye of the observer took in the view even as the view was constructed in almost photographic detail. Much of Powell's prose is marked by a similar concision and controlled use of descriptive metaphor. The very visuality of the Colorado Plateau region could not, according to Powell, be described adequately in mere words. Yet here, and in numerous other passages, Powell did achieve a sustained and highly charged visual language that was characterized by a calm, authorial self-assurance and measured pedagogy. In these instances clarity of prose, resistance to hyperbole, and a poised but not complacent sense of self inhabit the narrative.

Another passage, which concluded the chapter "From Flaming Gorge to the Gate of the Lodore," affords a further sense of how Powell interwove romantic aesthetics, a precise attention to descriptive detail, and a measure of anticipation to create a suspenseful narrative. These words foreshadow the loss two days later of the *No Name*, one of the four boats taken down the river. As an apt portent of the disaster that was to occur, the passage from the *Report of Exploration* put into writing what might be called the metaphysics of expectation:

When we return to camp at noon the sun shines in splendor on vermilion walls, shaded into green and gray where the rocks are lichened over; the river fills the channel from wall to wall, and the canyon opens, like a beautiful portal, to a region of glory. This

evening as I write, the sun is going down and the shadows are settling in the canyon. The vermilion gleams and roseate hues,
blending with the green and gray tints, are slowly changing to
somber brown above, and black shadows are creeping over them
below; and now it is a dark portal to a region of gloom—the
gateway through which we are to enter on our voyage of exploration tomorrow. What shall we find?[17]

The paragraph begins with bright noontime sunshine and ends with an
ominous image of darkness and gloom. The shift in emphasis is not only
from light to darkness, but from openness to closure and from wonder
to worry. All of Powell's exploration narrative takes place between these
poles, and his writing, like the journey itself, was constructed so as to
negotiate a course that is never predetermined. In this sense there is a
poetic quality to the narrative as it mediates uncertainty, expectation,
chance, hope, myth, fact, superstition, surety, anticipation, fulfillment,
result, and process. When consumed as the day-to-day progression of
the team downriver, the narrative does not appear to readers to have
been written retrospectively; instead it reads almost as a spontaneous
commentary freshly relayed from the scene as events unfold. Through
cultivating the anticipatory mode of perception and lending a measure
of page-turning suspense to the narrative, Powell endeavored to
dramatize entering the unknown through "a dark portal to a region of
gloom." That the account can be read so as to largely conceal its own
textual inventiveness is, of course, testimony to Powell's abilities as a literary writer.

Complementing the use of suspense was Powell's subtle, painterly
touch in the composition of literary landscapes. The play of light on the
canyon's steep vermilion walls, in the above passage, revealed more than
just color, texture, and flora. In addition, noontime light enabled clearsightedness and rational meditation on what lay ahead. At such points the
indices of Powell's descriptive prose are to be found in his geological picturing and explanation, in his dynamic descriptions of a water-sculptured
landscape, in his yoking together "the glamour and witchery of light and
shade" in the same sentence, in his appeal to architectural form in describing rock formations, and in his recourse to explaining the uniqueness of
the canyonlands terrain through contrast with the "verdure-clad hills" of
the eastern United States.[18]

In considering the language of the *Report of Exploration,* we must recognize the dual legacy today's readers inherit from the text. On the one hand, the narrative can be regarded, together with the writings of Henry David Thoreau and John Muir, as one of the key texts of nineteenth-century American nature writing. Powell's exploration took him into a geological wonderland where the nakedness of rocks allowed him to read the earth's natural history as an open book, and he used a combination of aesthetic imagery and scientific rationalism to express the singularity of the canyonlands. On the other hand, even at its most romantic Powell's writing in the *Report of Exploration* carried with it an appropriative edge, and as with so many literary romances it anticipated the demise of what it represented, in this case the wild Colorado.

During the years in which the Geographical and Geological Survey of the Rocky Mountain Region operated, Powell made repeat visits to Washington, D.C. Respect for his work as a scientist followed his celebrity as an explorer, and he grew steadily more influential through the 1870s. His culminating act as a scientist active in the western field was to consider the ways in which the arid lands of the West should be incorporated into the nation. Marked by clearsightedness and a corresponding clarity of prose, Powell's *Report on the Lands of the Arid Region of the United States* (1878) attempted to dismantle prevailing beliefs about how the public domain should be settled in the arid and semiarid regions of the far West. Essentially Powell made an environmental argument in which he advocated settlement of land in terms of the forms of activity it could reasonably be assumed to sustain; thus geography and climate needed thorough study before land could be utilized efficiently. In the ensuing political debate Powell's recommendations were attacked in the main by congressmen and territorial representatives from the West, and were largely ignored in legislation on the settlement of public lands. The balance of power in legislative circles was not in favor of a land policy based on careful planning, equal distribution of resources, and cooperative endeavor.[19]

By the end of the 1870s, Powell had completed his fieldwork in the West and begun his climb to a point of considerable influence in government bureaucracy. He held the position of director of the BAE from its inception in 1879 until his death in 1902, while the USGS was only two years old when in 1881 he succeeded Clarence King's short-lived tenure as director. Powell resigned from this post in 1895. As director of the USGS he aimed to survey thoroughly the natural resources of lands throughout the country, and to use this information in advocating environmentally informed development policies. Simultaneously, as head of the BAE, he practiced the systematic study of North American Indian cultures. Representative of a historical period in which civilian agency largely took over from military authority in both mapping the country and conducting Indian affairs, Powell sought to consolidate knowledge derived from the field by influencing suitable federal policy decisions and sensitizing the public at large to the problem of how to develop the nation's natural resources. The decade Powell spent visiting the Colorado Plateau was a period in which the lines of modern academic disciplines were established, new bureaucratic procedures were put into action in policy-making circles, and professionalism began to take on a dominant cultural currency in the United States.[20] It is now time to take a closer look at how Powell wrote about the indigenous people of the Colorado Plateau and to consider how this writing contributed to his thinking about the states of "savagism" and "civilization."

Expunged and Embodied: Powell among the Hopis and the Numic-Speaking People of the Great Basin

During the years Powell traveled to the Colorado Plateau, scientific research and government bureaucracy started to become professionalized. Simply put, Powell's activities in the far West were underpinned by his activity in Washington, D.C., which in the latter part of the nineteenth century became the locus of the American scientific community. It was through the coalescence of expert opinion, academic specialization, and institutional ties, and in the midst of the development and consolidation of a series of inceptive professional communities, that Powell's reputation and authority grew. The historian Curtis M. Hinsley Jr. notes that in his tenure as head of the BAE, Powell drew on two older anthropological traditions that at once pointed toward professionalized science and barred its fulfillment. From the natural history exploring tradition, of which the four western surveys of the late 1860s and 1870s were the culmination, Powell drew his emphasis on discovery and description. Careful organization and systematic research procedures were required, along with specialized individuals to develop and test hypotheses. The emphasis was upon both the individual for initiative and a supporting structure to back up research; however, in the midst of building the resources needed to support advanced work, more efficient bureaucratic practices were developed that threatened the autonomy of the individual. From the broader realm of eighteenth- and nineteenth-century moral philosophy, via the influence of Lewis Henry Morgan, Powell made it the role of the cultural philosopher to span disciplines and synthesize diverse information in order to make moral judgments on society and human evolution. As Hinsley puts it:

> In contrast to the believer in the natural-science survey, the conjectural historian sought an all-embracing account of man's mental, social, and moral evolution based on comparative observations and organized in various series of stages. Where the naturalist/explorer emphasized descriptive taxonomy and (some of them) regional holism, the goal of the comparative method was boundless, overarching synthesis—universal laws of human development.[21]

Bearing in mind these formative influences on Powell's own ethnological studies and his directorship of the BAE, how should we view his writing about Native Americans in the first half of the 1870s, before he became based in Washington, D.C.?

The remainder of this chapter will investigate the space between Powell's popular narratives of travel and his more "serious" reportage by juxtaposing a travel article, "The Ancient Province of Tusayan," published in *Scribner's Monthly* in 1875, and a report to the Commissioner of Indian Affairs on the Numic-speaking Indians of the Great Basin region made by Powell in collaboration with George W. Ingalls in 1874. Chronologically close and thematically related, the two pieces diverge in their modes of address, assumption of authority, and expected readership. "The Ancient Province of Tusayan" was a travel article specifically tailored for a popular readership in the East, while the report was an officially sponsored document addressed to the administrators of Indian Affairs and members of Congress. Although the texts differ in their subject matter, purpose, and manner of audience address, they do share a thorough grounding in the practice of an emergent ethnography. Both pieces proceeded through the *bodying* of inquiry and knowledge formulation. The travel article featured all manner of commentary, adventure and early ethnographic discourse existing side by side. Meanwhile the report recorded the very process of substantiating information on the seminomadic tribes of the region—here Powell sought to contain textually the Numic-speaking peoples of the Great Basin region.

Published in the December 1875 edition of *Scribner's Monthly*, "The Ancient Province of Tusayan" described first the survey of a supply route from Kanab, Utah, to the Colorado River at the mouth of the Paria River and then a journey to the Hopi mesas in northern Arizona.[22] Powell visited the Hopi mesas with Jacob Hamblin, the so-called Buckskin Apostle, who acted as guide and advisor to Powell's team in the vicinity of the Colorado River, and as Mormon missionary and peacemaker to local tribes of Indians. Covering the late summer and fall of 1870, the events recorded in the article took place between Powell's first trip down the Colorado in 1869 and the second, more organized and "scientific" survey of the Green and Colorado Rivers made in 1871–72. The article makes for fascinating reading today precisely because of Powell's open enthusiasm and the diversity of his commentary. In the space of twenty pages, many of them partly taken over by illustrations, Powell moved across great stretches of cultural and geographical terrain. What the article lacks in methodological rigor it gains in energy and eclecticism: from the often barren canyonlands north of the Colorado to the glowing Vermilion Cliffs, from informal census-taking to tasting "Virgin hash" (prepared through mastication), from observing Oraibi's domestic arrangements to dressing down to nakedness in order to take part in a sacred ceremony, Powell's writing derived from spirited viewing and the pleasure of reconstructing the scene for the purpose of reportage.

The article began with a brief allusion to Powell's previous travels in the Colorado Province, written up in earlier numbers of *Scribner's Monthly*, and quickly moved on to describe the Kanab River and its canyons and the curiousness of its intermittently wet and dry course. Journeying up the river, Powell and his team came upon a small Mormon settlement named after the river, which gave him an opportunity to air his enthusiasm for the Mormons' communal farming practices. After a few paragraphs of discussion, Powell stated: "Altogether, a Mormon town is a strange mixture of Oriental philosophy and morals, primitive superstitions and modern inventions."[23] Only a few years after Mark Twain had lampooned the *Book of Mormon* in *Roughing It,* Powell enthusiastically observed how Mormons had adapted their practice of agriculture to the arid environment.[24]

While waiting to rendezvous with another section of his team, Powell busied himself with learning the Southern Paiute language, watching the Kaibabit men and women hunt and gather during the day, and observing a "feverish" dance at night. Imagination alive on all fronts, Powell conveyed a vivid impression of his party's journey across "a desert, but a painted desert; not a desert plain, but a desert of hills, and cliffs, and rocks—a region of alcove lands."[25] Powell employed the familiar language of the picturesque aesthetic to bring to life southwestern landscapes. For example, he used the motif of landscape as architecture to launch into a highly charged description of cliff walls near the meeting point of the Little Colorado River and the Moencopi, a small stream:

> These cliffs are rocks of bright colors, golden, vermilion, purple and azure hues, and so stormcarved as to imitate Gothic and Grecian architecture on a vast scale. Outlying buttes were castles, with minaret and spire; the cliffs, on either side, were cities looking down into the valley, with castles standing between; the inhabitants of these cities and castles are a million lizards: great red and black lizards, the kings and nobles; little gray lizards, the common people, and here and there a priestly rattlesnake.[26]

Halfway through the article, Powell described reaching Oraibi on Third Mesa, one of the seven Hopi villages. He arrived with a group of "white men, Kai-bab-its, Navajos, and Shi-nu-mos," an intercultural group that appeared to have suspended any mutual animosities in order to communicate across linguistic barriers. Powell then stated: "We remained nearly two months in the province, studying the language and customs of the people; and I shall drop the narrative of travel, to describe the towns, the people, and their daily life."[27] Here the emphasis in Powell's writing moved from the record of travel to ethnography, and while what follows cannot be called ethnographic thick description, it did, nevertheless, pay close attention to key aspects of Hopi life. Geographical placement, town architecture, domestic economy, agriculture, food, play, arts, clothing, religious rituals, and belief systems were all given a quick run-through in order to round out the picture of life in Oraibi. While value judgments are apparent—"[t]he exterior of the house is very irregular and unsightly, and the streets and courts are filthy; but within, great cleanliness is observed"—for the most part Powell appears open-minded in his account of local practices.[28]

As early as 1803, when Thomas Jefferson instructed Meriwether Lewis to bring back information about the indigenous peoples beyond the Mississippi, there was an ethnological element to government-sponsored exploration of the continental land mass. In addition, frontier journals, Indian biographies, linguistic studies, records of customs and tribal lore, archaeology, and amateur historical societies all contributed to quasi-official and popular discourses on Indians in the nineteenth century. In conducting work with his survey team in the Colorado Plateau prior to the BAE's founding, Powell followed the instruction of Joseph Henry, secretary of the Smithsonian Institution, to avail himself of every opportunity to study local Indians in his exploration of the Colorado Plateau. From 1868 on, Powell made linguistic records of the Indians he met in the region.[29] All the four western surveys, with the exception of King's, studied tribes encountered in the field, although none other with the enthusiasm of Powell. In 1870, when the trip to the Hopi mesas took place, Powell had only just begun to study Indians formally. Over the next decade, he created many vocabularies, grammars, records of oral tradition and cosmology, censuses, and collections of material goods. While he failed to complete a formal treatise on the Numic-speaking peoples, experience in the field was an integral part of his larger anthropological thinking. As we will see, Powell's earlier opportunistic approach to ethnography fed his later, totalizing summaries of social evolution.[30]

At one point of the journey described in "The Ancient Province of Tusayan," Powell met a party of Kaibabit Indians. This encounter provided an immediate opportunity to conduct research:

> During the evening I was very much interested in obtaining from them a census of their tribe. They divided the arithmetic into parts, each of four men taking a certain number of families. Each sat down and counted on his fingers and toes the persons belonging to the families allotted to him, going over them again and again until each finger and toe stood in his mind for an individual. Then he would discuss the matter with other Indians, to see that all were enumerated, something like this:

"Did you count Jack?" "Yes; that finger stands for Jack." "Did you count Nancy?" "Yes; that toe is Nancy." Each of the census takers becoming satisfied that he had correctly enumerated his portion, he procured the number of sticks necessary to represent them, and gave them to me. Adding the four together, I had the census of the tribe—seventy-three. Then I set them to dividing them severally into groups of men, women and children, but this I found a hard task. They could never agree among themselves whether certain persons should be called children or not; but, at last, I succeeded in obtaining the number of males and females.[31]

A personable man, willing to sit and squat with Indians on equal terms, Powell appears to have been viewed favorably by the Kaibabit, a tribe with whom he freely fraternized. The informal census that Powell made proved a little confusing to Indians not used to quantifying their number according to the white man's logic. Powell's own act of near "literal" translation—the Jack and Nancy exchange—comes across to the modern reader with a certain comedy that Powell himself probably did not intend.

"The Ancient Province of Tusayan" reveals much about Powell's response to the Indians of the Colorado Plateau. Written for a popular audience, Powell's prose is characteristically concise and conveys a vivid sense of time and place. The article lies at the juncture of aesthetic and scientific discourses. As a travel narrative, the piece rendered the operations of exploration and survey as a journey into the heart of foreign territory populated by native inhabitants seen as different from Powell's own ethnicity. Placed between popular and scientific discourses, the article enacted the transitional phase from amateur to government-sponsored knowledge gathering and dissemination; overall it embraced the beginnings of official ethnology for which Powell would gain greater authority through his directorship of the BAE. The travelogue amounted to another form of mapping the region—not as formal in either intent or procedure as the ethnographic document, but certainly a participating factor in the overarching operation of rationalizing cultural and geographical knowledge about the peoples and landscapes of the Colorado Plateau.

From a contemporary perspective we can see how Powell represented a multicultural experience at a point prior to the more intrusive forms of white settlement and the intense scrutiny of Indians by tourists starting at the beginning of the twentieth century. All the same Powell found it hard to view rituals. Only after a council among Hopis at Oraibi was Powell allowed into a kiva to view a ritual for Muingwa, the god of rain, which took place immediately after the harvest. He accompanied priests from Oraibi, Shipualovi, Shongpavi, and Mishongnovi into the kiva, where they were joined by three generations of women, a grandmother, daughter, and grandchild. Powell wrote:

> The men were entirely naked, except that during certain parts of the ceremony they wrapped themselves in blankets, and a blanket was furnished me at such times for the same purpose. The three women were naked, except that each had a cincture made of pure white cotton wound about the loins and decorated with tassels. Event followed event, ceremony ceremony so rapidly during the twenty-four hours, that I was not able on coming out to write a very definite account of the sacred rites, but I managed to carry away with me some things which I was afterward able to record in my notes from time to time.[32]

It is important to note how interactive the occasion was; for Powell to observe he had to be incorporated into the ceremony. In this instance Powell could not be a dispassionate observer, but had to participate in events to a certain extent. Shorn of clothes and divested of notebook and pencil, he strove to memorize his experience later. However, in the aftermath of the ceremony he admitted to profound gaps in understanding: "My knowledge of the language was slight, and I was able to comprehend but little of what was said; but I think I obtained, by questioning and close observation, and gathering a few words here and there, some general idea of what they were doing."[33] At such points, we find the beginnings of participant observer ethnography, which, as the anthropologist James Clifford notes, relies for much of its interpretive procedures on the visualizing capacity of the observer—"culture was construed as an ensemble of characteristic behaviors, ceremonies, and gestures susceptible to recording and explanation by a trained onlooker."[34] At this point, though, Powell was only in the early stages of his ethnological studies, which were always carried out in piecemeal fashion, and, not surprisingly, "The Ancient Province of Tusayan" found him striving to articulate an integrated portrait of Hopi life in a speculative rather than systematic fashion.

The experience recorded in the article, then, was anything but reified. At a point prior to more prolonged research into Hopi culture by early ethnographers such as Alexander M. Stephen and Jesse Walter Fewkes, Powell's account of a relatively short amount of time spent among the Indians of the Hopi mesas foregrounded the discursive situation through which he gained information on tribal culture.[35] To what extent was he author of his own experience here? How reliable an observer was he? Did his informants tell him the truth about the order of the proceedings he observed and reformulated on the printed page? Could the resulting text contain the very Indian voices it articulated? Here I wish to emphasize the openness of his initial response to Hopi culture, an openness that, curiously enough, was diluted in a revised version of the same visit.

In 1895, the year Powell resigned as head of the USGS, he published a popular book-length edition of his trips down the Colorado River for the first time. Contained in the four hundred pages of *Canyons of the Colorado* is a short chapter titled "Over the River," a rewritten version of "The Ancient Province of Tusayan." The book is suffused with drawings, engravings and photographs collected in the field. Bountiful and eclectic, the collection of these objects and their translation into visual images motivated and sustained the work of Powell and his many associates in the ethnological field, institutional laboratories, university lecture halls, and debating rooms of scientific clubs. Now the images had been removed from an archival context in the annals of the BAE and put into Powell's popular volume.

In the revised chapter Powell describes the very process by which the reproduced objects (pottery, fetishes, implements, basketry, dance paraphernalia, trays, and ceremonial headdresses) came into his possession to begin with. Their reproduction appeared to substantiate the proprietary right of Powell to either own or have archival access to them. Powell's collection of "arts" thus had gone through an elaborate process of purchase, inventory, shipping, archival categorization, and institutional display that decontextualized from their cultural context the very objects that came to populate the pages of the narrative. Objects were reassembled as images on the printed page via processes of mechanized reproduction. In the process of this transformation the process of representation came full circle as what had been taken away in one context was put "back" with methodical care and considerable ingenuity in another context.

Although a large part of the 1895 chapter either replicated or was very close to the first version of Powell's trip to the Hopi mesas, there were some noticeable changes to the later piece. To linger over some of the revisions made is to gain a sense of how Powell's thinking about tribal cultures evolved in the twenty years between publication of the two texts. For example, in the revised account of entering Oraibi, Powell wrote:

> This is my first view of an inhabited pueblo, though I have seen many ruins from time to time. At first I am a little disappointed in the people. They seem scarcely superior to the Shoshones and Utes, tribes with whom I am so well acquainted. Their dress is less picturesque, and the men have an ugly fashion of banging their hair in front so that it comes down to their eyes and conceals their foreheads. But the women are more neatly dressed and arrange their hair in picturesque coils.[36]

Powell continued by giving a factual description of Oraibi's geographical setting and physical layout. Notably his writing proceeded by virtue of cultural translation. The woman who baked bread for the collective meal became a "good housewife" (rather than a "good woman" as in the earlier piece), while the bread itself became a "work of art." Innocuous as these comparisons may seem at first glance, the changes in the later text demonstrate a greater tendency toward ethnocentrism. Elsewhere, the lightly intoned observation of children at play in the 1875 piece—"it is a merry sight to see a score or two of little naked children climbing up and down the stairways and ladders"—is transformed in the 1895 chapter to a much darker image as the children are likened to "herds of monkeys." There is no escaping the ideological coloring of the later remark, but how are we to account for it?

As we have seen, much ethnological fieldwork in the late nineteenth century pivoted about the tension between impartial observation and subjective sympathy (or antipathy) that close proximity to the objects of inquiry necessarily involved. As head of the BAE, Powell was wary of his workers' losing their scientific detachment from the tribes they were studying and falling prey to emotional attachment. Hinsley explains Powell's capacity, especially in his later years, seemingly to renege on his less judgmental pronouncements on the virtues and vices of savagism by insisting that a form of high morality always lay at the heart of Powell's and the BAE's work: "the underlying moral and political question of BAE anthropology was the justice of the Indian's fate."[37] Thus wide-ranging questions of education, progress, and the quality of civilization that invariably underlay the work of the BAE had to be asserted at the end of the day. Hinsley writes:

> Ill-equipped or unwilling to face the realities of growth, power, and destruction in their own society, Powell and his followers sought to rise above immediate experience by appeal to the categories of scientific understanding. In short, the insistence on the large vision, the "great truths," over immediacy and sentimental attachment was an appeal and escape from history to scientific abstraction.[38]

And so the larger, historicizing mission of the BAE becomes clear to readers today: to study diverse Indian cultures was simultaneously to specify advances made through the passage from savagism, through barbarism, to civilization. When too much sympathy came into the ethnographic equation there was a risk of the assumptions on which such inquiry rested being undermined. The virtues of objectivity, dispassionate observation, and the rigor of science had to be resolutely reasserted.

Comparing the endings of the two pieces reveals a similar functioning of ideological revision at work in the later chapter. The *Scribner's* article concludes with a speculative answer to Powell's own question: "Who are these people?" After discounting the proposition that the Hopi are the descendents "of some ancient invading race from the Eastern Continent," Powell resorts to linguistic evidence to support his thesis that they were related to regional nomadic tribes with whom they once made a "great family": "now, but a remnant of this branch is left; but there was a time when they were a vast people."[39] As far as he ever let himself slip into an elegiac tone he did it here when describing the myriad "vestiges of ancient life" to be found in the ruins dotted throughout Nevada, Utah, Colorado, New Mexico, and Arizona. Imaginatively fired to reconstruct the historical decline of the predecessors to contemporary Pueblo Indians, Powell the archaeologist of native cultures explained that intruding bands of Navajo and Apache Indians, prior to the advent of Spanish colonialism, destroyed "town after town, hamlet after hamlet," while in succeeding years the Spanish conquerors did the rest of the damage. Of sixty towns remaining at the time of the first invasion by the Spaniards, only thirty stood as Powell wrote; of the former inhabitants of these destroyed pueblos, he hypothesized that many had reverted to nomadism.

This narrative contrasts with "Over the River," in *Canyons of the Colorado,* which concludes with a description of an exchange of articles between Powell's party and Oraibi's inhabitants, a procedure described as having a happy mutuality to it. Although there is an airy quality to Powell's prose at this point, the emphasis on the material process of ethnographic collection at the end of the article reminds the reader of the more serious rationale behind the travel narrative. For Powell and his team to collect materials and send them back to Washington, D.C., was to transform tribal artifacts into cultural property. As soon as these artifacts left the possession of the Hopi they were claimed as part of the social evolutionary heritage of the United States.

We turn now to another kind of text through which Indians of the Colorado Plateau and the Great Basin were represented, namely an official report that was submitted to the Commissioner of Indian Affairs in 1874. Compared to Powell's account of his first visit to the Hopi villages, the *Report of Special Commissioners J. W. Powell and G. W. Ingalls on the Condition of the Ute Indians of Utah; the Paiutes of Utah, northern Arizona, southern Nevada, and southeastern California; the Northwestern Shoshones of Nevada; and Report Concerning Claims of Settlers in the Mo-a-pa Valley, Southeastern Nevada* is a somber document that records visits made to the Numic-speaking groups of the Great Basin region. Where the earlier trip was characterized by Powell's opportunism and signs of mutual accommodation between him and his Hopi hosts, his later trip was more overtly political. How, then, did ethnography, federal Indian policy, and moral philosophy intersect in the report?

Powell, as Special Commissioner of Indian Affairs, and George W. Ingalls, Agent for the Southern Paiutes, were together charged with the responsibility of reporting on the condition of the Numic-speaking people of the Great Basin region. The many bands of Northern Paiute, Southern Paiute, Chemehuevi, Northern Shoshone, Eastern Shoshone, Western Shoshone, Bannock, and Ute Indians were spread across a 420,000-square-mile area that included "the greater part of Idaho, nearly two-thirds of Oregon, nearly one-fourth of California, the entire

State of Nevada, and the Territory of Utah, one-fifth of Arizona, and one-sixth of Wyoming."[40] The report's census put their total population at 5,522. Yet even this surprisingly low number of people had come into repeated conflict with white settlers over the loss of traditional hunting and grazing lands. In their initial statement to Edward Smith, the Commissioner of Indian Affairs, Powell and Ingalls stated that a number of the tribes they had spoken with realized a viable livelihood could no longer be sustained through hunting, fishing, and gathering. Compelled to scatter over wider areas for subsistence, and in the process losing both the cohesiveness of the band and tribe, many of these people had become impoverished and destitute.

In order to stave off the prospect of further conflict between whites and Indians, and to offset the morally debilitating effects of prostitution and, it is implied, sexual abuse of Indian women by Anglo men, the commissioners asserted: "Nothing then remains but to remove them from the country, or let them stay in their present condition, to be finally extinguished by want, loathsome disease, and the dissent consequent upon incessant conflict with white men."[41] The argument hinged on a logic of inevitability, not only of moral and physical decline but also of cultural death. Through a form of neomissionary work, Indians had to be saved from themselves in the midst of their association with the worst elements of white society, and saved also from their own lack of discipline. The argument ran: because their tie to a nomadic life necessarily must be broken, and if left to prevail their existing livelihood is in a fragmented and utterly compromised manner, which can only lead to further degeneration and dissension between Indians and settlers, then removal and assimilation must be their future.

Having advocated a complete policy of removal in the initial stage of their commission of inquiry, Powell and Ingalls were told to follow up their initial statement with a thorough report on the condition and suitability of existing reservations, the legalistic status of current Indian treaties, and the classification of Numic speakers according to their linguistic traits. In compiling the information for the report, Powell and Ingalls, both separately and together, covered an enormous amount of ground through the summer and fall of 1873. Along the way, Powell added to his Indian vocabularies and employed his survey team photographer, Jack Hillers, to photograph the tribes visited. Many of these images were used later as the basis for engravings in Powell's travel writing. The primary purpose of the special commission was to enumerate and describe the social organization and condition of each tribe. Running throughout the report was a call for an end to nomadism: put a stop to their wandering, their parasitism and petty crime, through the development of self-sustaining agriculture and they would be converted "from vicious, dangerous savages to civilized people."[42]

Toward the end of their report, Powell and Ingalls stated:

> They are broken into many small tribes, and their homes so interspersed among the settlements of white men, that their power is entirely broken and no fear should be entertained of a general war with them. The time has passed when it was necessary to buy peace. It only remains to decide what should be done with them for the relief of the white people from their petty depredations, and from the demoralizing influences accompanying the presence of savages in civilized communities, and also for the best interests of the Indians themselves.[43]

The precondition of the provision of welfare was obvious: surrender and you will be provided for. The exact constituents of the Native Americans' "best interests" were outlined in an eight-point package of "suggestions concerning the management of reservations." Recommendations included strong inducements to work; provision of fabric rather than ready-made garments; the preparation of houses to replace tents; the supply of a cow to each family "to enable them to start in the accumulation of property"; outside expertise to help develop irrigated agriculture and teach how to become blacksmiths, carpenters, and saddle and harness makers; and "an efficient medical department" to offset the "bad" influence of the "medicine-man." Powell also called for the creation of schools to teach English, for "into their own language, there is woven so much mythology and sorcery that a new one is needed in order to aid them in advancing beyond their baneful superstitions; and the ideas and thoughts of civilized life cannot be communicated to them in their own tongues."[44]

It is with such statements that the bedrock beneath Powell's ethnographic investigations is revealed to modern readers. In terms of the regional Indian "problem," the report demonstrated a surefooted pragmatism in dealing with a highly charged clash between the Great Basin's residual population and incoming miners, ranchers, and settlers who, respectively, sought out the most promising claims for mineral speculation, grazing, and agriculture. For Powell, the choice involved in such situations was not between the respective rights of Indians and of white settlers to the land, but between destructive and constructive ways of removing Native Americans from their homelands. He explained his vision of what a reservation should be:

> The commission does not consider that a reservation should be looked upon in the light of a pen where a horde of savages are to be fed with flour and beef, to be supplied with blankets from the Government bounty, and to be furnished with paint and gew-gaws by the greed of traders, but that a reservation should be a school of industry and a home for these unfortunate people. In council with the Indians great care was taken not to implant in their minds the idea that the Government was willing to pay them for yielding lands which white men needed, and that as a recompense for such lands they would be furnished with clothing and food, and thus enabled to live in idleness. The question was presented to the Indian something in this light: The white men take these lands and use them, and from the earth secure to themselves food, clothing, and many other desirable things. Why should not the Indians do the same? The Government of the United States is anxious for you to try. If you will unite and agree to become farmers, it will secure you permanent titles to such lands as you need, and will give you the necessary assistance to begin such a life, expecting that you will soon be able to take care of yourselves, as do white men and civilized Indians.[45]

Within the civilization or extermination binarism that was so common in Anglo thinking at this time, Powell displayed some flexibility in demonstrating how tribes should be assigned to reservations by paying close attention to the linguistic and familial relationships of Numic-speaking Indians. For Powell, the future of federal policy toward the indigenous peoples of the continent at the point when "there is now no great uninhabited and unknown region to which the Indian can be sent" was dependent upon the systematic and scientific understanding of tribal cultures. He justified the expense of making reservations into "schools of industry" by contrasting the high costs of troop occupation of disputed territories and military solutions of unrest with the comparatively low costs of "feeding, clothing, and civilizing the Indians." He also reminded the reader that "[w]e beg leave again to mention that these remarks apply only to conquered tribes."[46]

Powell's appeal to economics was not only financial but moralistic, and the rationale behind his moral economy was made clear when he wrote of the Western Shoshone:

> The condition of these Indians does not differ materially from that of the Pai-Utes and Go-si Utes which have been heretofore mentioned, though it should be stated that the more southern tribes are in an exceedingly demoralized state: they prowl about the mining camps, begging and pilfering, the women prostituting themselves to the lust of the lower class of men. There are no Indians in all the territories visited by your commission, whose removal is so imperatively demanded by consideration of justice and humanity, as these Shoshones of Nevada.[47]

Not merely concerned with the question of savagism versus civilization, the report also alluded to, rather than grappled with, what was understood as the mutually degenerative aspects of interracial contact. Removal in such instances was justified in terms of saving Indians from both their own "worst" instincts and the base "lust of the lower class of men."

The report and his subsequent guidance of the BAE demonstrated that Powell's enlightened humanitarianism was of a thoroughly paternalistic sort, albeit run through with scientific rigor. For in building a body of statistically corroborated information about Native Americans, Powell in this report and in his later work confirmed that Indians would have to change their lives immeasurably if they were to survive in the modernizing nation. Through linguistic maps that traced the territories of absent Indians, institutional archives that built a huge corpus of intelligence as a means of salvaging their vanishing presence from the land, and museum displays that brought scientifically certified interpretations of tribal cultures into the general public's field of vision at public expositions such as the Chicago World's Fair of 1893 through a form of cultural taxidermy, Native Americans across the

United States were given corporeality even as they were expunged from the territories. Displacement, then, augured the incorporation of tribes into the greater body of the United States.

We must take care, though, not to judge Powell by standards more germane to our historical period than his. For despite making distinct value judgments about Native American cultures that may strike today's readers as ethnocentric and outmoded, Powell was one of the more enlightened thinkers of his day on the obligations of the United States toward Indians. Similar to the manner in which he campaigned for the quantification and planned use of natural resources in the West, so he implored his peers that concerted ethnological study was necessary for the implementation of an effective reservation system. Pragmatic solutions to the so-called Indian problem were underpinned by Powell's conviction that all humankind developed through the successive stages of savagism, barbarism, and civilization. Indians, he thought, would have to move through these stages of human development more quickly than Europeans had, but since they had enlightened Americans to teach them there was ample opportunity for Indians to learn civilized ways.

We turn now to a woman, Helen Hunt Jackson, who became one of the great campaigners for the reform of federal Indian policy in the late nineteenth century. Unlike Powell, she deliberately brought a great deal of romance and sentimentality to the Indian question.

CHAPTER THREE

Travel Writing, Sentimental Romance, and Indian Rights Advocacy: The Politics of Helen Hunt Jackson's *Ramona*

DISMISSED AS "SENTIMENTAL SLOP" by Raymond Chandler during the 1950s, Helen Hunt Jackson's novel *Ramona*, published in 1884 to dramatize the plight of Indians displaced from their southern California homelands, has long been criticized as a politically conservative portrayal of California society in the aftermath of the U.S.-Mexican War.[1] According to the logic of this argument, Jackson, through her representation of elite Californios living a threatened yet still idyllic pastoral existence in the state's southern counties, helped forge a vision of southern California that was used by Anglo boosterists to represent the region as the ideal home for a genteel, Mediterranean-style culture in the late nineteenth century. A key element of both Jackson's novel and the promotional rhetoric built about it was the mythologization of the Spanish colonial mission system through which thousands of California Indians had been pulled into the work regimes of twenty-one Franciscan missions set along the coast between San Diego and Sonoma. The historian Mike Davis contends that "[t]he mission literature depicted the history of race relations [between Californios and Indians] as a pastoral ritual of obedience and paternalism. . . . Any intimation of the brutality inherent in the forced labor system of the missions and haciendas . . . was suppressed."[2] Although such a view of interracial contact is broadly supported by recent scholarship, Davis's polemical stance regarding the "sunshine" rhetoric of Los Angeles boosterists—guilty of producing "a comprehensive fiction of Southern California as the promised land of a millenarian Anglo-Saxon racial odyssey"[3]—fails to account for the ways in which *Ramona* challenged Euro-American racism toward Indians in the late nineteenth century.[4] Indeed, while Jackson did celebrate the Franciscan missionary effort to incorporate Native Americans as citizens into Spanish colonial society, she also criticized sharply the federal government's removal and reservation policies from the 1830s on for keeping Indians separate from the general population of non-Indians and thus maintaining their marginal status on the fringes of American society. That George Wharton James considered *Ramona* in 1913 "a constant missionary, ever silently, but potently, preaching the beautiful doctrine of the humanity of *all* men, regardless of the color of their skin, and the *Universal Fatherhood of God*," indicates the way in which Jackson was appreciated in the years after her death in 1885 for having striven to break down reified notions of race and ethnicity by promoting a transcendent and nondenominational vision of benevolent Christianity working for the benefit of collective humanity.[5] Set alongside James's contention that the novel had "awakened public sentiment and public conscience on behalf of the Indians" and helped bring about "a decided change in the attitude of the better class of politicians towards these, their helpless wards," we find that the very novel disparaged by Chandler and dismissed by Davis was still viewed twenty years after its publication as a politically engaged social reform fiction.[6]

Reading *Ramona* today in a way that enables us to see at close hand how Jackson sought to write a novel that would represent to the American public at large both the particular misfortunes of California Indians and by implication the collective fate of Native Americans in the late nineteenth century helps counteract the critical prejudices toward the novel that I have just outlined. Simultaneously though, we must recognize that there has been good reason for critics since World War II to question Jackson's representation of "a picturesque life, with more of sentiment and gayety in it, more also that was truly dramatic, more romance, than will ever be seen again on those sunny shores," for to look back uncritically on such a romanticized vision of California life implicitly validates not only the social and economic inequalities on which elite California society was based before and immediately after the U.S.-Mexican War but also the social and economic inequalities that prevailed in late-nineteenth-century American society.[7] One of the earliest commentators to make this point was Carey McWilliams, who became an expert on southern California history and culture during the three decades he dwelled in the state. Between 1922 and 1951, when he moved east to work for and later edit *The Nation*, McWilliams "lived" the wide-ranging events he wrote about in his 1946 book *Southern California: An Island on the Land* through working for the *Los Angeles Times* newspaper, studying toward a degree in law at the

University of Southern California, specializing as a lawyer in civil liberties cases, becoming a prominent part of intellectual circles, and taking up the cause of the migratory field worker in his book *Factories in the Field* (1939).[8] He argued in *Southern California* that civic boosters of Los Angeles and southern California followed Jackson's lead in mythologizing the Spanish colonial mission system and sentimentalizing the figures of California señors and señoras by positioning them as leisured souls in an idyllic setting. The "Spanish fantasy heritage" not only suppressed any discontent Indians may have had about being colonized but also provided a retrospective myth of national and racial ascendancy whereby nineteenth-century Californios were said to have accepted that since their culture was on the wane it was inevitable that American energy and culture-building would prevail in California. McWilliams also noted that for Euro-Americans the then recently restored mission in Santa Barbara was "a much better" and "less embarrassing" "symbol of the past than the Mexican field worker or the ragamuffin *pachucos* of Los Angeles." McWilliams concluded *Southern California* by envisioning a potentially triumphant future in which Los Angeles would become "the most fantastic city in the world" and California would outgrow its "strident cultural nativism" to emerge a truly cosmopolitan state. Simultaneously he balanced his utopian investment in the dynamism, opportunism, and creativity of Californians in the immediate postwar period with the perception that Anglo racism toward Indians prevailed in renewed form in the mid twentieth century: "the brutal treatment of Indians in Southern California in large part explains the persistence of an ugly racial arrogance in the mores of the region of which, alas, more than a vestige remains."[9] This emphasis on a history of racial oppression in California—which McWilliams saw as including Euro-American racism toward Mexican Americans and immigrants from Latin America, China, Japan, and the Philippines as well as toward African Americans and Native Americans—helps explain why he considered *Ramona* largely ineffectual in persuading Anglos to revise the ways in which they regarded and even interacted with Indians: "nothing much came of Mrs. Jackson's work in Southern California, for the region accepted the charming Ramona, as a folk figure, but completely rejected the Indians still living in the area."[10] For him Polonia, a blind Indian who wore an old blanket and walked the streets of Los Angeles during the 1850s and 1860s, was a more apt symbol of the dispossession of California Indians than the main characters of Jackson's novel.[11]

Given this contestatory stance toward *Ramona*—a critical evaluation amplified by Davis in his influential cultural history of Los Angeles, *City of Quartz*—the reader might well ask what is to be gained by reevaluating a novel that has been demythologized for substantial reasons. I contend, though, that both McWilliams and Davis have been unduly hasty in dismissing Jackson's passionate stand against the dispossession of California Indians and, by implication, Native Americans in general during the nineteenth century. Rather than moving toward a firm conclusion about the success or failure of the novel in dramatizing the marginalization and victimhood of Indians, this critique frames the novel as a site of interpretation in which the possibilities of Indian reform and the position of Native Americans within U.S. society were debated. I trace the ways in which Jackson altered her rhetorical strategy to convey her campaigning to distinct yet overlapping audiences and seek to recognize the ways in which the novel both challenged and concurred with prevailing sentiments regarding the place of Indians in American culture during the late nineteenth century. It is precisely because *Ramona* dramatizes complex issues of race, ethnicity, gender, class, citizenship, and nationhood without reconciling them that the novel provides fascinating reading today. The discussion that ensues is divided into three main parts. First, I ask how did Jackson, as a nineteenth-century author and Indian rights activist, set about writing a novel that "would do for the Indian a thousandth part that *Uncle Tom's Cabin* did for the negro"?[12] Second, I discuss *Ramona* in detail and clarify how the novel carried within its own pages the possibility for readings that largely ignored its Indian reform initiative. Third, I investigate the legacy of the novel immediately after Jackson's death by discussing Constance Goddard DuBois's report to the Women's National Indian Association on the progress of missionary efforts among southern California Indians and almost thirty years after its publication by examining George Wharton James's *Through Ramona's Country*, a book through which James endeavored to authenticate the "real life" events on which *Ramona* was based and thus foreground again its Indian reform initiative. James's book provided an ironic recognition of Indians' cultural survival even as he employed stereotypical language to describe their "vanishing" lifeways. I contrast these Euro-American perspectives with the story told by Delfina Cuero, a Kumeyaay Indian, of how her people were displaced from their homes in San Diego around 1900 and found refuge south of the U.S.-Mexico border in Baja California around the time of World War I. Through writing her autobiography in collaboration with anthropologist Florence Shipek, Cuero strove to authenticate her claim for U.S. citizenship during the late 1960s while also providing a stark account of an indigenous people's marginalization and their attempts to continue hunting and gathering well into the twentieth century. In the chapter's conclusion, I address the question of how today we can read *Ramona* to inform our understanding of contemporary debates over multiculturalism, *mestizaje* (or racial mixing), and the politics of identity in the United States. In sum, this interdisciplinary critique of *Ramona* and Jackson's Indian rights advocacy establishes the context in which the novel was written and foregrounds the role literature can play as an agent of social change.

Travel in Southern California:
The Romantic Past and the Urge to Reform

Born in Amherst, Massachusetts, in 1830, the young Helen grew up with her parents, Deborah and Nathan Fiske, in a household that stressed the value of religious service and educational endeavor. Her father was a Congregational minister and a professor of philosophy and languages at Amherst College who died when Helen was twelve years old. After pursuing her education at various schools in the East, Helen graduated from Abbot Institute in New York City, continuing there as a teacher until she relinquished her position in 1860 to move to Washington, D.C., with her new husband, Lieutenant Edward Bissell Hunt. Within five years, she was to experience dramatically changed circumstances as a result of her husband's death while testing the prototype of submarine weaponry during the Civil War. Of the couple's two children, a baby boy died several months after birth, while their son Rennie died at the age of nine years. It was at this point that Helen Maria Fiske Hunt began writing professionally. She moved to Newport, Rhode Island, and there received the literary guidance and personal friendship of Thomas Wentworth Higginson. During a visit to Colorado in 1873 to improve her health, Helen met William Sharpless Jackson, vice president of the Denver and Rio Grande Railroad. Two years later they married. Although Jackson found new subject matter in Colorado for articles and stories, she also felt isolated in the West. Significantly it was through returning to the East that she discovered a renewed sense of what she could accomplish in the West.[13]

In November 1879, Jackson attended a lecture in Boston given by Chief Standing Bear and several other members of the Ponca tribe. He told of the Poncas' loss of land and settlement on an inadequate reservation in their native South Dakota, their subsequent forced removal to Indian Territory, and the attempts of groups of Poncas to leave their Indian Territory reservation for first South Dakota and later Nebraska, where they endeavored to join Omaha kinfolk.[14] In previous years Jackson had shown little inclination for taking up moral causes such as abolitionism, temperance reform, and female suffrage, with which many women activists of the time were identified, but she did rally to what she perceived as Standing Bear's great dignity in the face of adversity. Jackson's biographer, Ruth Odell, claims that at this point she "was fired with the indignation that was to be the motivating factor in everything she did or said or thought or wrote for the rest of her life."[15] Shortly after hearing Standing Bear, Jackson went to work on her book *A Century of Dishonor,* a severe indictment of federal Indian policy that was published in January 1881. The book's muted reception, despite each member of Congress's being sent a personal copy, concerned Jackson deeply. Thereafter she became preoccupied with the problem of how to reach a wider audience that would share her enthusiasm for Indian reform. Until her death from stomach cancer in 1885 at fifty-five years of age, Jackson campaigned strenuously for the rights of Indians, focusing her attention on the welfare of the "Mission" Indians of California.

Although Jackson's education into the dispossession of Native Americans began in Boston and continued in New York City, where she conducted research for *A Century of Dishonor* at the Astor Library, it was on the West Coast that she concentrated much of her reform work. She traveled through California in the winter of 1881–82, having been commissioned by *Century* magazine to write a series of four travel articles that were published in 1883 and reprinted in the book *Glimpses of California and the Missions* (1902). During her only prior visit to California in 1872, Jackson had taken small notice of Indians, although she did express interest in writing a series of travel sketches on the Franciscan missions. But on her return a decade later, Jackson had developed her concern for the welfare of Indians while maintaining her interest in writing about the Spanish missions. Indeed, her knowledge of Indian welfare was deemed sufficient for an appointment to serve as special agent to report to the Commissioner of Indian Affairs on the livelihoods of "Mission" Indians of California in 1882. The following year, in conjunction with Abbot Kinney, founder of Venice, California, and a well-to-do reformer, Jackson presented her *Report on the Condition and Needs of the Mission Indians of California* to Commissioner Hiram Price. That Jackson had already written a travelogue and published her *Report* before setting out to write *Ramona* indicates the need for these texts to be considered in tandem.

Jackson's season of West Coast travel in 1881–82 included trips to Oregon, written up for *Atlantic Monthly*, and to San Francisco, where she visited the Bancroft Library to conduct research for the *Century* articles, in addition to her tour of Los Angeles, Santa Barbara, Franciscan missions, and numerous Indian villages in southern California. She returned to her home in Colorado Springs to complete the articles for *Century*, describing them in a letter to a friend as "hav[ing] far more real value & substance than anything merely 'descriptive' I have ever done."[16] Jackson had developed her enthusiasm for travel and her disciplined writing schedule in the aftermath of her first husband's death in 1865 when she became a professional writer. Having gained longstanding commercial success through her poetry, travel writing, short fiction, and novels— published under the titles *Marah, H.H.*, and *Saxe Holme*—by the early 1880s Jackson was in a position to interpret editors' suggestions freely and to suggest the subject matter for her travel writing. Thus she used the last of her articles for *Century*, "The Present Condition of the Mission Indians in Southern California," which largely echoed her official report, to forward documentary evidence of abuses toward Indians to a popular readership as well as to government officials in Indian affairs. That Jackson felt compelled to write an article of "real value & substance" suggests the experience of traveling through Indian villages in southern California was transformative and placed her in a different relationship to her human subjects than had been the case in her previously published travelogues. Going off the beaten track into the backcountry of southern California, Jackson witnessed at first hand the grim reality of Indians' social and geographical marginalization and in the process put herself in a position of ethical responsibility to provide for their welfare.

"The Present Condition of the Mission Indians" was written after Jackson traveled throughout southern California visiting Diegueños (or Kumeyaay), Gabrieliños, Juaneños, and Luiseños (all named after the missions with which they had become associated after Spanish colonization), as well as Cupeño, Serrano, Ipai, and Cahuilla groups.[17] She saw Indians collectively as "long-suffering . . . people who are in . . . immediate danger of being driven out from their last footholds of refuge, 'homeless wanderers in the desert,'" and stated unequivocally that it was the moral duty of the U.S. government to act fast and "give them lands and protect them in their rights" in a time when "there is only a small remnant left to be saved."[18] Jackson had very good reason to be concerned, for the impact on California Indians of Spanish colonization and the massive influx of Euro-Americans during the Gold Rush had been devastating. The population decline of the state's Native peoples during the late eighteenth and nineteenth centuries is truly shocking. Today historians agree that there were around 300,000 indigenous people living within the borders of California when the Spanish began colonizing the territory in 1769. At the time of Mexican independence in 1821, the Indian population had fallen by 100,000, and it fell a further 50,000 during the years of Mexican rule. The population dropped precipitously after American conquest in 1846 and the discovery of gold two years later, to the point where in 1860 only 30,000 Indians survived in California.[19] The sharp decline in numbers in the 1850s was largely due to the impact of the Gold Rush. As the historian Albert Hurtado notes, "disease, starvation, homicide, and a declining birthrate for native people took a heavy toll" at a point when the state was saturated with Euro-American incomers.[20] The 1900 census recorded a population of only 15,377 California Indians.[21]

In light of devastating population losses among Native Americans in California and throughout the United States, Jackson felt impelled to write a novel that would rally readers to the cause of Indian reform.[22] First published in serialized form in *The Christian Union,* the novel was composed at a feverish pace between December 1883 and March 1884 while Jackson was residing at the Berkeley Hotel in New York City. Wanting her readers to "swallow . . . a big dose of information on the Indian question without knowing it," her aim was to use the novel to educate readers into an acknowledgment of the humanity of American Indians and the corresponding need to provide effective means for their welfare.[23] The novel pointed to the severe injustice of institutional power toward Native Americans and articulated a withering assault on the male-identified violence of Anglo settlers encroaching on Indian lands. Traveling through southern California, Jackson had heard stories not only of Indians' displacement but of Anglo males sexually abusing and taking Indian women captives as "wives." Clearly such stories, although they were not replicated in *Ramona,* helped fuel the novel's negative image of frontier whites in contrast to the "half barbaric, half elegant, wholly generous and free-handed life" of Californios.[24] To comprehend more fully how Jackson came to characterize the pastoral livelihoods of elite Californios in this way, we must turn to the novel's opening pages before considering her travel writing for *Century* magazine.

Ramona opens in the household of Señora Gonzaga Moreno, widow of an elite California general killed in the culminating battle for possession of California during the U.S.-Mexican War. Describing life on the Moreno ranch as "picturesque" and "with more of sentiment and gayety in it, more also that was truly dramatic, more romance, than will ever be seen again on those sunny shores," Jackson claimed, unaware of how southern California's "Spanish fantasy heritage" would grow in popularity over the following two decades, that the "aroma" of that way of life remained and would "last out its century."[25] In romanticizing a way of life that appeared to belong to the past, Jackson played upon stereotypes of California indolence that, as we saw in the first chapter, first became commonplace in Anglo representations of California in the decades before the U.S.-Mexican War.

Before composing *Ramona,* Jackson wrote, in addition to her article "The Present Condition of the Mission Indians in Southern California," three further travel articles on southern California for *Century:* "Father Junipero and His Work," "Echoes in the City of Angels," and "Outdoor Industries in Southern California." Through these articles Jackson celebrated Junipero Serra and the missionary efforts of his fellow Franciscans, narrated the settlement of Los Angeles by Spanish settlers and its subsequent development, and meditated on the future of southern California. Reading these essays provides copious evidence of how Jackson echoed not only Dana's ambivalence toward Californios in *Two Years Before the Mast* but also his pleasurable mournfulness for the passing of old ways in his journal "Twenty-Four Years After," which was written on his return to California as a tourist in 1859.[26] According to Jackson in "Echoes in the City of Angels," California indolence began early on in the effort to colonize the territory. The original settlers of Neustra Señora Reina de los Angeles were twelve Spanish soldiers and their families who settled twelve miles from Mission San Gabriel. "Their homes were little more than hovels," they had only hoes for agricultural labor, and "evidently they did not work,—neither they, nor their sons, nor their sons' sons after them; for, half a century later, they were still living a life of almost incredible ignorance, redeemed only by its simplicity and childlike adherence to the old religious observances."[27] She commented on the "primeval peace" of Los Angeles before the "turmoil" of the Mexican years, telling of dances, old entertainments, and men, both reverent and irreverent, who were "a variety of centaur" because they so rarely dismounted from their horses. Passing through the old Mexican plaza where "idle boys and still idler men" sat, Jackson discovered survivors of the city's past, including the granddaughter of Moreno, one of the twelve original soldiers, and declared much of the place "bewilderingly un-American." In one house she saw a lock that took on symbolic value: "There was also one old lock, in which the key was rusted fast and immovable, which seemed to me fuller of suggestion than anything else there of the sealed and ended past to which it had belonged." At Mission San Gabriel Jackson met an old woman "worth crossing the continent to see" whom she described as living in poetic poverty and barely making a living through the sale of embroidery and providing folk remedies for illness. It was precisely this sort of impressionist representation of local color details run through with the "indefinable, delicious aroma from the old, ignorant, picturesque times" that would feature throughout *Ramona* and account, along with its sentimental plot, for much of the novel's popularity with readers.[28]

"Echoes in the City of Angels" also features the characters of Don Antonio and Doña Mariana, who lived in a "low adobe house, built after the ancient style."[29] Jackson recounted Don Antonio's stories of the past—his family's removal from Mexico City to California when he was child, battling against the United States during the war, finding a new vocation as a teacher in later years—and characterized him as an anachronistic presence in a modernizing culture:

> Full of sentiment, of an intense and poetic nature, he looks back to the lost empire of his race and people on the California shores with a sorrow far too proud for any antagonisms or complaints. He recognizes the inexorableness of the laws under whose workings his nation is slowly, surely giving place to one more representative of the age. Intellectually he is in sympathy with progress, with reform, with civilization at its utmost; he would not have had them stayed or changed, because his people could not keep up and were not ready. But his heart is none the less saddened and lonely.
>
> This is probably the position and point of view of most cultivated Mexican men of his age. The suffering involved is inevitable. It is part of the great, unreckoned price which must always be paid for the gain the world gets when the young and strong supersede the old and weak.[30]

This passage characterizes westward expansion, the U.S.-Mexican War, and the subsequent difficulties Californios experienced in holding onto land grants that were supposed to be upheld by the United States under the terms of the Treaty of Guadalupe Hidalgo in 1848 as part of a predestined and inescapable process of Euro-American settlement and democratization in North America. Nevertheless Jackson sympathized with men such as

Don Antonio—the real-life Antonio Coronel—who had experienced profound change in their lifetimes. The article ends with the image of an
orange tree beside her hosts' porch. The "twenty-five hundred oranges, ripe
and golden among the glossy leaves," along with abundant gifts of flowers
and fruit heaped on Jackson by Don Antonio and Doña Mariana, created
an image of natural abundance that Jackson could not help mythologizing:
"Fables are prophecies. The Hesperides have come true."[31]

The image of mythological plenitude that concludes "Echoes in the
City of Angels" also resonates in another of Jackson's articles for *Century,*
"Outdoor Industries in Southern California," in which she ponders the
fact that there should be any industry at all in a place where the air is
"sunny, balmy, dreamy, seductive" and fruits and grains grow abundantly
and "tak[e] care of themselves."[32] She encapsulates the charm of the
Californios' lifestyle by stating:

> Simply out of sunshine, there had distilled in them an Orientalism
> as fine in its way as that made in the East by generations of
> prophets, crusaders, and poets. With no more curiosity than was
> embodied in "Who knows?"—with no thought or purpose for a
> future more defined than "Some other time; not to-day,"—without
> greeds, and with the unlimited generosities of children,—no won-
> der that to them the restless, inquisitive, insatiable, close-reckoning
> Yankee seemed the most intolerable of all conquerors to whom they
> could surrender. One can fancy them shuddering, even in heaven,
> as they look down to-day on his colonies, his railroads, his crops,—
> their whole land humming and buzzing with his industries.[33]

For Jackson, then, Californios were both "children" and "poets,"
indolent and charming, culturally backward and of the Old rather than
the New World. As we have seen with Dana, this mixture of condescension and romanticized praise was not new, although the simple fact that
Jackson wrote over thirty years after the U.S. conquest of northern
Mexico helped make it easier to be sorrowful about the plight of older
Californios who could remember the days when they commanded a far
greater degree of political power and social prestige.

Today it is easy to see how such writing serves as a form of imperialist nostalgia, the process whereby members of a colonizing society come
to mourn the passing of the formerly autonomous culture their society has
defeated and incorporated.[34] It was safe to sympathize with Don Antonio

and interpret his courteous manners and bonhomie as a sign of his fate-
fulness regarding Californios' political and economic disempowerment in
the aftermath of the U.S.-Mexican War. Indeed Coronel thrived on playing the role of a gentlemanly Don, and his image—wearing old-style
clothing, playing guitar, dancing with his wife Doña Mariana—was
reproduced in much Euro-American art and photography of the time.[35]
The literary critic Rosaura Sanchez regards such behavior as evidence that
Coronel had become "a co-opted Californio."[36] She further contends that
behind the outward celebration of Mexican-era California in Hubert
Howe Bancroft's *California Pastoral* (1888)—a project that drew heavily on
the written and oral testimonials of Coronel and many other
Californios—lay "an absolute disdain for the Californios, a typically racist
portrayal drawn from disparaging remarks about lack of ambition, lack of
industriousness, and lack of a desire for power and domination in men
capable of standing tall only over cattle." Justified as this assertion may
well be regarding Bancroft's historiography, should it apply equally to
Jackson's representation of Coronel and what she saw as the inevitable end
of California culture? For while it is clear that Jackson to some extent
shared the romantic emplotment structuring Bancroft's interpretation of
"California Pastoral"—emplotment, according to Sanchez, used "to both
deride the conquered and substantiate the flaws that led to their fall"[37]—
Jackson's writing conspicuously lacks the elements of disdain and tri-
umphalism that, arguably, are present in Bancroft's narrative.[38]

As is indicated by Jackson's imagining Californios as "shuddering" at
the prospect of the Yankee's "restless" and "insatiable" appetite for industrial, agricultural, and urban development, she appears to have identified
with the nostalgia of Californios such as Antonio Coronel and Guadalupe
Vallejo. In an article published in the journal *Century,* Vallejo wrote: "In
these days of trade, bustle, and confusion, when many thousands of people live in the California valleys, which formerly were occupied by only a
few Spanish families, the quiet and domestic life of the past seems like a
dream. We, who loved it, often speak of those days, and especially of the
duties of the large Spanish households, where so many dependents were
cared for, and everything was done in a simple and primitive way."[39] These
words when combined with the article's opening statement—"it seems
there never was a more peaceful or happy people on the face of the earth
than the Spanish, Mexican, and Indian population of Alta California
before the American conquest"—amount to an ideologically loaded celebration of California culture through which Vallejo proclaims the loyalty

of "Spanish Californians" to the U.S. flag while simultaneously asserting their pride in the past, particularly "the long pastoral age before 1840."[40] Vallejo thus used similar terms to Jackson's in her reference to California Orientalism to produce an image of bucolic charm that rhymed with Anglo representations of California society in travelogues and histories after the Civil War and also articulated a renewed sense of identity among Californios during the 1880s through taking pride in their collective past. This observation helps us understand that what McWilliams labels the Spanish fantasy heritage was not merely an invention of Anglo writers. By playing upon the elite status of their families and stressing the social obligations of Californio patriarchs to an extended network of family members and workers in the decades before and after the U.S.-Mexican War, Vallejo and others of his class strove to legitimize their claim for a place in bourgeois American society. Since Vallejo's article for *Century* appeared in 1890, six years after the publication of *Ramona,* one suspects that the opportunity to publish his article was at least partly facilitated by readers' attraction to the novel's celebration of semifeudal relations in California. In turn, Jackson had written *Ramona* after consulting archival sources, including the Californio testimonials, in Bancroft's library. These details help contemporary readers of the novel appreciate the ways in which *Ramona* was created through dialogue with Californio sources that did not necessarily concur with Jackson's view that Californio culture in the 1880s was merely "old and weak."

Turning to Jackson's representation of the Franciscan missionary effort in the Spanish colonial era, notably she placed a "halo of exalted sentiment and rapture" about the heads of Franciscan friars in her article "Father Junipero and His Work."[41] Later I will discuss Jackson's representation of the missions in greater detail and point out how Californios in the 1870s both criticized and supported such an image of Franciscan saintliness, but here I wish to stress that Jackson's inclusive vision regarding the position of Indians in American society helps explain her valorization of Franciscan efforts to "civilize" Native Americans. Significantly, the Indians characterized in *Ramona* are far closer in origin to the victimized figures of Indian reform reportage than to the demonized figures of captivity narratives and the noble savages of James Fenimore Cooper's Leather-Stocking Tales. Yet lurking behind Jackson's characterization of Ramona and Alessandro are her own childhood fear of Indians—"it was one of my childish terrors that Indians would come in the night and kill us"[42]—and her stereotypical response to seeing Indians on her first trip to California in 1872. Ruth

Odell notes how on this trip Jackson "found the Indian extremely picturesque, 'his scarlet legs gleaming through the sage,' and she 'fairly rioted'
over the Indian names in Yosemite, but she [also] frequently applied to all
Indians such terms as 'loathsome,' 'abject,' and 'hideous.'"[43] Ironically,
similar terms are used in *Ramona* only to describe the conditions in which
Indians are forced to live after being deprived of their land and to represent
the acts of whites who squat on Indian lands and set about dispossessing
them on spurious legal grounds.

Having detailed the circumstances leading up to Jackson's writing of
Ramona and having suggested that much of its content was drawn from her
report to the Commissioner of Indian Affairs and her travel writing for
Century, I now want to clarify how Harriet Beecher Stowe's antislavery novel
Uncle Tom's Cabin (1852) provided an example for Jackson not merely of how
a woman novelist might pursue humanitarian causes through fiction writing but also of how to capture a large readership that could be persuaded, in
turn, to promote the cause of reform espoused in the novel. Jane Tompkins
argues that mid-nineteenth-century sentimental fiction by American
women writers should be understood "as a political enterprise, halfway
between sermon and social theory, that both codifies and attempts to mold
the values of its time."[44] According to this interpretation, although in
Uncle Tom's Cabin neither Tom's nor Little Eva's death appears to change
the political and economic "facts" of slavery, the sacrifice of each is
an essential means of bringing to the fore in American culture a redemptive
Christianity that, in Tompkins' words, "would destroy the present economic and social institutions."[45] Tompkins' critique helps contemporary
readers understand a key difference between Jackson's reportage about the
Mission Indians and her fictional treatment of Native Americans in
Ramona. While Jackson's article for *Century* and her report on the condition
of the Mission Indians call for pragmatic and immediate action to be taken
to protect lands and resources and to provide sustenance for people in a des-
perate situation, her novel only focuses on the dispossession of Luiseños
after a series of chapters in which the idyllic qualities of pastoral Californio
existence, albeit in the years after the U.S.-Mexican War, are represented.
We have already seen how compelling this image of natural abundance and
human harmony with landscape proved for readers and promoters of southern California in later years. But it should also be stressed that in addition
to providing a romantic image of the state that, in echoing her travel writing for *Century* magazine, would draw readers into the novel before they
were confronted with the misfortunes of Alessandro, his fellow Luiseños,

and the Cahuillas later on—dispiriting events that if featured earlier may not have engaged many readers—Jackson also appealed to values that she thought transcended material culture in order to make universal statements about the common humanity of Indians and Anglos. Although Jackson lacked the religious conviction and, it seems, the confidence in domestic values that sustained Stowe's critique of antebellum America to provide an alternative, woman-centered vision of moral and political power in the late nineteenth century, nevertheless Jackson designed the novel to engage readers' sympathy for dispossessed and exiled Indians by dramatizing the main characters' forbearance and dignity under duress and the eventual disintegration of their homemaking and child-rearing capability as external circumstances overwhelm them.

Ramona

Ramona is a sentimental romance whose action pivots about the intertwined fates of its heroine, Ramona Ortegna, and hero, Alessandro. Ramona is the stepchild of the widowed Señora Gonzaga Moreno, while Alessandro is a Luiseño Indian, one of a band of Indians formerly tied to Mission San Luis Rey, located in the northern part of San Diego County. Ramona's father was Angus Phail, a once prosperous Scots trader who died in her infancy, and her mother an unnamed Indian woman whom he had married during his decline into poverty and self-abuse. Away on his final trading voyage before settling down to life on the land, he was betrayed by his betrothed, Ramona Gonzaga, Señora Moreno's sister. She married another, Francis Ortegna, but it was a loveless and childless marriage. The aptly named Phail visits Señora Gonzaga, twenty-five years after she betrayed his trust, in order to give her the infant Ramona, who has been removed (perhaps forcibly, perhaps voluntarily) from her mother. The señora raises the small child as her own until her death; thereafter Señora Moreno, who hates her charge's Indian ethnicity but is compelled to maintain the tradition of family honor, adopts Ramona and raises her as a privileged member of the Moreno household.

Ramona, then, is the product of "base" intermarriage, but while there is some indication of her mixed-race ancestry in her physical appearance, there is small evidence of either her Indian ethnicity or her father's improvidence in her character. She has her father's "steel-blue" eyes, her mother's heavy black hair, and "just enough of olive tint in complexion to underlie and enrich her skin without making it swarthy."[46] Innocent, joyous, generous, and industrious, she is also childlike and without intellectual depth. Likewise Alessandro is a two-dimensional character, a "simple-minded, unlearned man" who sings beautifully and plays the violin—skills learned as a child at Mission San Luis Rey. He is the son of Pablo, "chief" of a band of Luiseños that in the aftermath of secularization has settled on former mission land in Temecula Valley. Alessandro, we are told, is "old before his time" with worry over the plight of his people, who "knew his goodness, and were proud of his superiority to themselves."[47]

The couple meet when Alessandro attends the annual sheep shearing at the Moreno rancho, quickly fall in love, and go into exile after the señora discovers their forbidden relationship. Before leaving the rancho they already know that Anglo settlers have preempted the Temecula Valley land on which Alessandro's people are settled. A number of the dispossessed Luiseños remove to San Pasqual Valley, where the couple go after their marriage in San Diego. After a year and a half of living in that village, white settlers again displace the Luiseños. Ramona and Alessandro journey into the mountainous interior of southern California, first settling in the village of Saboba, home of Serrano Indians, where Ramona's first child dies, and then moving further into the Mount San Jacinto "wilderness," where they eke out a tenuous existence prior to Alessandro's death.

Jackson intended her novel to be a fictional dramatization of factual events. In her travels about southern California she had heard of a doomed interracial affair between an elite Californio woman and an Indian male, and she combined this story with the plight of a Cahuilla Indian named Juan Diego. In her *Report,* Jackson recounted his story as an example of the exercise of arbitrary justice by whites in southern California. Diego "had been for some years what the Indians called a 'locoed' Indian, being at times crazy; never dangerous, but yet certainly insane for longer or shorter periods."[48] He lived in a remote mountain area with his wife and child, and cultivated a small plot of land. One day he returned to his family, after trying to find work as a sheepshearer, on the wrong horse; he had mistaken the horse of a white American, Sam Temple, for his own and had ridden off on it. Temple pursued Diego and killed him: "After Juan had fallen on the ground Temple rode closer and fired three more shots in the body, one in the forehead, one in the cheek, and one in the wrist, the woman looking on."[49] The murderer rode away, gave himself up to a justice of the peace, and was later acquitted of any wrongdoing, his justification for the killing being self-defense. Juan Diego's sad demise became that of Alessandro in *Ramona*.

In the novel the character Jim Farrar is a fictionalized version of the real-life Sam Temple. Through murdering Alessandro, Farrar destroys the interracial relationship between the mestiza Ramona and her full-blooded Indian husband. Traumatized by the death of her daughter and husband, Ramona takes refuge in a Cahuilla village and grows gravely ill, only to be saved through the folk remedies of Aunt Ri, a Tennessee matriarch. Finally Felipe comes to Ramona's rescue, and after her return to the Moreno family the novel concludes with her and Felipe marrying, leaving for Mexico, and having a child there.

In key respects Aunt Ri, the strong woman at the heart of a "contented, shiftless, ill-bestead" migrant family from Tennessee and at the center of the poor San Bernardino community the family settles into, is the novel's figure of hope in the present and for the future. Through her friendship with Ramona, Aunt Ri learns, in her own words, "a lesson 'n the subjeck uv Injuns" and is transformed into an indignant critic of white racism.[50] That Aunt Ri's succeeding message of racial tolerance contrasts boldly with Temple's murderous bigotry demonstrates the way in which Jackson's fiction provided a woman-centered critique of stereotypical images of Anglo male heroism in representations of conflict between whites and Indians.[51] Echoing Jackson's real-life conversion experience, through personal contact Aunt Ri quickly revises her preconceptions of Indians. Thus on the occasion of Aunt Ri's first meeting with Ramona and Alessandro, Jackson undermines popular stereotypes of Indians as Aunt Ri, Ramona, and Alessandro sit together:

> Aunt Ri was excited. The experience was, to her, almost incredible. Her ideas of Indians had been drawn from newspapers, and from a book or two of narratives of massacres, and from an occasional sight of vagabond bands or families they [her family] had encountered in their journey across the plains. Here she found herself sitting side by side in friendly intercourse with an Indian man and Indian woman, whose appearance and behavior were attractive; towards whom she felt singularly drawn.[52]

The literary critic Michele Moylan sees Aunt Ri as the novel's implied reader in whom a liberal transformation is meant to take place over the issue of Indian reform, and in an apt turn of phrase describes Aunt Ri's movement "from hillbilly to cultural pluralist."[53] Thus Jackson strove to counteract the negative portrayal of Indians in frontier narratives that, she reckoned in the conclusion to *A Century of Dishonor*, had "produced in the average mind something like an hereditary instinct of unquestioning and unreasoning aversion which it is almost impossible to dislodge or soften."[54] Not surprisingly, however, Aunt Ri's cultural pluralism is premised on the perception that she, and other poor Anglo emigrants, share their worship of a universal and benevolent God, their practice of domestic values, and their belief in agrarian individualism with Ramona and Alessandro. While it would appear that acculturation of American Indians to European lifeways during the years of Spanish colonization and missionization was the precondition to Indian reform campaigning in the 1880s—and I shall return to this issue shortly—it is important to note that through her characterization of Aunt Ri, Jackson clearly saw women as the most effective agents of social change.

Next to Aunt Ri, Anglo male administrators of Indian affairs, along with the Agency doctor who is unwilling to treat Ramona's sickly child, are seen as not only reactionary in their attitudes toward Indians but also ineffectual, and at worst corrupt, in acting on behalf of their charges. This critique of Anglo males compounds Jackson's representation of Farrar, of the corrupt judicial system that acquits him of any wrongdoing, and of the first Anglo character to appear in the novel, a "human brute" who preempts Indian lands, moves into Alessandro's former home in Temecula, and in a half-drunken state dominates his "kindly" yet "weary and worn" wife.[55] Through such images Jackson creates an ironic reversal by emphasizing the inhumanity of Anglo males rather than that of the iconic demonized Indian who had haunted the popular American imagination for decades.

Regarding Ramona and the Cahuilla Indians, significantly Jackson fails to provide a happy ending for the Cahuillas, with whom Ramona is staying when Felipe finds her in the San Jacinto "wilderness." As Ramona is taken away to resume an economically and socially privileged life with Felipe in Mexico, the Cahuillas are left in a "void":

> The gulf between them and the rest of the world seemed defined anew, their sense of isolation deepened, their hopeless poverty emphasized. Ramona, wife of Alessandro, had been their sister,— one of them; as such, she would have had share in all their life had to offer. But its utmost was nothing, was but hardship and deprivation; and she was being borne away from it, like one rescued, not so much from death, as from a life worse than death.[56]

Ramona, then, concludes by appearing to reinforce the racial and class lines between the novel's heroine and the Cahuilla women. As Felipe takes Ramona away from San Jacinto and restores her to a "European" identity in Mexico, so the Cahuilla women seem to disappear into invisibility. (I use the term "European" with appropriate wariness because Ramona does not suddenly lose her mestiza identity at the end of the novel, and I will return in the chapter's conclusion to issues of class and caste alluded to here.) To a degree Jackson was correct to leave the future of the Cahuilla women uncertain in her fiction for this was an accurate reflection of their marginalized and enclaved status during the 1880s, although fortunately the situation of Cahuillas and other southern California Indians did improve somewhat after Congress passed the Act for the Relief of the Mission Indians in 1891, which, in turn, had been created in response to Jackson and Kinney's *Report* of 1883.

Before considering in greater detail the legislation that affected the livelihoods of southern California Indians in the late nineteenth century, it is necessary to consider the question of why it became possible for readers to sideline or even ignore Jackson's Indian reform advocacy in *Ramona*. To accomplish this, we need first to consider the biases at work in Jackson's representation not merely of Alessandro and his fellow Luiseños but of Spanish efforts to acculturate the so-called Mission Indians to a new regime of labor, religious practice, and bodily discipline. We then need to analyze the gap that emerged between Jackson's intention for the novel and its reception in the years immediately after publication when local history and promotional writers rhapsodized about the novel's depiction of the pastoral life of Californios in the years before the U.S.-Mexican War.

Earlier I referred to Jackson's article "The Present Condition of the Mission Indians in Southern California," in which she called for the government to protect the lands and rights of Indians at a point when "there is only a small remnant left to be saved." The language of this excerpt suggests that Jackson strove to appeal to the consciences of enlightened citizens by stressing the geographical and cultural marginalization of Native Americans. Jackson hoped that she could appeal to her readers' humanitarianism not only by stating the need for immediate measures to be taken to save lives but also by alluding to the need to save Indians' souls. Such thinking about how best to provide for the welfare of Indians was widespread in the years after the Civil War and prepared the way for the implementation of a series of practical measures—among them formal education of Indian children, the Dawes Severalty Act of 1887, the promotion of agriculture on reservations, and restrictions on the practice of Native religions—that were designed to assimilate Native Americans into U.S. society. In time, government officials thought, Native Americans would break out of a pattern of dependency and provide for themselves. Not surprisingly this did not occur, and the "ethnocentric paternalism" at the heart of the government's administration of Indian affairs in the late nineteenth and early twentieth centuries now appears naive and anachronistic.[57] Of the failure of federal Indian policy to assimilate Native Americans into U.S. society during this period, the historian Francis Paul Prucha concludes: "A communal rather than an individualistic spirit, an emphasis on sharing rather than on accumulating, a relation with nature that did not accord rapid exploitation of resources for profit—these traits meant that the seeds of the civilization programs frequently fell on barren ground."[58]

Turning to *Ramona,* it is important to bear in mind Jackson's paternalism when considering, on the one hand, her characterization of Ramona and Alessandro and, on the other hand, her beatification of the Franciscan missionary effort in California. As I have mentioned already, Ramona is the product of intermarriage gone wrong; that is, her father, Angus Phail, was supposed to marry into an elite Californio family but instead married an Indian woman of whom Jackson tells her readers almost nothing. Significantly Ramona grows up without knowing her Indian ethnicity, but once it is revealed to her the affection she feels for Alessandro blossoms into love. However, despite Ramona's heartfelt affinity for Alessandro, the Luiseños, and the Cahuillas, she remains by virtue of her upbringing in a Californio household their intellectual superior. This is made clear when Jackson writes: "Alessandro was undeniably Ramona's inferior in position, education, in all the external matters of life; but in nature, in true nobility of soul, no!"[59] Although Alessandro has merits of his own, it is necessary to qualify Jackson's tacit acknowledgment that a certain equality exists between Ramona and her Indian spouse by realizing that Alessandro was made into an exceptional Indian by Jackson, and that in making him exceptional she downplayed the attributes of his fellow Luiseños. Rather than stress the resistance, resourcefulness, and cultural survival of Luiseños in the face of both Spanish colonization and American settlement, Jackson dramatized their poverty, displacement, and cultural demise as a consequence of the loss of their former home, Mission San Luis Rey.

Indeed Jackson was notably dismissive of the subject of Indian lives in the precontact period, concentrating her energy on representing the supposed benefits of the Franciscan missionary effort in both *Ramona* and her articles for *Century* magazine. She heaped praise on Junipero Serra, founding father of the Alta California missions, as one who traveled selflessly to bring civilization to the region's heathen savages. Jackson described the missionary effort as beginning in "wretched poverty" and culminating in "final splendor and riches":

> From the rough booth of boughs and reeds of 1770 to the pillars, arched corridors, and domes of the stately stone churches of a half-century later, is a change only a degree less wonderful than the change in the Indian, from the naked savage with his one stone tool, grinding acorn-meal in a rock bowl, to the industrious tiller of the soil, weaver of cloth, worker in metals, and singer of sacred hymns.[60]

She further contended that since acts of confrontational resistance to missionaries were relatively uncommon, Indians acquiesced to the Franciscans' efforts to change their livelihoods. Such claims, echoed in many travelogues and local histories well into the twentieth century, have been contested in more recent historical accounts. The historian George Harwood Phillips argues that Indians were coerced into laboring at missions and that large numbers of them became fugitives rather than suffer Spanish colonial discipline, noting also that many Indians who remained attached to the missions resisted acculturation by refusing to learn Spanish, only nominally following Christian practices, and holding onto their own customs.[61] Concentrating on the ideals of Franciscans rather than the deleterious impact of Spanish colonization on Indian communities closest to the missions, whose collective population fell from 72,000 to 18,000 during the mission period of 1779–1833, Jackson displayed little interest in recognizing the profound cultural and ecological changes Indians had experienced during the mission period.[62] Despite displaying blinkered vision regarding the complexity and achievements of California Indians prior to Spanish colonization, Jackson nevertheless campaigned strenuously for the rights of Indians fifty years after the Secularization Act, arguing that once removed from the tutelage of Franciscan fathers, Indians had been "forced to labor on the mission lands like slaves" and "hired out in gangs to cruel masters."[63]

When considering the precipitous population decline of California Indians between 1769 and the 1880s, it is important to bear in mind that the impact of American settlement on Indian communities was greatest in northern California, where mining activity was most intense. In parts of southern California, though, Indians were in a comparatively stronger position to resist the encroachments on their land of American settlers, many of whom came into the state along the southern emigrant trail. In 1851, for example, Cupeño leader Antonio Garra attempted to unite diverse groups of southern California Indians into collectively attacking American settlers. Garra's attempt to forge pan-Indian resistance failed in large part because most Indian leaders did not share his perception of the danger of American occupation. Stimulated by the prospect of what pan-Indian unity might achieve, Garra advocated nothing less than the complete removal of Americans (but notably not Mexicans) from California. Such acts of resistance were ignored, downplayed, or rejected as the work of fanatical Indians in Jackson's writing on the "Mission" Indians.[64] Why is this so?

There are several reasons. First, Jackson, similar to the great majority of Indian reformers during the 1880s, wished to promote an image of Indians as possessing an innately good character that would gain from the benefits of "civilization." That is, Native Americans in the abstract possessed the "true nobility" of soul that Jackson attributed to Alessandro in *Ramona*. Second, to claim otherwise and stress the essential difference of the Indian from Euro-Americans in both racial and cultural terms not only had the potential to perpetuate old hostilities toward Native Americans but also threatened to undermine the humanitarian ideals of citizens who saw it as their moral duty to "raise up" Indians so that they also might partake of the nation's progress. Such idealism helps us understand today why Native Americans were featured prominently in many late-nineteenth-century celebrations, such as parades at the Centennial Exposition at Philadelphia in 1876 and the Los Angeles Fiesta in 1895 or in encampments at the Chicago World's Fair in 1893.[65] Third, we must recall Jackson's debt to Harriet Beecher Stowe's novel *Uncle Tom's Cabin* and note a certain similarity in the way that each author envisages the political purpose of her reform-minded fiction. To stress the violent resistance of Indians against the missionary effort of both Franciscans and late-nineteenth-century reformers would mitigate against Indians' incorporation into the body politic.

As mentioned at the beginning of this section, in the years after *Ramona*'s publication readers soon learned to prize Jackson's romantic representation of elite Californios' lifeways. After Jackson's death in 1885 the novel lived on in such locations as Camulos, a Santa Barbara rancho that was the supposed model for the Moreno home, and the Estudillo

Home, in San Diego. According to the travel writer Margaret Allen in 1914, visiting the Estudillo Home, advertised as "Ramona's Marriage Place," made "the scenes in the story realistic to eastern visitors that have read *Ramona* as a part of their preparation for a winter's trip to Southern California."[66] Publications such as Charles Fletcher Lummis's *The Home of Ramona* (1888), Edwin Clough's *Ramona's Marriage Place* (1910), and George Wharton James's *Through Ramona's Country* (1913) were designed to appeal not merely to a burgeoning market of tourists drawn to southern California, but also to southern Californians themselves.[67] In striving to trace local lineage back to "noble Spain," these writers participated in a collective effort among Californians of a certain social standing—many of them well-educated, wealthy, and in positions of civic authority—to search for a usable past by forging a myth of their own cultural origins in the region. They fell into an elegiac mode of perception when describing the Spanish and Mexican past of California. Represented as a culture in irretrievable decline, the passing of Californios could be safely mourned and saved in the pages of travel articles and the sentimental romance. Although in 1884 Jackson could not have foreseen how her novel and its characters would be appropriated by southern California boosterists for their promotional purposes, she risked such co-optation by creating a romanticized story that conveyed a highly picturesque image of pastoral Californio life.

Through Ramona's Country

Given the misguiding stereotypes of both Indians and Mexican Americans that appear in *Ramona* and the promotional literature of the early twentieth century, together with stage and film adaptations of the novel in succeeding decades that have focused on the romance plot rather than its social reform message, it is tempting to be dismissive of *Ramona* in the way of McWilliams and Davis.[68] Yet taking this view ignores a counter-tradition of writing about *Ramona* and southern California Indians that stresses the novel's Indian rights advocacy and the need for continued reforms in the administration of regional Indian affairs. One uses the term "counter-tradition" with caution because the writers discussed here came to very different conclusions about the position of Native Americans in U.S. society and how the interests of southern California Indians were best served by reform efforts. In the aftermath of Jackson's death in 1885, Indian rights advocate Constance Goddard DuBois described the efforts of the Women's National

Indian Association (WNIA) to continue Jackson's campaigning work in southern California by opening the "Ramona Mission" among the Cahuilla Indians; three decades later, George Wharton James, a resident of Pasadena and along with Charles Fletcher Lummis one of the chief popularizers of California and the Southwest in the late nineteenth and early twentieth centuries, searched the Southland exhaustively for evidence of the actual occurrences on which *Ramona* was based in order to back up his claim that the novel "is a work of essential truth";[69] while during the 1960s, as mentioned earlier, Delfina Cuero, a Kumeyaay Indian, collaborated with anthropologist Florence Shipek to produce an autobiography that helped authenticate her claim for legal residency in the United States. With the assistance of Rosalie Robertson, a Kumeyaay who acted as translator, Shipek and Cuero completed Delfina's autobiography in 1968 so as to document the movements of Kumeyaay Indians who had traveled south of the international border after being displaced from San Diego and its surrounding valleys around 1900. Because the traditional homelands of the Kumeyaay stretch north and south of the international border, it was not surprising that a number of Kumeyaays who resided in the north of their territory took refuge in the south when Anglo settlers preempted the lands of San Diego County. Shipek also produced a comprehensive review of Native land use and reservation land tenure that has proved an invaluable resource for comprehending and confirming the legal rights of contemporary Indians since the 1960s. Taken together, these texts indicate the diverse ways in which the fortunes of Native Americans have changed since the publication of *Ramona.*

Not surprisingly, since she wrote only four years after Jackson's death and also advocated direct action to be taken by Euro-American reformers, DuBois shared many assumptions about the welfare of southern California Indians with Jackson. In the conclusion of a report published by the WNIA in May 1889, DuBois outlined the missionary work that needed to be conducted among the Cahuillas and other Mission Indians: "Christian instruction, Sunday schools, sewing schools; temperance, industrial, domestic and sanitary teaching; house-to-house visitation; a hospital department, and indeed whatever help and light are needed for Indian elevation, Christianization and general well-being."[70] Paraphrasing a report by regional Indian agent Colonel J. W. Preston, DuBois commented that "there is no reason why they [Indians] should not be on a level with the average of agricultural laborers if proper surveys and well defined limits can be had to give them a feeling of security." DuBois's report implied that if indeed missionaries could educate Indians into knowledge of the rights promised them under the provisions of the Treaty of Guadalupe Hidalgo, whereby they could become full U.S. citizens, then their place within American society, albeit at the lower end of the social scale, would be assured. With the benefit of hindsight, we can see that DuBois's endeavor to apprise her audience of Indians' need to be defended "by those wiser and stronger than themselves" rested on paternalist thinking about Indian welfare that was typical of reformers at the time. Nevertheless it is important to stress that along with Jackson she advocated an inclusive vision of Indians' place in American society and also that in time her vision of the terms under which Indians were to become incorporated into the United States would be challenged.[71]

Evidence of the shifting ground on which Euro-Americans represented Indians during the early twentieth century can be found in James's book *Through Ramona's Country.* Although it was dismissed by McWilliams as the work of a man "who did much to keep the Ramona promotion moving along,"[72] the book is actually less straightforward and more complex—and even convoluted—than an initial perusal of its pages might suggest. This is not to say that James meant the book to be complex, for his basic intention was clear, namely to remind readers of why Jackson had felt compelled to write *Ramona* and to educate them into a more profound understanding of Native Americans. In this regard the book functions as a form of salvage ethnography through which a comprehensive account of the vanishing lifeways of Indians is recorded and made available to a dominant culture through archives and publications of anthropology and folklore, museum displays, and large-scale expositions such as world's fairs.[73] Although James verified the presence of Indians in southern California through visiting villages, collecting basketry, preserving folk knowledge, and taking photographs, he did not see Indians as possessing a viable future in which the "old ways" would continue. Instead he reckoned that education at schools such as the Sherman Institute with its "Ramona Home" would alienate children from traditional culture, intermarriage would impair racial "purity," and the existing administration of local Indian affairs, unless remedial measures were made immediately, would also contribute to the continued demise of the Indian population through what he thought amounted to a policy of criminal neglect. Thus he concurred with Jackson in regarding Indians as a residual population whose welfare was the responsibility of government officials, but he was not optimistic that efforts to assimilate Indians would prove successful.

When we consider James's reflection on the cultural and environmental transformation of Los Angeles and its locale—specifically the way
that Mexican pueblos had changed in the span of a lifetime from a state
of "sleepy, lazy happy-go-luckiness" to "active, bustling, shoving, money-
grasping, pleasure-seizing, American arenas of local trade, far-reaching
commerce, modern education and strenuous civilization"—it is easy to
see how marginal and anachronistic Indians must have seemed to the
majority of Anglo settlers who moved to the Southland from other areas
of the country at the turn of the century.[74] The immigrants' travel to and
residency in southern California had been facilitated by momentous
changes in the economic and social fabric of American society that
involved large-scale industrialization, the building of a nationwide network of railroads, the growth of a corporate economy, mechanization of
agriculture, and widespread urbanization—in sum, the process described
by Alan Trachtenberg as the incorporation of America.[75] Contrasting the
image of the carreta and slow, tedious, and uncomfortable travel during
the Mexican years with the speed, efficiency, and ease of the modern electric car, James celebrated the conquest of nature and the compression of
time and space in Los Angeles and its satellite communities. Likewise he
bragged about the agricultural riches of southern California, boasted of
the desert's being made productive, and gloried in the "tunneling,
damming and piping" that had secured the water of the Owens River for
irrigation and the growth of metropolitan Los Angeles.[76]

So much of *Through Ramona's Country* is written in the affirmative
that James appears to have seen no contradiction between concluding the
book by celebrating the promotional cult that had grown about *Ramona*
in the years after its publication and his intention at the outset to provide
information about Indians that would "aid in deepening the practical
sympathy of the American people for an unfortunate and dying race."
Throughout the book James claims Indians are essentially good people
who have been victimized by their colonizers, although by focusing his
criticism on aggressive settlers and negligent government agents for
wrongful treatment of Indians he avoids stating the obvious subtheme
of his book, namely that Indians are not merely victims of "Anglo Saxon"
racism and neglectful administration but of the very forces of modernization he vigorously celebrates in the latter part of the book. Or put another
way, the continuation of distinctively "Indian" livelihoods far into the
twentieth century was thought by James to be incompatible with
the social and economic development of southern California. Hence, on

returning to the subject of Indians, he concludes that "a few scattered remains are to be found in the far away mountain or desert valleys" but overall "nearly all [are] gone—swept away by man's cupidity."[77]

Actually James exaggerated the demise of southern California Indians, for although competing pressures on Indian lands prevailed throughout the second half of the nineteenth century, the 1891 Act for the Relief of the Mission Indians helped stabilize their situation by withdrawing from the public domain lands they used and occupied and by providing for the purchase of alternative land in situations where the title to land occupied by Indians was held by ranch owners and settlers.[78] Much of the damage done to Indian communities had taken place by 1891 through the combined impact of land loss, depopulation, and social and political disorganization, so that while Indian communities continued to struggle through poverty and demoralization when James visited them in the early 1900s, nevertheless they were surviving as semiautonomous groups.[79] Typical of many Anglo commentators on Native cultures at this time, James frowned on "civilization" as he saw it manifested in Indian cultures: "They are growing civilized into a money-grubbing, whiskey-drinking materialism which scoffs at the mysticism, the simple-hearted supernaturalism of the older members of the tribe, and many a time has a story been stopped in my hearing by the sarcastic and scoffing voice of a young school Indian, whose respect and veneration have been civilized away to give place to a veneer of white man's learning, vices and trousers."[80] Such words illustrate James's ambivalence toward Indians while also echoing the comments of missionaries and government agents from the earliest days of the Republic onward. Implied in the passage is a recognition of how incorporation and dependency necessarily exacerbate the colonized subject's awareness of his or her marginality and disempowerment. James records, for example, how in the midst of a long process of land loss, drought, and removal to land unsuitable for ranching, agriculture, and hunting, Saboba Indians also lost faith in the capacity of rituals to provide for their collective welfare. But the dilemma over how Sabobas might go about regaining faith in their ability to comprehend and thus change their circumstances for the better is not addressed by James. I suggest that although such a silence can be interpreted to indicate how James was unable to imagine a future for the Sabobas and other southern California Indians in which they could become successfully bicultural, this silence can also be read as a recognition of the space in which they had the capacity to reimagine themselves as Indians. That is to say, James implicitly suggests the need for Indians to allow themselves to become educated into white ways and decide for themselves, as far as possible, how to negotiate the limited social and economic alternatives open to them in the "white" world while simultaneously remaking their cultural traditions in light of the increasingly bicultural aspects of their lives in the twentieth century.

There is no doubt that one has to read James against the grain in order to come to this conclusion, but ironically his account of meeting the "real" Ramona provides evidence to support the claim. Ramona Lubo (or Lugo) was the widow of Juan Diego, the model for Jackson's Alessandro, and, according to James, "settled down to the dull and uneventful life of a Cahuilla Indian" until people started seeking her out in the aftermath of *Ramona*'s publication. Revealing a typical combination of sympathy and exploitation, after seeking out Ramona, James prompted her to show her husband's grave and photographed her as she wept by its side: "It seemed almost a sacrilege to make a photograph of her at this moment, yet I trust she and the recording angel will consider the kindliness of my heart towards her and her people in balancing the amount of my culpability." James continues his account by describing Ramona as "squat, . . . fat and unattractive," paying particular attention to her "low forehead, prominent cheek bones, wide nostrils, heavy lips" and concluding that "she appears dull, heavy, and unimpressionable." What should we make of such a representation? On the one hand James's attention to physiognomic details appears crudely racist, equating the Cahuilla Indians' facial and bodily appearance with physical languor and mental torpor. (James comments later that the Cahuillas "possess the full-blooded corpulency of the negro, rather than the slim nervous habit of some tribes.") But in also noting that Ramona is "uncommunicative" and that "her features seem to have crystallized into an expression of indifference, dislike to the whites, and deep sadness," James is forced to acknowledge her individual agency. Indeed, after quoting a *Los Angeles Times* article of 1907 that states Ramona's "baskets bring phenomenal prices, as well as her photos and lace work," James credits her with exclaiming: "Nobody love me here, white people no love me, Indians no love me, only Condino [her son] love me and I heap tired." Through these details a more detailed image of Ramona emerges. It appears she became keenly aware on the one hand of how the curiosity value invested in her image and crafts by visiting whites lacked a larger humanitarian dimension in which her full personhood was realized, and on the other hand how the commodity value of outsiders' interest in her figure helped strain her relations with fellow Cahuillas. Although it is tempting to say that Ramona Lubo thus became caught between cultures, in fact the shifting fortunes of her life indicate more generally the ways that interactions between Cahuillas and Anglo society were changing at the turn of the last century.[81]

In a chapter titled "The Indians of *Ramona's* Country," James comments on several aspects of Cahuilla life in his account of a visit to a reservation near San Jacinto around 1900. After locating great granite boulders that feature in oral storytelling, *morteros* that he thinks are neglected but still may be used occasionally for grinding and pounding, and rock art that he confesses to not understanding, James then notes that some of the Cahuillas are "keen and sharp in trade." Specifically he refers to the work of women who in addition to gathering and preparing food and making limited amounts of pottery are "fairly expert basket weavers." Thus James hints at the way Cahuillas have adapted to a cash economy and taken advantage of Anglo interest in crafts that hitherto had a utilitarian and ceremonial function within Cahuilla society. James's response to the cultural survival of Cahuillas and other Indians is typical in its ambiguity, for even as he wishes the Indians he visits to be good, simple, childlike, and uncorrupted, logic forces him to recognize the ways in which they have been drawn into the white world. When James comments that "reservation life is not exciting" and explains that "men are shepherds, cattlemen, cowboys, and engage in all simple and pastoral industries," one senses that he was far more enthused by imagining Indian lives free of Anglo influence than by the prospect of "actual" Indian life. And yet in noting that Cahuillas, despite being "nominally Christian," continue to "indulge in their ancient dances, whenever the old anniversaries come around," James demonstrates, in effect, the resourcefulness of Cahuillas in adapting to changed circumstances.[82]

Having stressed the resourcefulness of Cahuillas in this discussion, I must announce a note of caution for, as the anthropologist Lowell John Bean points out, many southern California Indians in the twentieth century have had "the status of Orwellian non-persons."[83] Delfina Cuero became such a non-person when the record of her baptism at a church was burned accidentally. Later in life she struggled, with the assistance of anthropologist Florence Shipek, to gain official recognition of her own U.S. citizenship and thus also convey to the children to whom she had given birth in Mexico legal standing as U.S. citizens. As Shipek points out, during the 1960s Cuero agreed to participate in the writing of her autobiography after she had moved back across the international border and wished to prove that she had been born in San Diego County and thus had the right to remain in the United States as a permanent resident. Despite the autobiography's candid details of poverty, domestic abuse, and personal loss, it is a life-affirming story of cultural survival against the odds. Cuero tells the story of how small groups of Kumeyaay struggled to survive after being displaced from their homes in and around San Diego at the beginning of the last century. She recalls that her parents and grandparents lived in San Diego's Mission Valley but had not been brought up in the Spanish mission after which the valley is named: "There was nobody living there any more; just some Indians and their families living there and Indians all up and down the Valley."[84] Her parents were forced to move away from land their ancestors claimed they had always lived on when Americans and Chinese immigrants moved into the area. Along with fellow displaced Kumeyaay, Cuero's parents settled east of the developing city in locations that were also claimed by incoming Anglos. At Jamacha, to where Cuero's parents had removed at the time of her birth, the family lived in brush shelters in a canyon and received food and old clothing in payment for clearing ranchers' land. The women added to meager food supplies by gathering wild cherries and other foods. Years passed and the family continued to move away from San Diego, eventually settling in a small Kumeyaay village located in the mountains twenty miles south of Tecate, Mexico. There Cuero spent the later years of her childhood and the duration of her first marriage. Finding it hard to provide for her children—hunger is a recurrent motif in the autobiography— Cuero agreed to sell her twelve-year-old son, Aurelio, to a Mexican in return for food given to her other children. Aurelio was worked like a man, beaten, and paid for his labor only with the provision of food. In the meantime Cuero returned to the mountains with her baby son and three daughters after a futile trip to Tecate to find food, because in the mountains "at least we had what wild food we could find."[85]

Although Cuero's account contains further distressing details of her family's breakup, her own and her daughters' abusive relationships with men, and the growing difficulty Indians experienced as they sought to hunt and gather on mountainous lands in the northern part of Baja California that became coveted by Mexicans, nevertheless her story is one of endurance and survival. The autobiography provides ample evidence of the range and depth of Cuero's cultural memory, conveying a vivid and imaginative portrayal of Kumeyaay culture in which myriad details of subsistence, cosmology, and oral tradition are relayed. Kumeyaay Indians forged an independent livelihood for many years after their displacement from lands in the San Diego locale not only out of sheer necessity to provide sustenance for their community but also because they continued to understand themselves as a distinct people. But as the years passed and Kumeyaay existence became even more marginalized and tenuous, traditional religious practice that in the past had formed an integrated system for the education, moral instruction, and ethical behavior of community members gradually weakened. Although this integrated system had already been impacted by missionization during the late eighteenth and nineteenth centuries, it appears that both during and after the mission years Kumeyaay Indians were able to maintain a long-held interdependent relationship between ritual behavior and food resources.[86] When Cuero tells of favorite locations for food gathering and of the stories associated with those places and practices, readers learn something of how knowledge production within Kumeyaay culture changed during the twentieth century. For instance, after informing readers of the rich and varied seafood diet Kumeyaay Indians enjoyed when visiting coastal areas, she alludes to a story about how olivella shells were babies that fell out of the "'dipper in the sky' [the Big Dipper] when it was too full." However, Cuero relates, "There was more to it but I am not a story teller and that is all I can remember. They used to name all the stars and tell stories about them, and explain why the Dipper is lying differently in summer and winter." Elsewhere she comments, "I only remember a few of the stories now; it is so long since I have heard them."[87] These words testify to the specialized function of the storyteller in Kumeyaay culture while also hinting, through the use of the past tense, at the way "traditional" knowledge grew fragmented and partial in the second half of the twentieth century. One should add that the very fact that Cuero collaborated in the writing of an autobiography also indicates ongoing cultural change.[88] The autobiography ends with Shipek's noting that although a number of Kumeyaay Indians like Cuero maintained their independence through decades in which the federal government forced Indians into dependency, "[n]ow they are asking, 'Can our grandchildren go to your schools? There is no longer any room for hunters and gatherers! We can no longer teach them how to survive. They must learn the new skills from you!'"[89]

To some extent Delfina Cuero's life story confirms James's observation in the early 1900s that only "a few scattered remains" of Indian cultures were to be found in mountain and desert areas of southern California that incoming Anglos had not developed. Through moving south of the border into Baja California onto land the Kumeyaay considered part of their territory, Cuero's family continued to eke out a living by using traditional patterns of subsistence and by participating only to a small extent in a cash economy. However, this way of life could not be sustained and so the autobiography ends with the paraphrased voices of Kumeyaay Indians who wished to be incorporated into the United States. For Shipek, the autobiography relates not only "the destruction of Indian self-sufficiency on the land, of Indian society, culture, and religion" but also the "much, much slower pace of Indian integration into modern society."[90] Cuero's narrative also departs from James's narrative in key respects, not least in providing an insider's perspective on what it means to be part of a so-called "dying" culture. Although the autobiography is a record of profound loss and irrevocable change, it is also a document of cultural persistence and cultural renewal, as is demonstrated by Cuero's stated wish for her people to learn new skills and to take up educational opportunities in order to participate more fully in U.S. society. That desire for greater integration does not mean forsaking the old ways is demonstrated by the way that Cuero remembers places and natural features that have been transformed during the twentieth century, especially after World War II. She helps readers envision San Diego's Mission Valley—now a thoroughfare for Interstate 8 and the location of numerous shopping malls, commercial offices, and residences—when Kumeyaay Indians still subsisted in that environment. Elsewhere she comments on the San Diego neighborhood of Ocean Beach: "There are so many houses here now I can't find my way any more," adding, "[e]verything looks so bad now; the hills are cut up even."[91] These words, combined with Cuero's intricate details of subsistence, function in several ways at once. They articulate an indigenous memory of what long-transformed landscapes used to look like and how people used to live on them; in so doing they levy a cultural claim not so much on the land itself as on storytelling about the land. Thus Cuero calls into question the hierarchy of progressive and capitalistic social and economic values that have proved instrumental in facilitating urban development during the twentieth century. In addition, through remembering past activities Cuero forges a link between older and younger generations and provides for the persistence of Kumeyaay culture.

Cuero's autobiography demonstrates how Native American storytelling, both oral and written, plays a central role in articulating the ties among individuals, communities, and the places they inhabit. As is indicated by the subtitle of Cuero's autobiography—"her ethnobotanical contributions"—

Native storytelling is often also a rich source of information about the ways in which the local ecology has changed as a result of human intervention. The writer and literary critic Louise Jeffredo-Warden, a southern California Indian who prefers the term *Poyomkawish* to "Luiseño" when describing her ethnicity, explains how her culture's songs are constructed about metaphors, known as "ceremonial couplings," which are as interrelated and inseparable as the elements of an ecosystem.[92] Generalizing from this particular example of how Native storytelling articulates a holistic understanding of the world, she argues that tribal stories are "metaphoric avenues through which our elders articulate, teach, and reinforce the balance and cyclical interrelationship in power and being, in elements—aged and young, human and non-human, female and male, spiritual and material—of this world."[93] Such stories in the present help bind tribal people together and forge a collective sense of identity while also, insofar as tribal elders wish the stories to reach a larger audience, contributing a land-based ethical viewpoint to regional debates on environmental change.

While Jeffredo-Warden suggests the ways in which tribal storytelling helps foster a discrete sense of identity that strongly differentiates between Poyomkawish ethnicity and non-Indian cultures, interestingly Cuero's life story demonstrates that although there is a phenomenon we call Kumeyaay cultural persistence, there is not necessarily such a thing as an "essential" Kumeyaay cultural identity. Thus Cuero's life story dramatizes its narrator's individual agency, draws attention to changing gender roles in Kumeyaay culture, and demonstrates the ways in which in a culture under duress reinvention is necessary. Indeed, the literary critic Phillip Round argues that the personal self and collective identity conveyed through the pages of Cuero's autobiography are created dynamically through the dialogic form of narrative, and so the life story both records and helps to create "a discursive history of performative interaction and struggle."[94] I would argue there is a compatibility between Round's interpretation and Florence Shipek's claim that southern California Indians "have a tradition of a constant search for new forms of beneficial knowledge and new forms of income."[95] For both commentators stress the vitalism and adaptability of southern California Indians and in this they each convey a keener awareness of the precise ways in which Native cultures have striven to remain "true" to themselves while reinventing themselves as tribal peoples, as pan-Indian cultures, and as U.S. citizens, a welcome phenomenon that neither Constance Goddard DuBois nor George Wharton James could have anticipated.

The Legacy of *Ramona*

Having discussed James and Cuero, it is time to return to *Ramona*. We should recall that Carey McWilliams saw emerging out of the Spanish fantasy heritage of southern California certain damaging consequences for Mexican Americans. In his view *Ramona* helped create an image, almost endlessly reiterated in subsequent travel narratives, local histories, and boosterist writings, that consigned Californios to the past and did not account for the continued presence of Mexican Americans and Mexican immigrants in California and the larger Southwest. From the signing of the Treaty of Guadalupe Hidalgo in 1848, through the reign of dictator Porfirio Diaz, and to the Mexican Revolution and beyond, huge numbers of Mexicans migrated to the Southwest. Historians estimate that between 1900 and 1989 2.4 million Mexican nationals with formal papers immigrated to the United States, while perhaps as many as twenty million people traveled as undocumented individuals.[96] This constitutes one of the great mass migrations in recent world history.

Although a more considered analysis of Mexican immigration to the United States and of the twists and turns of U.S. immigration policy over the past hundred or so years is outside the scope of this discussion, *Ramona*'s publication at a time when many Euro-Americans subscribed to racialist assumptions about the superiority of "Anglo Saxons" to people of other "races" is significant in two respects. First, regarding Jackson's characterization of Ramona, who we should recall leaves California for Mexico with her "brother"/husband Felipe at the end of the novel, it is important to note that Jackson appears to imagine more tolerance for the mestiza in Mexico than in the United States. In an ironic turn of phrase, Mexico is imagined by Felipe as the "new world" that possesses vibrant possibilities for "a new life" free of the "boasted successes," "brigandage and gambling" he associates with "the fast incoming Americans."[97] For the literary critic Carl Gutiérrez-Jones, though, Ramona's marriage to Felipe at the end of the novel in a manner that suggests incest—and necrophilia insofar as Ramona has "died" in the aftermath of the deaths of her husband and child—and the way in which she is insulated within a high-caste "Spanish" family suggest that Ramona's mestiza identity is denied. Gutiérrez-Jones further contends that "the mestiza population and all the potentially threatening sexuality that it represents," is the novel's symbolic center.[98] This is a persuasive interpretation of the novel's ending, and one that is only confirmed when bearing in mind the intolerance of politicians and other cultural commentators in the late nineteenth century who warned their fellow citizens of the dangers of "Anglo-Saxon" purity's being corrupted through interracial relationships and the perceived encroachment, primarily in eastern cities, of darker-skinned and non-Protestant immigrants who were not deemed assimilable into American society.[99]

There is a second point to make regarding the position of *Ramona* in relation to discourses on race and ethnicity in the 1880s. It should be stressed that while Jackson clearly subscribed to racialist assumptions in her dramatization of both Indian and Mexicano characters, nonetheless she challenged her own culture's more conservative propositions about the character of the American nation and its people. To illustrate this point I refer to William Makepeace Thayer's *Marvels of the New West*. Published in 1888 by an author who was renowned for "preach[ing] the gospel of virtue and success,"[100] *Marvels of the New West* is one of a number of grandiose and richly illustrated volumes published in the late nineteenth century to convey a holistic picture of the West. The book was designed to appeal to a white, Protestant, and eastern audience and celebrated, in a decade when large-scale conflict with Native Americans was over, "the marvels" of nature, race, enterprise, mining, stock-raising, and agriculture incorporated into the United States through westward expansion. Thayer concluded his book by stating: "This race has laid the foundation of our Western empire, and started it off in a career of unexampled prosperity; and its grip upon the masses will not be relaxed as the battle for unity and right waxes hotter; but will rather tighten its hold and increase its power, until language, custom, and purpose are one, under the control of Liberty, Education, and religion."[101] Such rhetoric appears to carry to an extreme the will to nullify through incorporation anything that stands in the way of "Anglo-Saxon supremacy over the New West," and to a contemporary reader, these words, despite their sinister connotations, appear outlandish because the image of American culture they promote is so obviously skewed and unrealizable.[102] Indeed, their very exuberance suggests an anxious need among elite Americans to protect their class interests against the reality of ethnic and cultural diversity in the late nineteenth century. In relation to this sort of writing—racist, self-aggrandizing, and myopic—Jackson's Indian reform politics appear liberal and visionary, and *Ramona*, despite the shortcomings noted throughout this chapter, can be read as a novel that campaigns not only for Indian reform but for more improved interracial relations generally while simultaneously calling into question, through its impassioned critique of frontier violence, the rhetoric of Manifest Destiny that undergirded Thayer's writing about the so-called New West.

I conclude with some observations regarding *Ramona* and Jackson's Indian rights advocacy. When regarding Jackson's characterization of Native Americans, we must remember that in striving to elicit the sympathy of readers she was consciously avoiding damaging stereotypes of Indian savagism. Furthermore, as an Indian reformer she worked within an ongoing rhetorical tradition in which victimhood and oppression rather than resistance were stressed. Related to this observation, most Indian reformers of the late nineteenth century considered accommodation and acculturation were to be the key to Indian survival. They tended to see Indians as caught in a civilization-or-die binarism and that it was in Indians' best interest to assimilate as far as possible into American society. Concerning the promotional appropriation of *Ramona* and the co-optation of the novel's reform message, it is significant that writers such as Charles Fletcher Lummis and George Wharton James, who wrote voluminous amounts of travel-related literature about southern California and the Southwest, considered themselves Indian rights advocates. For such people promotional writing was not necessarily at odds with a genuine concern for Indian rights. Taking a larger view of Indian reform initiatives, we must see *Ramona* within a larger history of Indian reform initiatives and note that during the 1930s there was a fundamental reorganization of Indian affairs after the appointment of John Collier as Commissioner of Indian Affairs in Franklin Delano Roosevelt's administration. Collier's "Indian New Deal" provided for Native American tribal government and promoted economic self-determination, a significantly different approach to the administration of Indian affairs than that practiced between the early 1880s and the 1920s.[103] Finally, we do well to recognize *Ramona* as an ethically-minded fiction that commands our attention today precisely because we can learn from the limitations of Jackson's social and political vision regarding Indian reform and interculturation.

1. Richard H. Kern, "Hosta, Governor of Jemez Pueblo." From Lieutenant James
H. Simpson, *Journal of a Military Reconnaissance, from Santa Fe, New Mexico, to
the Navajo Country, Made with the Troops under Command of Brevet Lieutenant
John M. Washington, Chief of Ninth Military Department, and Governor of New
Mexico, in 1849* (Philadelphia: Lippincott, Grambo and Co., 1852). Courtesy
Huntington Library, San Marino, California.

2. View of a Caravan, Santa Fe Trail. From W. W. H. Davis, *El Gringo; Or, New Mexico and Her People* (New York: Harper and Brothers, 1857). Courtesy Huntington Library, San Marino, California.

3. Arrival of the Caravan at Santa Fe. From W. W. H. Davis, *El Gringo; Or, New Mexico and Her People* (New York: Harper and Brothers, 1857). Courtesy Huntington Library, San Marino, California.

4. View of the Colorado River. From John Wesley Powell, *Report of the Exploration of the Colorado River and Its Tributaries* (Washington, D.C.: Government Printing Office, 1875).

5. View of the Grand Canyon. From John Wesley Powell, *Report of the Exploration of the Colorado River and Its Tributaries* (Washington, D.C.: Government Printing Office, 1875).

6. "Paiute Chief Tau-Gu and John Wesley Powell, Kaibab Plateau, near Grand Canyon, Arizona." John K. Hillers, Powell Survey, c. 1872–73. Courtesy National Anthropological Archives, Smithsonian Institution, Washington, D.C.

THE LAND OF SUNSHINE

VOL. 3, No. 1.   LOS ANGELES   JUNE, 1895

SAN JUAN'S DAY AT DOLORES.

BY CHAS. F. LUMMIS.

AY! Never was fiesta fair as good
    San Juan's today—
A thousand souls at mass this morn,
    and what a glory when
They ran the chicken-races! How
    Felipe swept away
The squawking prize—first cavalier
    among a hundred men!

How like a rock from off the cliff he thundered
    down the plain!
And how the chase behind him roared in a
    tumultuous flood!
And how he beat the grapplers off,
    with feathered blows amain!
And how
    his white teeth
laughed thro' bronze
    besplashed
with manly blood!

7. "San Juan's Day at Dolores," from *Land of Sunshine* 3, no. 1 (June 1895).
Courtesy Huntington Library, San Marino, California.

8. Charles Fletcher Lummis on horseback. Courtesy Huntington Library, San Marino, California.

COPYRIGHT 1902,
BY C.F.LUMMIS. 1337.

9. Charles Fletcher Lummis at work in his study in his home El Alisal, Los
Angeles. Courtesy Huntington Library, San Marino, California.

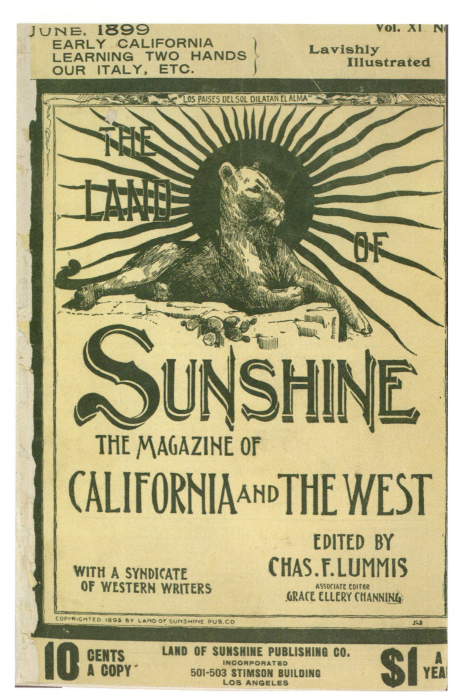

10. *Land of Sunshine* cover (June 1899). Courtesy Huntington Library, San Marino, California.

11. Advertisement for Campbells Curio Store, Los Angeles, featuring a photograph by Charles Fletcher Lummis of a young Isleta women, which appeared in *Land of Sunshine* 2, no. 5 (April 1895): unpaginated advertisements. Courtesy Huntington Library, San Marino, California.

12. Elbridge Ayer Burbank, *Chief Geronimo (Apache, Chiricahua, Fort Sill, OT)*, 1899. Oil on canvas, 13" x 9". Courtesy Butler Institute of American Art, Youngstown, Ohio.

13. Elbridge Ayer Burbank, *O-bah (Moqui, Keams Canyon, AZ)*, 1898. Oil on canvas, 13" x 9". Courtesy Butler Institute of American Art, Youngstown, Ohio.

SI·YOU·WEE·TEH·ZE·SAH. ZUNI.

From original Painting by E. A. Burbank — Copyrighted, Brush & Pencil, Chicago, 1899

October 1899	SUN	MON	TUES	WED	THUR	FRI	SAT	Santa Fe Route
							1	
	1	2	3	4	5	6	7	
	8	9	10	11	12	13	14	
	15	16	17	18	19	20	21	
	22	23	24	25	26	27	28	
	29	30	31					

Zuñi pueblo is in New Mexico, and is reached by stage from Wingate, a station on the main line of the Santa Fe Route to California. The Zuñis have a number of strikingly picturesque ceremonies peculiar to themselves.

14. Atchison, Topeka, and Santa Fe Railroad, *Aztec Calendar,* 1899. Courtesy Edward Everett Ayer Collection, The Newberry Library, Chicago, Illinois.

15. Elbridge Ayer Burbank, *Tube-eh (Hopi, Polacca, AZ)*, 1905. Conté crayon drawing. Courtesy Edward Everett Ayer Collection, The Newberry Library, Chicago, Illinois.

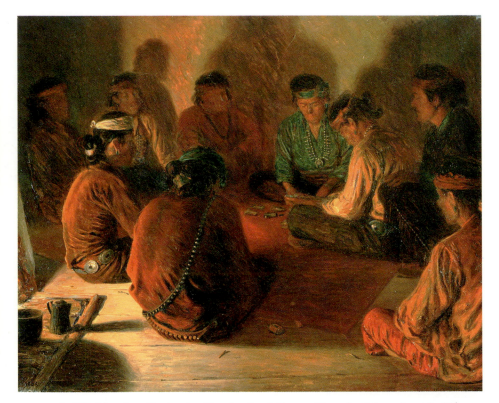

16. Elbridge Ayer Burbank, *Navaho Card Players (Ganado, Arizona),* 1908. Oil on canvas, 16" x 20". Courtesy Edward Everett Ayer Collection, The Newberry Library, Chicago, Illinois.

17. Elbridge Ayer Burbank, *Edward Everett Ayer,* 1897. Oil on canvas, 32" x 25". Courtesy Edward Everett Ayer Collection, The Newberry Library, Chicago, Illinois.

18. Adam Clark Vroman, "Walpi Village from the Northeast," from his
"Photo-Diary of the Hopi Snake Dance," 1895. Courtesy Huntington
Library, San Marino, California.

19. Adam Clark Vroman, "Our Home on the Mesa," from his "Photo-Diary of the Hopi Snake Dance," 1895. Courtesy Huntington Library, San Marino, California.

20. Sumner Matteson, "Self-Portrait with Snake," ca. 1900. Courtesy Beinecke Rare Book and Manuscript Library, Yale University, New Haven, Connecticut.

21. Frederick Monsen, "Navajo Blanket Weaver," ca. 1905. Courtesy Huntington
Library, San Marino, California.

22. Frederick Monsen, "Navajo Indian Children," ca. 1905. Courtesy Huntington Library, San Marino, California.

23. *Indian Detours* (New York: Rand McNally and Company, 1933). Courtesy Edward Everett Ayer Collection, The Newberry Library, Chicago, Illinois.

24. Martin Padget, "Taos Pueblo" (c. 1993).

Travel, Exoticism, and the Writing of Region: Charles Fletcher Lummis and the "Creation" of the Southwest

ON SEPTEMBER 11, 1884, Charles Fletcher Lummis embarked on a self-styled "tramp across the continent" from Cincinnati, Ohio, to Los Angeles, California. The trek ended on February 1, 1885, after 143 days and 3,507 miles of walking. Planned as both a personal endurance trip and a publicity stunt, the "tramp" was a deliberate attempt to step outside the boundaries of Eastern society and engage in a frontier existence in the Southwest. It was also a sporting adventure, a masculinist athletic trial, an escape from Lummis's home in malarial Ohio, a symbolic departure from the perceived decadence of Eastern society, a chance to separate temporarily from his first wife, Dorothea, and the means of securing the position of city editor at the young *Los Angeles Times* newspaper. En route Lummis sent one series of letters to the *Chillicothe Leader* newspaper in Ohio and another to the *Los Angeles Times,* which later formed the basis of his book *A Tramp Across the Continent* (1892). Travel westward for Lummis meant a deliberate move away from an East perceived as economically and morally corrupt, subject to race mongrelization and scourged by a cruel climate in which the full bodily and mental potential of the individual could not be realized. Yet the irony of southwestern travel was that while it was a self-conscious departure away from the perceived threat of immigration to Anglo-Saxon racial and cultural purity in the East, it was a move into one of the most ethnically diverse regions of the United States.

Travel and fiction writer, poet, journal editor, historian of "Spanish" America, explorer, archaeologist, ethnologist, folklorist, raconteur, and feisty eccentric, Lummis was one of a generation of Euro-American intellectuals who became fascinated with the Southwest in the late nineteenth and early twentieth centuries. A Harvard-educated Easterner who went on to live most of his life in Los Angeles, he was hyperbolic, self-aggrandizing, and relentlessly enthusiastic in his promotional writing. Between 1884, when he first "tramped" through Colorado, New Mexico, Arizona, and southern California, and his death in 1928, Lummis wrote voluminously about the region's natural landscapes and its populations of Native Americans and Mexican Americans. From the 1890s, when the bulk of his books on the Southwest were published, to the end of his life in 1928, Lummis was judged by his peers as one of the foremost writers on the Southwest.[1]

From the moment he entered the region, Lummis became engaged in mapping a new cultural geography of the Southwest. Through highly romanticized commentaries on the region's spectacular natural land-scapes, archaeological and anthropological antiquities, and "exotic" pop-ulations of Native Americans and Mexican Americans, Lummis transcribed selected parts of the Southwest into the bodies of written texts. His voluminous writings about the region both drew on and significantly differed from the work of the earlier writers discussed in the first chapter. Whereas W. W. H. Davis had been alienated by the strange-ness of Santa Fe in the 1850s, Lummis reveled in the "foreign" qualities of New Mexico three decades later. As we have seen in the case of Susan Wallace, Lummis was by no means the first writer to claim that American tourists should visit New Mexico in order to view people, architecture, and landscapes that were so different from the rest of the United States. But he was arguably the most influential popular writer of travel-related literature on the Southwest as a whole in the 1890s and early 1900s. Lummis's interest in the cultural antiquity of the region echoed the ongo-ing pursuits of pioneering archaeologists and anthropologists in the Southwest, foremost among them Adolph Bandelier, Frank Hamilton Cushing, Jesse Walter Fewkes, and Washington Matthews.[2] These indi-viduals developed both a greater personal and professional familiarity with the Southwest, and in the process of producing knowledge about the region's landscapes and peoples they helped rationalize the hitherto unfamiliar cultural terrain of the region for popular and professional audiences.[3] While there were significant differences between the texts written on the Southwest by ethnologists and by travel writers like Lummis, collectively their texts contributed to the process whereby the colonial frontier of the Southwest was claimed by intellectual authority and, in tandem with social and economic activities, transformed into a region of the United States.

Recent critics have noted that the incorporation of the conquered territories of the Southwest into the nation in the aftermath of the U.S.-Mexican War and the Civil War proceeded along aesthetic as much as economic and political lines.[4] Writers of turn-of-the-century travelogues and ethnological reports contributed to the process of cultural incorporation by exoticizing the livelihoods of contemporary Pueblo Indians and Navajos, and by romantically conjecturing on the pre-Columbian past of the Southwest. In representing dramatic natural landscapes such as the Grand Canyon, large-scale archaeological antiquities such as Pueblo Bonito (in Chaco Canyon, New Mexico), and the adobe-structured homes of Pueblo Indians, writers *produced* the Southwest for popular and professional readerships.[5] In the 1880s and 1890s, as travelers became attracted to the Southwest for the full exercise and expression of their physical and creative energies, their voices joined with regional boosterists to rhetorically construct the region as a land of enchantment. New Mexico and Arizona, in particular, were prized for the varieties of authentic experience they afforded. The historian Curtis M. Hinsley Jr. argues that late-nineteenth-century "aesthetic claim staking" in the Southwest "reflected . . . a widespread appetite in post–Civil War American society for varieties of authentic experience: authentic aesthetic/religious sensibilities, relations to landscape, modes of production, sexual identities, and social relationships."[6] He further argues that around 1900 these responses were commodified and that thereafter "the association of authenticity with the Southwest fed powerful market forces" that continue to impact the region.[7] Nowhere is the link between personal experience, authenticity, and promotion stronger in late-nineteenth and early-twentieth-century representations of the Southwest than in Lummis's texts.

In tramping across the continent, Lummis strove to embody and incorporate the geographical expanse of the United States through his athletic activity. Initial travel through the Southwest was an opportunity to escape what he saw as the debilitated culture of the East and to regenerate his personal and "Saxon" racial identity outside of the bounds of "civilized" society. After 1884, he demonstrated a lifelong commitment to the promotion of the racially invigorating qualities of New Mexico, Arizona, and southern California. Extensive travel through the region in subsequent years formed the basis of his knowledge of the history and cultures of the Southwest. Significantly it was Lummis's personal investment in the region that afforded him the expertise to make grandiose sweeping statements about its attributes, and this expertise was in large part founded on what he and many contemporaries saw as his authentic experience of place. Thus Lummis's chief capital in claiming authority on the Southwest became his own experience—"authentic" experience that was created and commodified through the act of writing.

This chapter examines Lummis's "creation" of the Southwest for popular readerships in both the East and the West in the late nineteenth and early twentieth centuries. His association with the Southwest in general, and New Mexico in particular, went through three distinct phases: initial encounter by way of the "tramp," participant observation through prolonged stays at San Mateo and Isleta Pueblo, and consolidation of his "expertise" after his return to Los Angeles. The discussion proceeds in three parts. First, I examine how Lummis wrote about the Southwest when first visiting the region. While embarking on the walk with fierce athletic intensity, he also labeled his account "the wayside notes of a happy vagabondizing."[8] His combination of almost tireless activity with the call for a less hurried and regimented lifestyle was central to Lummis's character and his work and was only seemingly paradoxical. As we will see, this combination was the site of a productive tension that was first evidenced in the "tramp" itself.

Second, I take the years 1888–92 as Lummis's period of participant observer ethnography in the Southwest. After arriving in Los Angeles in 1885 and expending himself in three years of characteristically frenzied activity at the *Los Angeles Times,* Lummis suffered a severe stroke and left the city to recover in New Mexico. For almost a year he stayed in or around San Mateo with the family of Amado Chaves, former Speaker of the New Mexico Territorial government. Out of his experience with the Chaves family grew a fierce regard for the beliefs and practices of the old Spanish colonial elite and a sympathetic, albeit patronizing, affection for the local population of "humble" Hispanos. Lummis then removed to Isleta Pueblo, where he lived for three years, eventually overcoming his paralysis. Lummis spent much of his time at the pueblo recording what he saw for publication. A flow of books, remarkable for their quantity if not their quality, issued from Lummis's pen, half of them published while the author was still residing at Isleta. *A New Mexico David* (1891), *A Tramp Across the Continent* (1892), *Some Strange Corners of Our Country* (1892), *The Land of Poco Tiempo* (1893), *The Spanish Pioneers* (1893), *The Man Who Married the Moon* (1894), and *The King of the Broncos* (1897) all drew from their author's intimate experience of locale, and combined travelogue, ethnology, archaeology, storytelling, and regional history in their exposition of southwestern themes.[9]

Written primarily for an Eastern audience, these texts trumpeted the Southwest as a "foreign" country within the United States. For Lummis it was the very difference of the region, measured in terms of landscape and population, that was its chief cultural asset. Thus he celebrated Pueblo Indian festivals, Navajo rug makers, "Mexican" shepherds, and Hidalgo Indian fighters, while also writing negatively about Native American beliefs in witchcraft and the activities of the Hispano Penitentes. In this section, I endeavor to unravel the complex web of ethnic, gender, and cultural relations in Lummis's representations of Pueblo Indian life and his disparaging portrayal of the Penitentes.

Third, I examine the writing Lummis produced after his move back to Los Angeles in 1893 by looking at how he edited the influential magazine *Land of Sunshine* (later renamed *Out West*). Initiated in 1894 as a promotional journal for Los Angeles and southern California, the magazine quickly took a more literary turn after Lummis assumed the editor's position in 1894. As editor and chief contributor, Lummis relentlessly praised the climate and culture of southern California, paying particular attention to the region's "Spanish" heritage by actively campaigning for the preservation of its mission buildings. El Alisal, Lummis's home on the outskirts of Los Angeles in Arroyo Seco, became a gathering point for southern California literati, artists, and politicians. He was visited by many contributors to *Land of Sunshine/Out West,* including the writers Mary Austin, Ina Coolbrith, Charlotte Perkins Gilman, and John Muir, and the artists Elbridge Ayer Burbank and Maynard Dixon.[10]

"The Wayside Notes of a Happy Vagabondizing"

On November 18, 1884, Lummis wrote from Alamosa, Colorado, the eleventh of twenty-four letters sent to the *Chillicothe Leader*. He described coming into La Veta, a small town lying at the foot of the Spanish Peaks, just north of the New Mexico territorial line:

> The day was full of interest to me, for in it, I stepped across the line from an alleged American civilization into the boundaries of one strangely diverse. Two miles out from little Cucharas, and on the willowy banks of Cucharas creek, I ran across a big plaza of Mexicans—Greasers as they are called out here. A Westerner would no more think of calling a "Greaser" a Mexican, than a Kentucky Colonel would of calling a negro anything but "nigger."[11]

He continued by characterizing local ranchers as "a snide-looking set, twice as dark as an Indian, with heavy lips and noses, long, straight, black hair, sleepy eyes, and a general expression of ineffable laziness." And added: "Their language is a patois of Spanish and Mexican. These may be poor specimens along here. I hope so. Not even a coyote will touch a dead Greaser, the flesh is so seasoned with the red pepper they ram into their food in howling profusion."[12]

Such brutal humor at the expense of rural Hispanos was hardly a new facet of Anglo travel writing on the Southwest; indeed, it appears that prior to first contact Lummis crossed the Spanish Peaks with his racial prejudice already formed.[13] Soon after writing from Alamosa, however, his opinion changed, and in his next letter to the *Leader*, written in Santa Fe, New Mexico, he praised "Mexicans" for their hospitality and personal warmth. Given the opportunity to revise his account of the "tramp" in later years, Lummis highlighted his earlier racism by asking a rhetorical question: "Why is it that the last and most difficult education seems to be the ridding ourselves of the silly inborn race prejudice?"[14]

This gesture of public penance was fully expressed in *A Tramp Across the Continent*, when he rewrote his entry into "a civilization that was then new to me" by explaining:

> In Colorado the Mexicans are much in the minority, and are frequently nicknamed "greasers"—a nomenclature which it is not wise to practise as one proceeds south, and which anyway is born of an unbred boorishness of which no Mexican could ever be guilty. They are a simple, kindly people, ignorant of books, but better taught than our average in all the social virtues—in hospitality, courtesy, and respect for age. They are neither so "cowardly" nor so "treacherous" as an enormous class that largely shapes our national destinies; and it would be a thorn to our conceit, if we could realize how very many important lessons we could profitably learn from them. I speak now from years of intimate, but honorable, personal acquaintance with them—an acquaintance which has shamed me out of the silly prejudices against them which I shared with the average Saxon.[15]

Rhetorically, the passage suggests a significant change in Lummis's interpretation of Mexican American culture. On the basis of personal contact, Lummis not only dismissed Euro-American stereotypes of Mexican

Americans but praised the "social virtues" of Hispanos in direct relation to the "unbred boorishness" of lower-class Euro-Americans. His succeeding writing on Hispanos, however, reformulated rather than overturned existing Anglo assumptions about Mexican American culture.

When writing about New Mexico after his return from Los Angeles in 1888, Lummis characterized the territory's charm as that of "the land of poco tiempo." This representation contributed to equally debilitating Anglo notions of Hispano backwardness, rustic simplicity, and a lack of competitive spirit measured in social, economic, and racial terms. Lummis's representations of Hispanos generally divided local people into two camps. On the one hand, he related a number of stories about *pobres*—the humble shepherds, farmers, and miners of the region—while on the other hand, he dramatized the lives of *ricos,* a privileged class of landowners and officials. These stories were often based on tales of Indian fighting and "heroism" told to him by Colonel Manuel Chaves of San Mateo. Emergent from this largely dualistic attention to character and deeds in New Mexico was storytelling that stressed fatalism, sentimentalism, heroism, and romance in the lives of Hispanos. Stories were nuanced so as to emphasize the perceived fatalism of *pobres* to the rigid social hierarchy of Hispano culture and the similarly passive acceptance among *ricos* of their diminished authority and wealth in Anglicized New Mexico. As we shall see in the next section, a significant exception to this general rule of representation is found in Lummis's fanatical pursuit of the Penitentes, whom he saw as a threat to the otherwise orderly incorporation of Hispano culture into American society.

Turning to Lummis's initial view of Pueblo Indians, it is ironic, considering his later period of residence in Isleta, that Lummis's first impression of the pueblo was hardly complimentary. In a letter to the *Chillicothe Leader,* he labeled the pueblo "tolerably interesting."[16] At that point of his account, Lummis was more concerned with describing details of his walk from Albuquerque to El Rito, New Mexico. Thus he wrote about lava beds, agates, the scarcity of water, and the loneliness of the country, before describing a meeting with cowboys (whom he saw favorably) and his arrival in the "tiny Indian town" of El Rito. In his next letter, however, he wrote with vigor about his appearance at Laguna Pueblo as "Pa-puk-ke-wis," wild man of the plains.[17] What Lummis claimed to have occurred was described with characteristic flamboyance:

My nondescript appearance as I climbed up a house and sat down on the roof, captured the whole outfit, as well it might. The

sombrero with its snake-skin band, the knife and two six-shooters in my belt, the bulging duck coat and long-fringed, snowy leg-
gins, the skunk skin dangling from my blanket-roll, and last but
not least, the stuffed coyote over my shoulders, looking natural as
life, made up a picture the like of which I feel sure they never saw
before and never will see again. They must have thought me Pa-
puk-ke-wis, the wild man of the plains. A lot of the muchachos
and muchuchas (boys and girls) crowded around me, and when I
caught the coyote by the neck and shook it, at the same time
howling at them savagely, they jumped away, and the whole
assembly was convulsed with laughter. An Indian appreciates a
joke, even if it be a rather feeble one.[18]

Here we see Lummis's relish for the drama of self-creation. In representing himself as "Pa-puk-ke-wis," he made himself more "wild" than
Indians. The act of dressing up and adopting the guise of a rough-edged
"Southwesterner" manifested a deep desire to go beyond the East in order
to revitalize the mind and body out West. Lummis assumed a new identity by "playing Indian." For all the spontaneity that may have attended
the first instance of dressing up in the Southwest, the act was quickly
commodified through the process of writing for popular readerships.[19]

In his combination of roles as tourist adventurer, enthusiastic athlete,
and professional writer, Lummis closely resembled his friend from
Harvard Theodore Roosevelt, who also wrote extensively on western
themes in the late nineteenth century. Roosevelt and others of his generation and elite social standing in the East, such as the artist Frederic
Remington and the writer Owen Wister, traveled west to shore up what
they saw as the threatened social identity of White Anglo Saxon
Protestants in the United States.[20] According to the literary historian G.
Edward White, they went west to experience for themselves the perceived
distinction between the West as an "agrarian, rural, egalitarian, and ethnically homogeneous" social order and the East as an "industrial, urban,
elitist, ethnically heterogeneous, and racially-mixed" social order.[21] To live
the outdoor life in the West was to partake of a stabilizing influence on a
social body threatened by economic depression, labor unrest, crises of
management, and large-scale immigration. Through his advocacy of the
rigorous western life, Roosevelt, by appealing to male, and particularly
youthful, readers in the East sought to invigorate what he saw as their
flaccid bodies. Nature, youth, manhood, and the state were conjoined in

Roosevelt's understanding of what constituted the health of the body politic, and it was through a symbolic reassertion of the primacy of man over nature that men grew strong again.[22]

Lummis shared with Roosevelt a passion for fierce athleticism, hunting, and the masculinist pursuit of rugged individualism. Letters from the tramp were filled with details of food and trophy hunting, trout fishing, and scrapes with mountain lions. Adventures that put a premium on quick thinking and sharp physicality taxed the body into an often-ecstatic expenditure. These adventures were, in turn, seen as a remedy for a social sickness identified by Lummis in the following terms: "Somehow, our civilization has always seemed to me to civilize backwards. Its whole tendency is toward laziness, for it is always inventing something to supplant work. . . . Yes, civilization is mighty fast ruining the race physically, and the mental and moral decay are inevitable corollaries of the bodily."[23]

These sentiments echoed a fear among middle- and upper-class Easterners at the turn of the last century that they were becoming both victims and perpetrators of decadence. The cultural critic Donna Haraway argues that decadence "threatened in two interconnected ways, both related to energy—limited, production systems—one artificial, one organic. The machine threatened to consume and exhaust man. And the sexual economy of man seemed vulnerable both to exhaustion and to submergence in unruly and primitive excess."[24] For Haraway, the establishment of Carl Akeley's African Hall in New York's American Museum of Natural History in the early twentieth century was an emblematic expression of Eastern anxiety over the threatened social superiority and racial purity of privileged whites in the United States—the museum was the "ideological and material product of the sporting life" advocated by Western enthusiasts.[25] Therein, the purity of nature was given manifest form through the art of taxidermy and the construction of dioramas that joined animals and man "in visual embrace."[26]

The ideological underpinnings of the institutional growth discussed by Haraway are much the same for Lummis's writing in the 1880s. Lummis's advocacy of the Southwest in succeeding years pivoted about a similar concern for the preservation of threatened manhood, the consolidation of Anglo racial identity, and the conservation of both natural and cultural resources for moral and exploitative purposes. Because the walk west was a means of recreating his personal identity in a way that stressed individualism and self-reliance in the most testing of circumstances, it is also significant that Lummis made little reference to his wife, Dorothea

Rhodes Lummis, in the letters sent either to Ohio or Los Angeles. It appears that Lummis's tramp was motivated in part by a desire to avoid confronting the reality of his failing marriage. Lummis's virtual silence concerning Dorothea in his public letters suggests that asserting his masculinist self meant marginalizing his involvement in the domestic scene.[27]

"The Land of Sun, Silence, and Adobe"

In *A Tramp Across the Continent*, Lummis wrote: "I have lived now in Isleta for four years, with its Indians for my only neighbors; and better neighbors I never had and never want. They are unmeddlesome but kindly, thoughtful, and loyal, and wonderfully interesting. Their endless and beautiful folklore, their quaint and often astonishing customs, and their startling ceremonials have made a fascinating study."[28] While residing in New Mexico between 1888 and 1892, Lummis used his informal participant observer ethnography of not only Isletans but also other Pueblo communities, Navajos, Utes, and Apaches to fill out his accounts of regional landscapes and peoples. Part travelogue, part regional history, part ethnology, part folklore, and part adventure storytelling, Lummis's articles and books on the Southwest all capitalized on his intimate experience of locale. These articles, largely published in Eastern magazines such as *Scribner's Monthly, St. Nicholas,* and *Harper's Monthly,* transported images of the Southwest across the country in the years that Lummis spent in New Mexico. The articles were incorporated wholesale or in revised form into Lummis's books, which, in turn, tended to resemble one another as passages in one volume were duplicated or amplified in a succeeding volume.

While residing at Isleta Pueblo, Lummis sent a number of stories to *St. Nicholas.* The magazine was published by Century Company of New York and designed for an audience of children. Similar to its parent publication, *Century* magazine, *St. Nicholas* was cosmopolitan in fare, featuring myriad stories and travelogues that described locations across the globe. Writing for *St. Nicholas,* Lummis capitalized on an existing market for stories and travelogues with "exotic" locations. He wrote two series of articles that described the landscapes and peoples of the Southwest and retold folktales from Isleta Pueblo. These articles were published in the magazine between 1891 and 1894, and later collected in the books *Some Strange Corners of Our Country* and *The Man Who Married the Moon* (later renamed *Pueblo Folk-Tales*). Aimed toward a young male audience, the articles jostled for readers' attention alongside many other adventure stories, travel narratives, and historical fictions. These items were joined by domestic fictions, sentimental poems (including several by Lummis's first wife, Dorothea), and college-girl romances that were designed to appeal to girls.

Singling out for attention one of Lummis's clutch of southwestern books enables us to examine the terms on which Lummis envisaged Native Americans and Hispanos becoming incorporated into the United States. *Some Strange Corners of Our Country* was published by the Century Company in 1892, most of its chapters having been published previously in *St. Nicholas.* Lummis began by chastising his audience for not taking greater pride in the natural wealth and historical drama of American culture. The Southwest was a part of the country that would cure Americans of their "unpatriotic slighting" of their own country:

> There is a part of America—a part even of the United States—of which Americans know as little as they do of inner Africa, and of which too many of them are much less interested to learn. With them "to travel" means only to go abroad; and they call a man a traveler who has run his superficial girdle around the world and is as ignorant of his own country (except its cities) as if he had never been in it. I hope to live to see Americans proud of *knowing America,* and ashamed not to know it; and it is to my young countrymen that I look for this patriotism to effect so needed a change.[29]

The writing that followed was relentlessly hyperbolic. Lummis's keywords were "wonder" and its variations: "curious," "marvelous," "astonishing," and "strange." The Grand Canyon, featured in the first chapter, was described as a "stupendous chasm," then an "unparalleled chasm," and later a "peerless gorge," before Lummis declared that he could not describe it at all. The "Great American Desert" was a "vast, arid waste," while throughout the book the author played upon the immensity of open terrain and the unrelenting indifference of mountains and deserts to the presence of humans.[30] Further chapters described such "strange" natural phenomena as the Petrified Forest and the natural bridge of Pine Creek in Arizona and the lava fields of El Malpais in New Mexico. In giving travel directions to many of these same "forbidding" landscapes, Lummis made it obvious to readers that a commercial infrastructure had been created that provided relatively easy access to most of the places described in the book.

Consequently, the first chapter of the book ended with details of travel, food, and accommodation costs for visitors to the South Rim of the Grand Canyon. Presumably these details, largely absent from the original articles in *St. Nicholas,* were included for the book's adult readers.

The bulk of the book related the customs of contemporary Hopi, Navajo, and Pueblo Indians, and speculated on the fate of the Pueblos' cliff-dwelling ancestors. Common to chapters on the Hopi Snake Dance, Navajo "superstitions," witchcraft, Navajo and Pueblo medicine men, and the Isleta Scalp Dance was Lummis's rhetorical wonder at the prevalence of practices in the modern United States that he thought properly belonged to another time and place. In setting the scene for an account of the Hopi Snake Dance, Lummis wrote: "It is in these strange, cliff-perched little cities of the Húpi ('the people of peace,' as the Moquis call themselves) that one of the most astounding barbaric dances in the world is held; for it even yet exists. Africa has no savages whose mystic performances are more wonderful than the Moqui snake-dance—and as much may be said for many of the other secret rites of the Pueblos."[31]

But the Hopis, Navajos, and Rio Grande Pueblo Indians did not belong to another time and place really, and Lummis knew it. Instead he realized they were a vital part of the Southwest's contemporary cultural geography, and as such were liable to be objects of fascinated viewing in the eyes of Euro-American visitors. Lummis played upon cultural antiquity, "quaintness" as well as alleged barbarism, and "exotic" practices among the Hopis and other groups of Native Americans, not simply to relegate their beliefs and acts to the past, but instead to make this textualized "past" their entry into the contemporary United States. It is no coincidence that *Some Strange Corners of Our Country* was published only a year before the opening of the Chicago World's Fair of 1893, for the book shared in the display and commodification at the fair of "primitive" peoples from different parts of the world. Similar to the fair, it might be said that the book erred less toward the pedagogical purpose of displays in and around the Anthropological Building, under the supervision of Frederick Ward Putnam and Franz Boas, than it partook of the character of the Midway Plaisance, that "jumble of foreignness" where quasi-ethnological types and exotic "curiosities" were exhibited.[32]

For Hinsley, borrowing from Walter Benjamin's analysis of the mid-nineteenth-century French poet Charles Baudelaire, the *flâneur* who walked the Midway was the newly emergent modernist type through whom the older P. T. Barnum-esque human freak show and the public service ideal of late-nineteenth-century museum-based anthropology were conjoined: "The eyes of the Midway are those of the *flâneur,* the stroller through the street arcade of human differences, whose experience is not the holistic, integrated ideal of the anthropologist but the segmented, seriatim fleetingness of the modern tourist 'just passing through.'"[33] I propose that Lummis's book itself amounted to a gallery of quickly sketched portrayals of racial, ethnic, and cultural differences that were designed to thrill as much as educate the reader. *Some Strange Corners of Our Country* thus shared with the fair the quasi-ethnological exposition of the lives of "primitive" peoples, although in this instance they all lived within the United States. This quasi-ethnological curiosity was piqued by taking a readerly stroll through the pages of a book full of suggestions, in the guise of travel directions, on how to purchase the experience of cultural interaction for oneself.

At the fair the commodity relation largely decided the nature of the exchange between Anglo visitors and those ethnic others brought in from the imperial (or internal colonial) periphery to the urban center of Chicago for the purposes of exhibition. Similarly, in succeeding years, travelers bent on following Lummis's directions to the Southwest would find that within the part of the country the author had labeled the domain of "still savage peoples, whose customs are stranger and more interesting than those of the Congo," there were indigenous people increasingly able to sustain their livelihoods by capitalizing on tourists' very desire to purchase authentic artifacts from them.[34]

Although Lummis's writing about southwestern American Indians exoticized their cultural practices and made them the object of a colonizing gaze, it is important to emphasize that incorporation was a complex and dynamic process of negotiation between dominant and marginalized cultures. The historian Edwin L. Wade notes that as early as 1880, when the Atlantic and Pacific Railroad (later the Atchison, Topeka, and Santa Fe Railway) reached Albuquerque, there was a developing infrastructure for the sale of local Indian wares at main depots in the Southwest.[35] Subsequently the arts and crafts trade at stations, hotels, and pueblos helped sustain many American Indian communities in the Southwest. By the late 1880s, Pueblo Indians and Navajos were able to capitalize on traditional crafts as a substantial source of income. In some cases Pueblo Indians left their homes to travel great distances in order to participate in Anglo cultural festivals such as the Los Angeles Fiesta, in which Isletans performed ceremonial dances, displayed traditional crafts, and participated in elaborately staged tableaux. The increasing numbers of tourists and curiosity seekers who viewed Native Americans performing their "authentic" selves helped further commodify Indian lives. Yet commodification neither a century ago nor today, when arguably the arts and crafts trade thrives more than ever, simply co-opted Native American "traditionalism." After much internal conflict over how to deal with the impact of tourism, Native American communities have learned to profit from Anglo interest in their arts, crafts, and homes.[36]

Turning to Lummis's representation of Hispanos, the terms of cultural incorporation proved different from those associated with Native Americans. In *Some Strange Corners of Our Country,* he praised the Spanish for making in the Southwest "a heroic history which is quite without parallel."[37] According to Lummis, elite Hispanos allegedly owed their nobility to "pure" European blood and their direct lineage to Europe; poor Hispanos were mestizos whose racial and cultural traits were confused.[38] Lummis both sentimentalized and demonized *pobres* in his travelogues and fictions. As noted earlier, Lummis claimed to have liberated himself from racialist assumptions about Mexican Americans after his initial arrival in the Southwest. His writing on the Penitentes, though, demonstrates both continued racialism and a fanatical obsession with making their activities into the cultural property of his readership. By taking a close look at how Lummis reinvented the Penitentes for public consumption, we arrive at a more solid understanding of how such representations were an integral part of constituting a cultural claim on the various peoples and landscapes of New Mexico and, indeed, the Southwest as a whole.

In several published articles and book chapters, Lummis wrote about the occasion on which he photographed the crucifixion of a Brotherhood member in San Mateo, New Mexico. The fullest account of this episode is to be found in *The Land of Poco Tiempo* (1893), in a chapter that plays upon images of attraction and repulsion.[39] For Lummis, the Brotherhood was a grotesque wonder of the Southwest whose acts of penance during the four weeks of Lent were to be highlighted and exploited for representational gain. In the chapter "The Penitent Brothers," Lummis described "a procession of flagellants . . . in which voters of this Republic shredded their naked backs with savage whips, staggered beneath huge crosses, and hugged the maddening needles of the cactus; a procession which culminated in the flesh-and-blood crucifixion of an unworthy representative of the Redeemer."[40]

The Penitentes were a subsection of the Hispano population of northern New Mexico and southern Colorado. "Penitentes" was a pejorative label, and officially their organization was named "La Fraternidad Piodosa de Nuestro Padre Jesus Nazareno" (The Pious Fraternity of Our Father Jesus Nazarite).[41] The Brotherhood's roots were in the late eighteenth century, and its influence on local folkways grew in the mid-1830s after the secularization of missions in Mexico. For the historian Marta Weigle, the Brotherhood was "a movement clearly within Spanish Roman Catholic tradition" that "took root because it fulfilled vital needs for social integration and individual spiritual security," particularly during the secular period when Franciscan friars were gradually replaced by secular priests.[42] Penitential observances were a frontier phenomenon, whereby generally poor settlers in areas remote from first Spanish and then Mexican centers of administration created their own folk religion. Many of its members, particularly after the American annexation of New Mexico in 1846, found a cultural refuge in the Brotherhood. Weigle explains: "As residents of a Territory of the United States, the Hispanic populace had to adjust to a new regime which separated the powers of church and state, to a new language, to important changes in Catholic Church administration, and to a growing influx of Anglo-American settlers who were largely Protestant."[43]

Lummis regarded the Brotherhood as an anachronistic and barbaric organization that had degenerated from a once noble heritage in Spain: "By slow degrees the once godly order shrank and grew deformed among the brave but isolated and ingrown people of that lonely land; until the monstrosity of the present fanaticism had devolved."[44] He claimed that until its suppression by the Catholic Church earlier in the nineteenth century, Brotherhood membership had numbered in "some thousands, with fraternities in towns of every county" of New Mexico. By 1888, however, Penitente activity was supposed to be limited to only three towns in the territory. He proceeded to recount activities he observed take place during 1891 in San Mateo, "the most *unreclaimed* village in New Mexico" [emphasis added]—a place, he also claimed, where witches were said still to be abundant.[45] By invoking the word "unreclaimed," Lummis tacitly acknowledged that his own purpose was to represent penitential activity as the remnant of an obstinate past that needed eradication.

Lummis's account represents bodily violence as the primary characteristic of penitential activity, hence references to "tortures," "long, bleeding cuts," and blows that "[ravish] from the back its tiny morsels of flesh."[46] Readers were warned of the danger of becoming too curious about the Brotherhood: "Woe to him if in seeing he shall be seen! A sharp-edged knife or flint shall be over-curious of his back, and across its bloody autograph a hundred fearful lashes shall lift their purpling wales—in barbarous hint to him henceforth to keep a curb between the teeth of inquisitiveness."[47] In describing the act of photographing the Penitente ceremony, it is clear that for Lummis the courting of such danger was itself a thrill. In fact as much of the chapter is given to Lummis's own risk-taking as it is to providing a quasi-ethnological account of the Penitentes' activities.[48] Made into a sensational spectacle, the Penitentes' stated capacity for bloody revenge upon the body of the outside viewer was made the very measure of Lummis's heroic escapology. Indeed, he followed the above statement by asserting: "[L]et him stalk his game, and with safety to his own hide he may see havoc to the hides of others."[49] Escapology, stalking game, anticipating pain with an almost masochistic delight— these were all vital elements of the account. But the central point of encounter between the Penitentes and Lummis was on the ground of technology. Lummis conveyed his eagerness for the final seven days of Lent to arrive by stating: "I had been watching feverishly for Holy Week to come. No photographer had ever caught the Penitentes with his sun-lasso, and I was assured of death in various attractive forms at the first hint of an attempt."[50] The camera, then, was for Lummis the primary means of exposing the "barbarous" practices of the Penitentes. His "feverish" desire to intrude on dangerous ground found him setting up a large-format camera in plain sight of processional officials and participants while receiving the protection of his friend, Don Ireneo Chaves, from a mob that was "openly hostile."[51] That evening Lummis successfully bribed processional officials so as to allow him to freely photograph the Good Friday crucifixion the next day.

Lummis described the culminating procession of the Penitentes in detail, again emphasizing the collective antipathy of the "ill-faced mob" toward him and the bodily endurance of the Brothers, two of whom carried heavy wooden crosses, while others lashed themselves "with a burro-load of *entrana* (buckthorn cactus)."[52] When it finally came to the actual crucifixion of a Brother, the *Hermano Mayor* (or Chief Brother) signaled that Lummis could take his photograph. In Lummis's words: "And there we stood facing each other, the crucified and I—the one playing with the most wonderful toy of modern progress, the other racked by the most barbarous device of twenty centuries ago."[53] Thus Lummis constructed the encounter between photographer and subject so as to set modernity against antiquity. By relegating Brotherhood practices to a stubborn past that refused to give way to what he considered correct behavior within the more egalitarian present, Lummis helped shape readers' perceptions of part of the Hispano population as backward, deluded, and in a state of willing submission to "fanatical" religious beliefs.

"Romance is the Chief Riches of any People": The Cultural Legacy of Conquest[54]

In 1892, having made a full recovery from his paralysis, Lummis left New Mexico to make an archaeological expedition to Peru and Bolivia with archaeologist and ethnologist Adolph Bandelier. Henry Villard, builder of the Northern Pacific Railroad, financed the expedition. Before leaving the United States, Lummis and his second wife, Eve, together with their four-month-old daughter, Turbese, moved to Los Angeles.[55] In a letter to his former wife, Dorothea, with whom he maintained ties after their divorce, he explained the South American trip: "I couldn't go on forever filling the public with New Mexico and Arizona: I could feel that my rope there was about to end."[56] There was, then, at this time a sense of exhaustion to Lummis's association with the Southwest. While the archaeological expedition was to falter in 1893 because of Villard's financial problems, Lummis used his experiences in Peru and Bolivia as the basis for further writings, such as the books *The Gold Fish of Gran Chimu* (1896) and *The Enchanted Burro* (1897) and celebratory articles on Spanish colonialism in the Americas.[57] On his return to Los Angeles in the autumn of 1893, "[e]verything had to be turned into money—articles, photographs, even cherished curios . . . Eve was frail then and undernourished, but her husband set her to printing hundreds of photographs to sell to tourists curious about the bronco-busting explorer, his scenes of the Southwest, and his collections."[58] These details suggest the consistently improvised quality of Lummis's association with the Southwest and the way in which the financing of his activities was often tenuous, there being no guarantee that much money would be made from his writing.

His doubts notwithstanding, Lummis did continue to exploit southwestern themes after his trip to South America. In 1894 he took over the editorship of the journal *Land of Sunshine,* continuing in that position for fifteen years. As editor and chief contributor to *Land of Sunshine,* Lummis advocated the development of southern California's commercial and cultural resources and extolled the virtues of what he called "the right arm of the continent." The historian Kevin Starr points out that Lummis was one of a number of boosterists in the 1890s who sought to capitalize on the romantic past of southern California in particular, and the Southwest as a whole, in selling the region to incoming investors, tourists, and prospective residents.[59]

Land of Sunshine (subtitled An Illustrative Monthly, Descriptive of Southern California) began life in June 1894 as a promotional magazine. Funded in large part by the Los Angeles Chamber of Commerce, the journal was designed to appeal to both California and Eastern readers, particularly "travelers, health seekers, and intending settlers."[60] When announcing Lummis as the new editor, writer Charles Dwight Willard characterized him as "one of the best known of the younger school of American writers."[61] Under Lummis's guidance Land of Sunshine quickly took on a more cosmopolitan character, although some of the promotional attributes remained. Stating the purpose of the journal in his first editorial, Lummis wrote that Land of Sunshine "aims to find out and bring out a literature and art local in color but broad in sympathy. It will make a modest but growing feature of short stories, poems, studies, sketches, all of characteristic flavor; the folklore and folksongs, the history and legends, the types of man and nature, and whatever else shall appeal to the intellectual."[62] We can see how this statement of intent informed the selection of material for the journal by briefly noting some of the articles that appeared in the December 1895 edition. The lead article on "California and Fremont," written by Jessie Benton Fremont, widow of John C. Fremont, was accompanied by a Joaquin Miller poem and articles on the oldest church in Los Angeles, Cahuilla Indian songs and dances, and the preponderance of Spanish words in (American) English. Thus, at the outset of his editorship, Lummis emphasized historical, romantic, and ethnological themes for the journal.[63]

Through the 1890s and the early 1900s, the cultural and geographical scope of the journal continued to broaden under Lummis's guidance. He used the pages of Land of Sunshine/Out West to pursue campaigning interests in the restoration of southern California missions through the Landmarks Club, in Indian policy reform initiatives through the Sequoyah League, and in the preservation of Native American material culture through the Southwest Museum. Lummis also endorsed a number of writers and artists who visited El Alisal, his home in the rustic environment of Arroyo Seco, a few miles northeast of Los Angeles. Special fascination, however, was reserved for what Lummis saw as the glorious

Spanish colonial heritage of southern California and New Mexico. "The Missions," he proselytized, "are, next to our climate and its consequences, the best capital southern California has."[64] He also praised the "Spanish-American face" as the "very poetry of evolution," noting that "through all [variations of the mestizo], individual or local, runs the inevitable dominant of Spain."[65] Southern California, according to Lummis, was to be understood "not only [as] the new Eden of the Saxon home-seeker, but part, and type, of Spanish America."[66] In southern California, then, Anglos had the opportunity to combine "Anglo-Saxon" energy with the aesthetic "beauty" of the "Spanish-American" past.

Several years after he first arrived in Los Angeles, and while he was still working as a journalist at the *Los Angeles Times,* Lummis published a small volume entitled *The Home of Ramona.* Following Jackson's novel by only four years, the book's publication was a bold attempt to cash in on interest generated by *Ramona.* It featured Lummis's own photographs of Camulos rancho in Santa Barbara County, the supposed home of Helen Hunt Jackson's heroine, and some poetry of dubious quality. For Lummis, Camulos was "The sweetest spot where e'er romance/ Above, or fancy strayed." The last stanza of the singularly sentimental verse "Camulos" reads:

> Untaint by greed of riches,
> That is our modern shame;
> Unchanged as in those far old days
> When Padre Serra came;
> Its white adobes face the sun,
> Its myriad wood-doves call—
> Its heart the heart of mother Spain—
> Of Spain before the fall![67]

When Lummis returned to Los Angeles in 1893 after recovering his health in New Mexico, he further capitalized on the romantic nostalgia inspired by *Ramona* through myriad articles, editorials, and books. He also helped organize southern California cultural celebrations of the 1890s, such as the 1894 Spanish Days Fiesta in Coronado and the 1895 Fiesta de Los Angeles. These festivals were organized and funded in the main by chambers of commerce, business elites, and railroads, and played a central role in revitalizing the economy of the Southland, which had stagnated in the aftermath of a real estate boom in the 1880s.[68] The following description of the Coronado event gives notice of how a sense of the region's "Spanish" past was conspicuously created for public consumption:

> The fiesta will be as nearly as possible a revival of the sports, tournaments, dances, and pastimes of the early Spanish Californians. In the dress of the participants, the presence of Indians and Mexicans in their native costumes, the trappings of the horses and the character of the games; the whole fiesta will be a scene from the ancient days, transplanted to delight a modern audience. Mexican and Spanish caballeros, Indian riders and American cowboys will compete for hours in horsemanship, and among other thrilling events will be a genuine Spanish bull-fight.[69]

Lummis used his ties with Isleta Pueblo to include Pueblo Indians in both the Coronado and Los Angeles fiestas. In a letter printed in the *San Diego Union* newspaper, he reported on the success of his recent negotiations with the Isletans: "I shall have to go for them, and shall bring you a full twenty, or two or three more. They will be the most representative band of Pueblos that ever went anywhere; and it may positively be reckoned a triumph to get such a showing."[70] The Pueblo Indians were to display traditional crafts and perhaps perform a dance, although the latter was to be understood as "a privilege and not a proposition." Meanwhile, at the Los Angeles Fiesta, Isletans were set to perform in "a Pageant of the Pacific, illustrating the aboriginal civilizations of the West Coast of America, the Spanish conquest, and the new era in California."[71] They were featured in a parade of floats that first dramatized the Spanish colonial conquest of Guatavita Indians, Incas, and Aztecs and then depicted "our own Southwest and its romantic prehistoric peoples." The description continues:

> An exact representation of one of the famous cliff-dwellings will be peopled with actual descendants of the Cliff-dwellers, repelling an attack of the Apaches. Next will come a correct model of one of the stupendous communal houses of the ancient Pueblos, accompanied by actual Pueblos in their picturesque national costume. In this tableau will be introduced the priest-scout Fray Marcos de Nizza [*sic*], who discovered New Mexico and Arizona in 1539; and that greatest of North American explorers, Francisco Vasquez de Coronado, who discovered the Grand Canyon of the

Colorado, most of New Mexico, Colorado, Indian Territory, and Kansas, 355 years ago.[72]

By appearing in a tableau that represented the "discovery" of New Mexico by Spanish conquistadors, it might seem that Isletans were complicit in a celebration of their own colonization. Yet things were more complex than at first they seem. The scholar Theodore S. Jojola notes that Isletans continued to perform at the fiesta until 1903, when, in an effort to quiet disruptive disputes over who was chosen to travel to Los Angeles, tribal officials prevented further participation.[73] These disputes were, in turn, part of a larger conflict within the Isleta community between "conservatives" and "progressives" over the degree to which the pueblo's government and social structure should change in the face of contact with Anglo outsiders.[74]

Perhaps some of those Isletans who traveled away from their home environment did so because they had become alienated from their "traditional" culture. Equally, however, Isletans may have become curious about the world beyond Isleta, and travel outside pueblo lands allowed them to explore Anglo culture for themselves. Regardless of the precise reasons why each individual made his or her way to Los Angeles, their movement back and forth between the pueblo and the metropolis was indicative of the larger dilemma for Isletans over how to engage with Anglo society and their incorporation into the United States.

Conclusion

By the turn of the last century, Lummis was an influential figure in the middle-class and elite culture of Los Angeles. His self-appointed expertise on matters ethnological and "Spanish" had become prized by a diverse audience of promoters, travelers, and general readers who wished to know more about the history and cultures of the Southwest. In Los Angeles Lummis proved one of the major promoters of the Southland's new urban culture as he capitalized on the southern California Mission Myth. The construction of a romantic Spanish colonial past by civic architects was both a sales ploy and an attempt to overlay the blatant commercialism of the booster ideology with a "greater" sense of purpose. By extolling the gentility of the old Californios and the romance of the Spanish missions, Lummis endeavored to provide the key to a hybridized future, where incoming whites could take the "best" of the culture that had preceded them while forging a strengthened mind and body through the vigorous, year-round outdoor life that

California's climate allowed them. Clearly such a picture manipulated both past and present realities (such as forced labor for Indians under the old Spanish mission system and racial conflict in post–Civil War Los Angeles) in order to render the illusion of a natural hierarchy of racial, ethnic, class, gender, and cultural values in the city and state.[75]

Racialist and class-biased assumptions were always at work in Lummis's promotional activity in both the Southland and the greater Southwest. Overall, his writing ended up servicing an oligarchic and repressive cultural ideal that is expressed most clearly in *Land of Sunshine,* when Lummis envisioned Los Angeles as "the latest and highest development of modern civilization, the climax of human achievement to date, the most radical and important experiment ever made by the race which just now stands at the head of the world."[76] For all of Lummis's profound interest in Native Americans and Mexican Americans, he imagined the United States as hierarchized along racial, class, and gender lines that clearly privileged forms of Anglo male authority.

And yet this is not the whole story. For in the course of traveling through, living in, and writing about the Southwest, Lummis contributed to Anglo audiences a simultaneously popular yet more complex understanding of human diversity in the Southwest. I have singled out Lummis for critical attention because in his roles as interpreter and promoter of the Southwest he played a significant role in popularizing the region's landscapes and peoples, first to largely Eastern audiences and in time increasingly to Western readerships. The challenge in reading Lummis today is not to be merely dismissive of his representations, but to criticize his texts in ways that counter the hierarchy of cultural values they establish. And further, to realize that even though Lummis played a significant role in promoting southwestern tourism and establishing institutions, such as the Southwest Museum, that attempted to fix Native American cultures through the dominant culture's gaze, the forms of cultural exchange associated with these sites have changed over time and are open to continued negotiation.[77]

CHAPTER FIVE

Burbank among the Indians:
The Politics of Patronage

IN MARCH 1897 the artist Elbridge Ayer Burbank traveled from his home in Chicago to Fort Sill, Oklahoma, to fulfill an assignment for his uncle, Edward Everett Ayer, a rich businessman who was president of the Field Museum of Natural History in Chicago. Ayer was in the process of building a private library of texts and images that documented Native American and European encounters in the Americas and had instructed his nephew to paint Geronimo, the renowned Chiricahua Apache shaman and iconic figure of Indian resistance. The portrait of Geronimo was to be added to the Ayer Library as a document recording the Chiricahua Apaches' incorporation into the United States in the aftermath of their final surrender to the army a decade before. Now that the aged Geronimo was imprisoned on the Fort Sill Reservation with three thousand fellow Apaches, Comanches, and Kiowas, it appeared that southwestern Indian resistance had been neutralized and that Native people were being pulled into the sphere of American society. This viewpoint seemed to be confirmed when Burbank reported Geronimo as saying that "he had got through being an Indian" and was "a white man now."[1]

Soon after arriving at Fort Sill, Burbank realized that Indian portraiture might well offer a vocation that provided new aesthetic challenges and commercial opportunities. He remained at Fort Sill for over two months, painting the portraits of Comanches and Kiowas as well as Apaches. He also claimed to have transcribed eleven pages of Geronimo's life story with the help of an interpreter. Energized at the prospect of painting not only the Indians at Fort Sill but populations of Pawnees, Wyandottes, Caddos, Shawnees, Pottawatomies, Cheyennes, Arapahoes, Wichitas, Chickasaws, and Choctaws elsewhere in Oklahoma Territory,

Burbank envisaged a new vocation as a painter of Native Americans. At the end of April he commented to Ayer: "Am sure I will have fine success with these Indian pictures as they make beautiful pictures so rich in color and the costume so artistic and then they have a historical value."[2] When Burbank returned to Chicago in early June, Thurber's Art Gallery hosted an exhibition of nineteen Indian portraits, seventeen of which sold quickly.[3] Thereafter Burbank was soon on the road again, first visiting Fort Yates, North Dakota, to paint Lakotas and then traveling to the Crow Agency in Montana from where he enthused, "I have struck a perfect paradise here."[4] He remained at the Crow Agency for a number of weeks because he had found "such saleable subjects among the Indians."[5] Soon he declared his intention to paint every single Indian tribe in America."[6] Explaining the profound change of direction in his artistic career later, he recalled: "Once in the Indian country, I was fascinated by the wildness and freedom of the West, and delighted with the rich and abundant material which I found at hand, practically untouched."[7] By 1909, Burbank had, according to his own calculation, visited 128 tribes. He went on to complete as many as a thousand oil paintings and thousands more red Conté crayon drawings of Indians living west of the Mississippi River.

Part of a generation of Euro-Americans who thought Indian cultures were dying out as the twentieth century loomed, Burbank sought to preserve Native people's identities in paintings and drawings. His principal sponsor was Ayer, to whom Burbank sold many hundreds of images and who also appears to have provided additional funds for travel and subsistence. Two other individual patrons played a great part in the artist's career. For almost two decades, Burbank sojourned at the home of J. L. Hubbell, the renowned trader who lived in close proximity to Navajos at Ganado, Arizona. Hubbell offered Burbank not only free accommodation and board while he stayed at Ganado but a regular source of income through purchasing the artist's paintings and drawings. Equally important, Hubbell provided him with easy access to Navajo subjects. Burbank was also supported by Joseph G. Butler Jr., a wealthy industrialist in Youngstown, Ohio, who made the largest single purchase of his art in 1902. The artist sold hundreds more images to private collectors and institutions such as the Field Museum of Natural History in Chicago and the Smithsonian Institution in Washington, D.C. Further works of art were purchased by the Atchison, Topeka, and Santa Fe Railway, which reproduced them in its annual calendar. These images joined the chromolithographs of Burbank's paintings that were distributed as newspaper supplements and as individual items for sale. The images were also featured in newspaper and journal articles written about Burbank's art.

Given the substantial body of work Burbank created between 1897 and 1917, the period in which he traveled extensively through the West, it is surprising that his work is not better known today. Until recently, it would be true to say that Burbank's art has attracted little academic criticism, and further, that the few contemporary critics who have looked at his art and life have done so in the context of broader discussions of representations of Native Americans and the role of philanthropists such as Ayer in supporting the creation and maintenance of museums and libraries that documented the lifeways of Native Americans at the turn of the last century.[8] Fortunately this critical neglect is giving way to renewed interest in Burbank's work. Recently a major retrospective of Burbank's art was mounted by the Butler Institute of Art and exhibited in venues across the United States with an accompanying catalogue of images and critical commentary.[9] Meanwhile today's visitors to the Hubbell Trading Post National Historical Site at Ganado, Arizona, on the Navajo Reservation, can view many of Burbank's paintings and drawings when they tour Hubbell's private home, which has been restored to its appearance in the 1920s.

Commentators at the beginning of the last century praised Burbank for the precision of his images of Native Americans. They sympathized with Burbank's sense of moral duty in representing the older generation of Native Americans who had, according to their viewpoint, been least compromised by their association with whites. And they perceived an implicit morality in representing Native Americans accurately whereby the artist bowed neither to the pressure to romanticize nor to demonize the American Indian. One critic stated in 1898: "His endeavor is literal accuracy in color, drawing, character, [and] every detail."[10] Two years later Charles Fletcher Lummis praised Burbank as America's best "historical painter of Indians."[11] Such accuracy was deemed important because the distinctive lifeways of Native Americans were understood by Anglos to be passing away as Indians were incorporated into American society. Burbank stated in a letter written in 1904: "It won't be many years before this Indian work will be a thing of the past. They are dying off so fast, the older ones and genuine Indians. . . . Now is a chance to get types of every Indian tribe in America."[12]

Burbank's language is typical of the time. Euro-American commentators assumed that Indians were "dying off" or vanishing, both in terms of

their actual number and their changing lifeways as a result of being corralled onto reservations. Thus it was the duty of concerned Anglo citizens
to create and collect images of representative Indians from tribes across
the United States before they were absorbed into American society.
Underlying this argument was the assumption that the only "genuine" or
authentic Indians were those people who did not have mixed-race ancestry and those who dressed in the most "traditional" fashion. Such assumptions on the part of Euro-Americans were not new; indeed they were
commonplace throughout the nineteenth century. But unlike, for example, James Fenimore Cooper's Leather-Stocking Tales, which, written
between the 1820s and 1840s, dramatized warfare with Indians as an
inevitable consequence of westward expansion, Burbank's art belongs to
the era in which Indians across the West were being physically incorporated into American society through the reservation system. He traveled
extensively in search of diverse Native American tribes only to participate
in the process of absorbing them into American society; he considered
himself a friend of Native Americans but could be dismissive of those people he did not think sufficiently "Indian"; and he spent copious amounts
of time among Native people, claiming them as friends, while working for
patrons who thought tribal cultures must inevitably come to an end.[13]

It is these very limitations in Burbank's vision and art that make him
such an interesting figure to consider today. If it is true that his images
fail to transcend their historical moment, this failure may well be because
they are so thoroughly embedded in it. A critical account of Burbank's
career enables us to explore in detail the tensions and ambivalences of a
period in which Anglos debated with particular vehemence the place of
the Indian in American history and contemporary society. The 1890s and
early 1900s were for Native Americans extraordinarily difficult years, and
particularly so for tribes in the West who in the aftermath of the Civil
War lost their homelands and were placed on reservations. Burbank
painted men such as the Lakota Red Cloud, the Nez Perce Chief Joseph,
and the Chiricahua Apache Naiche, who had led tribal resistance to
American encroachment between the 1860s and 1880s and then helped
move their people to a more conciliatory stance toward whites. As army
officers, Indian agents, and traders facilitated Burbank's movements
among Native people, so Burbank witnessed profound changes in Indian
livelihoods. Native Americans responded in different ways to his presence. While the artist often claimed that he earned the respect of his sitters by showing them copies of previously completed portraits, his letters

also refer to tensions and outright conflicts with Indians. Native people posed for various reasons: for the respect portraiture accorded them, for the cash paid for sitting, and because they were persuaded to do so by Indian agents. As is indicated by Burbank's observations in his letters, he met Native Americans at a point when their clothing, hair, and facial appearances had often changed greatly from the years in which their tribes lived autonomous lives. He saw that they lived in cabins, owned property, participated in a cash economy, practiced agriculture, and were migrant laborers. He valued the education of Indian children at off-reservation schools and he considered it inevitable that Indians would be absorbed into American society. And yet Burbank also expressed disappointment when he found it hard to find Indians who had not been greatly affected by white society.

Even though Burbank articulated the conventional logic that Native people's lifeways were fast disappearing and supported efforts to educate Indians into white ways, the very fact that he spent so much time with Indians rather than with whites, that he so obviously felt ill at ease in metropolitan society, and that he consistently praised Indians for many of their cultural practices suggests that the actual conduct of his life called into question the rhetoric he used to describe his activities. The remainder of this chapter will explore these inconsistencies and ambivalences in Burbank's ways of seeing not only Native Americans but also his own society.

Burbank among the Indians

When Burbank traveled to Fort Sill to complete the assignment of painting Geronimo for Ayer in 1897, he was thirty-eight years old and two decades into his artistic career. At the age of sixteen he had moved to Chicago from Harvard, Illinois, in 1874 to study art at the Academy of Design. He established a small portrait studio in St. Paul, Minnesota, in 1880, then traveled along the Northern Pacific Railroad to illustrate scenes for its publicity magazine *North-West* in 1885, and later moved to Munich, Germany, for a short time in 1886 and subsequently in 1888 for several years to further his studies with artists Toby Rosenthal and Paul Nauen.[14] On returning to Chicago in 1892, he opened a portrait studio. He made a name for himself painting sentimental portraits of African Americans, or "darkeys" as he labeled the images in letters to Ayer. These images, which are patronizing and even racist by today's standards, were semihumorous in design and proved popular with white audiences. One painting, entitled *American Beauty*—"a little Negro boy holding in his hand an American Beauty rose of the most perfect variety"[15]—was reproduced as a chromolithograph that was widely distributed with Sunday newspaper supplements in Chicago. The popular response to *American Beauty* and other images of African Americans helped earn Burbank the Yerkes Prize at the annual exhibition of the Society of Chicago Artists in 1893. This is not to say, however, that there was unanimous approval of Burbank's success. An article published in the art journal *Brush and Pencil* in 1898 to coincide with an exhibition of Burbank's Native American portraits referred to the days in Chicago when "no exhibition was complete without at least a half-dozen darkies in black frames casting a decided shadow on the wall" and suggested that Burbank's commercial success in the early 1890s had caused some jealousy in local art circles.[16]

Burbank's visit to Fort Sill was not the first time he had traveled extensively in pursuit of artistic images. In addition to journeying along the Northern Pacific Railroad in the 1880s, Burbank had spent a winter in the early 1890s near Nashville, Tennessee, painting "the Negro in all his simplicity of character and surroundings."[17] He made visits to the South in search of African American subjects up to Ayer's commission to paint Geronimo. Indeed Burbank appears to have continued to sell images of African Americans as his Indian portraiture gathered pace.[18] But Burbank's new sense of vocation rapidly developed after arriving in Oklahoma Territory in 1897. By January 1899 he could claim that "[t]he work I am engaged in now I expect to work at the rest of my life."[19]

Burbank began his artistic enterprise by seeking out Geronimo and other well-known Indians. Their portraits were highly valued by art patrons who wished to possess unique images "painted from life" and by people with more modest incomes who purchased widely distributed color reproductions of Burbank's paintings. The initial images of Geronimo feature him in profile and frontal poses and were designed to concentrate the viewer's attention on the subject's face. Burbank claimed Geronimo patted him on the back on seeing the first portrait and immediately showed it to fellow Chiricahuas.[20] Burbank employed a similar approach to the additional portraits he made of Geronimo over the following two years. The most striking of these images, made in 1899, shows Geronimo in profile, wearing a red blanket and a yellow bandana (plate 12). The painstaking detail in Geronimo's craggy face contrasts with the broad brushstrokes in the lightly colored neutral background and the bright red blanket wrapped about Geronimo's upper body.

Burbank's mindset at the outset of his new career is instructive. From Fort Sill in March 1897, he reported that Captain Scott, his conduit to Geronimo, had a large collection of clothing and accoutrements with which to dress Indians and then commented: "I won't paint the Indian with half American clothing on it as it spoils the whole thing."[21] Within two weeks of his arrival in Oklahoma, he declared his ability to make images that were correct in all details. "I won't have a Kiowa moccasin on an Apache Indian," he boasted.[22] Accordingly, Burbank's oils show subjects wearing tribal clothing, facial markings, and accoutrements such as headdresses, jewelry, scapulars, breastplates, pipes, presidential peace medals, and ceremonial masks. These figures are mostly represented from the waist up, in frontal, profile, and three-quarter poses. Burbank also made full-size portraits, although these images are generally not as successful because he tended to have trouble rendering the proportions of the human body accurately.[23]

In taking to the field, Burbank joined a long line of artists and photographers who represented Native Americans during the nineteenth and early twentieth centuries. His painting echoed the work of earlier American artists, including Charles Bird King, who made portraits of delegations of Indian leaders as they visited Washington, D.C., to negotiate with the U.S. government in the antebellum period. Unlike King's portraiture, which typically depicts "patriot chiefs" who represented at the least semiautonomous tribal cultures, Burbank's painting belongs to the era of the reservation, when Indian livelihoods across the West had been dramatically impacted by the government's attempts to incorporate Native Americans into the United States. Unlike King also, Burbank's portraiture was by no means restricted to well-known adult men; he painted women and children extensively. As a would-be artist-ethnologist, he followed the example of George Catlin, whose *Manners, Customs, and Conditions of the North American Indians* was published in 1841. George Wharton James, the writer, photographer, and self-styled expert on Native Americans, emphasized the link between Catlin and Burbank when he wrote: "The red races of America are fast perishing, and it is to be hoped that so sympathetic and successful a student of their lives, manners and customs as Mr. Burbank, will not allow himself to be lured back into civilization to take up a less important labor. May he continue and complete the work accomplished by Catlin for art and ethnology."[24] There was a circular logic and self-fulfilling prophecy to the idea that Native Americans were inevitably dying out. Such rhetoric echoed the distinction between "corrupted" and "uncorrupted" Indians that underlay Catlin's art and writing a half-century earlier. Catlin in turn had absorbed the cultural logic of the vanishing Indian that pervaded American society in the antebellum period. According to this logic Native Americans who had once been noble were degraded by prolonged association with whites, proving that they must inevitably fall before the advance of civilization.[25]

When in December 1901 Burbank declared his intention to use an interpreter and make a more pronounced effort to learn about the Indians he visited and thus be in a better position to write about his experiences, he was mimicking ethnologists such as George Dorsey, George Bird Grinnell, and Jesse Walter Fewkes whom he had met while traveling. That Burbank had started out by adding the names of subjects, their tribal identity, and the location and year in which their images were created to all his paintings and drawings indicates the influence of ethnology on his art. Similarly his use of profile, frontal, and three-quarter poses echoed "physical type" photography employed extensively for ethnographic study in this period.[26] It is no surprise, then, that Burbank's images were purchased by ethnographers at the Smithsonian Institution in Washington, D.C., and the Field Columbian Museum in Chicago. In this regard, Burbank's images joined a wealth of art and photography that was designed to preserve the arts, crafts, beliefs, and appearances of Native American cultures for anthropological research.

When critic Everett Maxwell appraised Burbank's images in 1910, he singled out for praise not only the accuracy of Burbank's images but also the rapport between artist and subjects that he considered crucial to the success of Burbank's art:

> The real secret of Mr. Burbank's success lies back of his hand and was never learned in art school. It is the response of the inner man, quickened to the appeal of kinship which exists between us and our forest brother. He does what few of our so-called civilized race have done—he does the red man the simple justice to understand him, to credit him with the attributes of a soul, a conscience, intelligence, a proud spirit, and a noble heart. This fact has won for the artist the warm friendship of the best tribes of the West, and has been an open sesame to a treasure trove which otherwise might have become extinct with the rapidly disappearing

race. Mr. Burbank acknowledges at once that he is endeavoring to paint the Indian exactly as he looks, in costumes and ornaments, authentically correct, and with painstaking fidelity to every detail of form and texture.[27]

How should today's viewers regard Maxwell's claims for Burbank's sense of kinship with Native Americans and his intuitive understanding of their cultures? Looking at several of Burbank's portraits in tandem with his written comments helps us come into a closer understanding of the circumstances in which the images were made and speculate on how Indians regarded the artist's presence among them. Because it was within Arizona, New Mexico, and California that Burbank traveled most extensively and sojourned the longest, it is only right that we take particular notice of his images of southwestern Indians.

In December 1897 Burbank visited the Hopi Reservation for the first time. From Keams Canyon he declared, "[t]his place is a paradise for me" and considered Hopis "the most interesting Indians have as yet visited."[28] The trader Thomas Keam provided Burbank with room and board and studio space, and, most importantly, used his influence among local Hopis to coax them into sitting for portraits. Over a three-month stay, Burbank completed twenty-six oil paintings, many of which were images of participants in the Antelope-Snake ceremony (which I discuss in the next chapter) and the many kachina dances that fill the Hopi calendar during the spring and summer months. Burbank explained to Ayer that he had worked over ten weeks to convince several men to sit for portraits with the masks they wore for kachina dances. One such image is that of O-bah (plate 13), who is represented as a Hemis Kachina. O-bah stands against a neutral background, the mask obscuring a large part of his person. Unlike the portraits of Geronimo, which concentrate the viewer's attention on facial detail, here the focus of attention is on the ceremonial costume rather than on O-bah himself. Burbank's skill at mimetic representation is clearly demonstrated in this image, the precise details lending credence to Maxwell's praise of the artist's "authentically correct" paintings. But, following Maxwell's lead, is it also the case that this image provides evidence of Burbank's understanding of Hopi culture and his "warm friendship" with individual Hopis?

Burbank commented in a letter written after leaving the Hopi villages: "I feel as though my stay there was a dream and that I have been on another planet."[29] He went on to describe a ceremony at which he was the only white man present and reported that he had been asked to join one of the kachina societies—"they are going to make a mask for me and teach me the dance and . . . I will have to strip naked [and] wear a breach clout."[30] Taken at face value, these words appear to support the claim that Burbank established a good rapport with Hopis. But it is far more probable that Burbank's activity was viewed warily by many Hopis because he sought the exposure of sacred knowledge. He noted that after he had painted portraits of O-bah and another man dressed as an Ogre Kachina, two elders "came to me and raised the very devil." Triumphantly, he reported that he had then convinced these two men to sit for portraits as well. In all likelihood the Hopi men considered they had little choice but to cooperate with Burbank in the matter. Having registered their opposition and then seen the artist continue painting regardless, they were forced to acknowledge where power lay in relations between the two parties. Hence what Burbank understood to be an invitation to participate in the activities of one or more of the kachina societies was more likely an uneasy, or even forced, accommodation on the part of Hopis to the Anglo desire to represent their ceremonies.

Significantly, Burbank provides a commentary on how O-bah reacted to having his portrait made:

> The God of rain before he sat for me went through a ceremony to bring the God back and when the picture was finished he washed all the paint from his body[,] removed the mask[,] took all the feathers from it[,] washed his face[,] and then made a short prayer[,] at the same time moved the mask around his head[,] then asked me to get on my knees and he moved the mask around my head[;] he then asked me to go out doors with him[,] and he moved the mask towards the East[,] threw some sacred meal and prayed[;] he then turned to me and says now the God of rain has gone to his home.[31]

This fascinating passage provides telling evidence of how Hopis sought to neutralize the disruptive influence of Anglos who wished to represent their ceremonies and depict individuals in ceremonial costume.[32] Tellingly Burbank does not appear to have fully understood the significance of O-bah's actions; instead—similar to his paintings—he represented the situation mimetically and without interpretation. In other instances, there was overt hostility toward Burbank's presence.

From Keams Canyon, Burbank went in search of Yumas and Pimas in Arizona and Mission Indians in California. By the time Burbank reached Needles, California, he had become discouraged in this endeavor. Having encountered Hualapais in Kingman, Arizona, who "have absolutely nothing on that belongs to an Indian" and Mojaves in Needles who did not wish to be painted—"when you talk picture to them they hold up their hands say no good no good"[33]—he decided to return to New Mexico. There he spent three weeks among the Zuni Indians. Here too his pursuit of picturesque subjects became thwarted when a number of Zunis took exception to his effort to paint them in religious costumes. Burbank described the situation in a letter to Ayer:

> They took me for a witch and if I hadn't managed things as I did they would have tortured me[,] but I just bluffed them and I talked terribly to them and they actually believed what I told them and they were afraid of me[,] but I was glad to get away[,] and the last picture I painted of them was an old woman witch that they would of [sic] killed if the troops hadn't interfered.[34]

Reading this long run-on sentence, one senses Burbank's unease as he recollected events at Zuni weeks after leaving the pueblo. Although here and elsewhere Burbank was dismissive of Indians' "superstitions," he was also forced to acknowledge Zuni opposition to his activities.

In spite of such resistance, Burbank considered that he left Zuni with a number of "good pictures."[35] Among them was an image of "Si-you-wee-the-ze-sah" (plate 14), a young man shown holding two ears of blue corn while wearing silver and shell necklaces over a tunic boldly patterned in blue and white with turquoise and red trimming. This portrait was featured in the Santa Fe Railway's *Aztec Calendar* for the second half of 1899 with five further images by Burbank of Hopis and a Laguna woman. The caption accompanying the image reads: "Zuñi pueblo is in New Mexico, and is reached by stage from Wingate, a station on the main line of the Santa Fe Route to California. The Zuñis have a number of strikingly picturesque ceremonies peculiar to themselves."[36] While it is highly unlikely that Burbank wrote this blurb, the association of his art with the promotion of the Southwest and its indigenous peoples as a destination for popular tourism is highly significant. Such writing shared the assumption underlying so much travel and promotional writing on the Southwest at the beginning of the last century that the cultures of Zunis, Hopis, and

Lagunas were accessible to the gaze of Anglo tourists traveling on the Atchison, Topeka, and Santa Fe Railway. As we shall see in the next chapter, the *Aztec Calendar* was published at the point when the Santa Fe's passenger department made more concerted efforts to use images of southwestern Indians to advertise the services of the railroad.

Writing to Ayer from Santa Monica in May 1898, Burbank reported that over the past seven months he had completed sixty-six portraits of southwestern Indians. He explained that he had traveled to Santa Monica because he had been working hard and felt run down. Praising the beauty and climate of the West Coast, he noted that his diet there consisted largely of fresh clams and oysters and that he had spent much of the time lying in the sun and bathing. Yet after only several days of rest, he was "getting tired of it" and reckoned "it was harder work trying to kill time than to paint Indians."[37] Within two weeks of sending this letter, Burbank had traveled to Yuma—where he complained of "awfully superstitious" Indians who are "too hard to handle"[38]—and moved on to Ignacio, Colorado, to paint Southern Utes.

This pattern of extended periods of travel and intensive work continued for almost two decades. During 1904 he sojourned for weeks and months at a time at the Hubbell Trading Post on the Navajo Reservation and at Keams Canyon and Polacca on the Hopi Reservation. After spending the first four months of 1905 living at Polacca and then briefer amounts of time at several other locations in Arizona, Burbank traveled to California. That year he sent forty letters to Ayer and sixty-seven more the following year. Moving south to north, these letters were sent from Pala in San Diego County, Ballarat in the Panamint Valley, Chico in the Sacramento Valley, Hoopa in Humboldt County, and Yreka in Siskiyou County.

At a first reading, Burbank's letters convey the impression that as an artist he largely labored alone in the field. However, it is more likely that Burbank simply did not mention some occasions when he met fellow artists and photographers. For example, in August 1904 he traveled from Ganado, Arizona, with Lorenzo Hubbell's family, four teams, and a cook to attend the biennial Snake Dance ceremony at the village of Oraibi. Writing about the event to Ayer, he mentioned no other Anglos in attendance apart from a group of Harvard students with their professor.[39] Almost certainly a significant number of other Anglos were there to photograph and sketch the ceremony. But this is not to say that Burbank did not refer to other artists at all. Writing from the Crow Agency in Montana in July 1897, he noted that the well-known painters Frederic Remington and George de Forest Brush had recently been there, thus confirming to him the wisdom of traveling to that location for subjects. He also spent time with the artist brothers Ed and Phil Sawyer at the Hubbell Trading Post and the Hopi mesas and referred to other painters, such as Louis Akin and Ferdinand Lundgren, he encountered in the Southwest. In Ukiah, California, he met Grace Hudson, whose paintings of Pomo Indians he much admired. When Burbank met George Wharton James in Yuma, Arizona, the writer boasted of having written three books on Native Americans and possessing twenty thousand negatives of Indian portraits and views.[40] Burbank also visited Charles Fletcher Lummis at his home in Los Angeles. One suspects that meetings with James and Lummis, both renowned for the daunting scale of their writing, photography, and travel through the Southwest and their overwhelming personalities, left Burbank in danger of nervous exhaustion.

As the months and years that Burbank spent in the field went by, so his portraiture changed. He struggled to maintain the close attention to costumes and ornaments that his contemporary commentators praised so highly. It was hardly surprising given ongoing acculturation efforts on reservations that many Native Americans no longer possessed traditional costumes and instead dressed in the "half American clothing" that Burbank had so disliked when he first visited Fort Sill. As early as 1898 he had diversified his output by creating Conté crayon drawings. These images maintained the fidelity to appearances that he considered a hallmark of his work and had the advantage of being created quickly and thus could be sold cheaply. This way Burbank could earn a higher rate of return on the investment of his time and capital in portraiture. Lest these comments suggest that Burbank was motivated to change his preferred medium solely out of pecuniary considerations, it is important to emphasize that for both Burbank and his patrons the images had an aesthetic appeal of their own. The portrait of "Tube-Eh" (plate 15), a Hopi girl drawn at Polacca in 1905, is typical of the drawings. By concentrating on the heads and shoulders of subjects, Burbank avoided the potentially tricky dilemma of how to dress them in what he considered appropriate clothing.

Both private patrons and institutions bought the Conté crayon drawings, Ayer being by far the largest single purchaser of original drawings. Given Ayer's mission to collect documentary evidence of Native American lifeways, his support for his nephew's endeavor should not be a surprise. After Burbank explained to his uncle that the quickness with which the drawings could be completed was an advantage over oil paintings if indeed he were to accomplish his goal of representing members of each tribe in the United States, Ayer instructed Burbank to represent as many different tribes as possible in this medium. Over the following seven years Burbank sent 1,236 drawings to his uncle. It does appear that at one stage Ayer grew impatient with his nephew for making what he considered too many images.[41] Burbank defended himself by explaining that at that point—December 1906—he had made portraits of only half of California's different tribes and that while traveling there he had been struck by the great linguistic variety of its Native peoples. He emphasized the continuing value of his work, claiming that while he had visited 101 tribes already there remained a huge amount of documentation to complete. "In a few years," he reminded his uncle, "nearly all the full blood Indian [*sic*] will be dead and when the old Indians are dead few full bloods will be left."[42] Burbank's argument won the day a month later when, in January 1907, he finalized arrangements with Ayer. Henceforth he would continue to make Conté crayon drawings at a rate of 200–300 images per year for a fee of $6 each.[43] Ayer appears to have remained sufficiently enthusiastic about the images after the First World War to urge his fellow bibliophile and art collector Henry Huntington, in California, to commission Burbank to copy the 445 images of California Indians housed in the Ayer Collection. Burbank completed these drawings, along with further copies of hundreds of southwestern Indian portraits from the Ayer Collection, between 1922 and 1930.[44]

After 1906 Burbank continued to travel extensively through the Southwest, spending much of his time at the Hubbell Trading Post and visiting Pueblo Indian communities in the Rio Grande Valley of northern New Mexico. In September 1909 he wrote to Ayer from Ganado, reporting the completion of a large and elaborate image of the Hopi Snake Dance containing twenty-three human figures and fourteen rattlesnakes and bull snakes which he later sold to Hubbell for $500.[45] After this the Ayer Collection contains only one further letter that Burbank sent to Ayer, from Oklahoma in 1914, but it is unclear what he was doing there or whether a financial arrangement between the two men continued beyond 1909. Ayer did purchase a final oil painting in 1908, a genre painting of Navajo men playing cards, but within a year the supply of Conté crayon drawings had come to an end. Significantly, *Navaho Card Players* (plate 16) is, at 16" x 20" in size, a larger-format image than all the other images Burbank sent Ayer. Indeed Burbank produced further larger-size genre paintings about this time, including two 30" x 40" paintings of the Snake Dance that were sold to Butler and Hubbell. Similar-size images of

Navajo men playing the card game "Koon Can" and of a typical scene within the Hubbell Trading Post were also sold to Hubbell. Collectively these images are different in subject matter, style, and scale from the great majority of Burbank's work and represent a notable change of direction in his painting. The three Navajo images reflect Burbank's immersion in the environment of the trading post, where he spent many hours observing Navajos come and go in his leisure time and while working as a clerk. Unlike the subjects of his portraits, who are abstracted from the physical circumstances in which they lived, the figures are shown in a particular place—the interior of the trading post—and as part of a vibrant community in which Navajos interacted with Anglos.

Burbank spent less time in New Mexico and Arizona after 1909. Letters sent to Hubbell in this period indicate that Burbank was actively pursuing commercial opportunities of his own. Writing from his hometown, Harvard, Illinois, in February 1911, he reported the sale of two full-length portraits he had painted in Ganado to the Santa Fe Railway. Living expenses, however, were high and revenue was low: "[I]n selling pictures it is hard to get a good price. And when sold it is hard collecting."[46] These practical difficulties, along with turmoil in his personal life, resulted in a complete breakdown in 1917. Burbank never again painted Indians "from life."

The Politics of Patronage

In 1929, two years after its subject died at the age of eighty-five, Frank Lockwood's *The Life of Edward E. Ayer* was published. The book had been commissioned late in Ayer's life and was designed to provide readers with a grand narrative of his exemplary business success and philanthropy. Lockwood associated Ayer's life story with the epic narrative of westward expansion in the nineteenth century and the fulfillment of the United States' destiny as a leading power in the world. Ayer, he stated, had played a key role "during the picturesque and strenuous period of railroad expansion in the West that followed the Civil War" and had helped build Chicago into a great city. Lockwood also praised Ayer for working in "philanthropic and constructive ways for the betterment of the American Indian."[47] In a book that never ceases to flatter its subject, Lockwood provides a full account of Ayer's remarkable career as an industrialist and private collector of documents and objects pertaining to Native Americans and the exploration and settlement of North America by whites.

It is instructive to set the clear sense of purpose and capitalist ambition that both Ayer and the industrialist Joseph Butler developed in the post–Civil War years in relation to the anxiety and discontinuity that so often characterized Burbank's existence. To what extent did Burbank share the views of his major patrons concerning social and economic progress in the United States? Why indeed did these men spend thousands of dollars purchasing art representing Native Americans? And how did they view "real-life" Indian people in the late nineteenth and early twentieth centuries? In contrast to Ayer and Butler, Burbank's third major patron, the trader J. L. Hubbell, had developed close personal ties to southwestern Indians. Whereas Ayer became active in the campaign to assimilate Indians into American society and Butler appears to have experienced only fleeting contact with "real" Native people, Hubbell lived in the midst of Navajos and regularly traveled to the Hopi mesas. His trading post at Ganado, Arizona, stood at the center of an expanding commercial fiefdom at the beginning of the last century. Undoubtedly Hubbell prospered greatly from consolidating his profitable trade with Navajos with land speculation, but this could only be achieved through entering into ties of mutual obligation with Native people. Hubbell provided Burbank with easy access to Navajos who were encouraged to sit for the artist. Similarly the English trader Thomas Keam, of Keams Canyon on the Hopi Reservation, provided access to Hopis. Burbank spent many months sojourning with Hubbell and with Keam until the latter's death in 1902.

When Ayer commissioned the portrait of Geronimo in 1897, he had been a successful businessman for three decades. Seventeen years older than his nephew Burbank, Ayer's fortune was built on supplying lumber to railroads. After serving in the Southwest with the Union Army during the Civil War, Ayer returned home to Harvard, Illinois, and began his commercial career by purchasing land and selling wood to fuel the locomotives of the Chicago and Northwestern Railroad. Then in 1867 he earned the first of many contracts to supply railroads with ties. After the Chicago and Northwestern ordered sixty thousand ties, Ayer supplied the Union Pacific with a further sixty thousand ties. By 1871 he was selling almost a million ties a year.[48] While Ayer's business success grew, his sister Annie remained in Harvard, where she married Abner Burbank and brought up their son, Elbridge, born in 1858. Unlike Ayer, Abner Burbank made no fortune from the railroad; instead he was employed as a station agent for the duration of his working life.

Lockwood presents Ayer as a man from a relatively humble back-ground who participated in key events of the nineteenth century—frontier settlement, sectional crisis, civil warfare, industrialization, and the incorporation of America—that had consolidated and developed American nationhood as the country moved into the twentieth century. Ayer's life was also narrated as an epic story of self-improvement. Ayer claimed that reading Prescott's *The Conquest of Mexico* while he was sta-tioned at Tucson, Arizona, during the Civil War was "absolutely respon-sible for the 'Ayer Collection' in the Newberry Library, Chicago."[49] Ayer used his growing wealth to purchase Native American objects. This collecting interest built on Ayer's personal experiences in the West. In 1859, at the age of eighteen, he set out for California with an emi-grant party and reported arriving in San Francisco with only twenty-five cents to his name. Quickly Ayer took a job working in a lumberyard, thus enabling him to claim later that he really had worked himself up from the bottom to the top of the lumber industry. In August 1861 he enlisted with the First California Cavalry Company E and was stationed at San Bernadino as a defense against the Confederate advance on the Southwest from Texas. During the Civil War he spent the bulk of his time in Arizona and New Mexico. As a second lieutenant in the First New Mexican Infantry he visited San Ildefonso Pueblo in New Mexico while recruiting Pueblo Indians for the Union and was greatly impressed by a ceremonial dance he witnessed. He also visited the Navajo Reservation as a member of a court martial committee presided over by General Kit Carson.[50] After the Civil War Ayer traveled exten-sively through the West, and particularly the Southwest and northern Mexico, while on business. During the late 1870s and 1880s Ayer sup-plied ties to the Atchison, Topeka, and Santa Fe Railway and the Mexican Central Railroad. He reckoned to have supplied the latter with between six and seven million ties.[51]

Ayer began his Indian collection by purchasing costumes and beadwork from Plains Indians in Denver, Colorado, and Omaha, Nebraska, in 1871. Soon he was also buying arrows, spears, shields, and tomahawks, indeed "everything that had to do with the life of the North American Indian."[52] Lockwood reported that when in 1880 Ayer returned to the plains he had crossed twenty years earlier en-route to California, he noticed profound changes in Indian livelihoods: "The game had vanished, and the Indians dressed differently from what they did in the old days. His observant eye saw that aboriginal life in America would soon be a thing of the past, so he set diligently to work collecting Indian material, wherever it could be found."[53] This material was first displayed at Ayer's summer home at Lake Geneva, Wisconsin, and then placed in a specially built library when a new home was built for Ayer in Chicago in 1887. Burbank painted Ayer in his library, surrounded by Native American arts and crafts as well as books and paintings (plate 17). According to Lockwood, Ayer's "whole career as a collector was based on the desire to know who was the first white man in every five hundred square miles of North America, how he treated the Indians he found there, how they treated him, who followed in exploration, and what became of the Indians."[54] As a trustee of the Newberry Library between 1892 and 1911, Ayer supported its founders' mission to create a privately endowed research library whose collections would be made available to the general public. In 1911, Ayer donated his private collection of fifty thousand books, myriad manuscripts, and hundreds of drawings and paintings to the Newberry.[55] He boasted of having spent over $700,000 on literature and art describing cultural encounters between Native Americans and Euro-Americans. He also spent over $100,000 on a collection of Native American material culture that he donated to the Field Museum of Natural History in Chicago.[56] The figures are important because they indicate that Ayer measured the success of both his business and largesse in financial terms.

Although Burbank completed a huge body of work for Ayer, his uncle by no means envisaged his nephew's paintings and drawings as taking the most prominent position in his collection of art. Ayer did not subscribe to what he considered interpretive studies of the Indian, maintaining instead his overriding interest in documentation of Native American lives and encounters between Indians and Euro-Americans. This aversion explains Ayer's refusal to purchase work by photographer Edward S. Curtis.[57] Ayer wanted Burbank's images to complement earlier portraits of Native Americans he owned by Karl Bodmer, George Catlin, and Charles Bird King. Significantly Burbank's images also stood alongside the work of Native American artists of the late nineteenth and early twentieth centuries. Indeed it was Burbank who helped purchase the work by several Indian artists for Ayer's Library. In May 1897 Burbank reported that he had the Kiowa artist Hawgone (or Silver Horn) "making Indian pictures in colors," a reference to what became a collection of over a hundred examples of Plains ledger-style art that he purchased on behalf of Ayer.[58] In addition, Burbank probably arranged for the purchase of paintings by the Chiricahua Apache leader Naiche. Ayer also collected 160 drawings by Indians at the Fort Yates Reservation in

North Dakota and paintings by Awa Tsireh from San Ildefonso Pueblo, New Mexico, and Monroe Frederick Quamahongiva, a young Hopi Indian.[59] Whereas many of the Fort Yates images, largely created by Hunkpapa Lakotas, depicted scenes of raiding and hunting and Awa Tsireh's paintings illustrated ceremonial dances, Quamahongiva's oils and watercolors appear to have been incorporated into the art collection as a sign of what Ayer considered to be advances in Native American education. An article in the Phoenix *Republican* explained that Ayer had been impressed by the sixteen-year-old boy's art on a visit to an Indian school and had arranged for his training in art in Chicago after the completion of his school studies. He had also commissioned Quamahongiva to paint fifteen images for $75.[60] Among these images are an oil painting entitled *After E. Irving Couse,* which shows two Indian males contemplating a painting of a turtle on an easel with firelight illuminating the scene, and a watercolor labeled *After Burbank,* a copy of a Conté crayon drawing of a Hopi woman by Burbank. Ayer does not appear to have appreciated the irony of instructing a young Hopi man to mimic romanticized and ethnological representations of Native Americans by Anglos.

Burbank's art was limited by the constraints of his uncle's often-functional attitude toward images of Native Americans. Bearing in mind Ayer's conservatism toward Curtis, it is hardly surprising that when Burbank claimed he was in the midst of completing a book that "would give the side of an Indian different from what has ever been written," his uncle offered no financial support and provided only words of caution against the enterprise.[61] In actuality Burbank's book was not completed until the final years of his life, although he did publish a number of illustrated accounts of his travels in newspapers and magazines that brought income in their own right and provided an advertising outlet for his art. In the earlier years when Burbank's Indian portraiture was still considered fresh and innovative, his oil paintings regularly sold for an average of over $150, suggesting that he could make a fairly lucrative living from his art. However Burbank had many expenses. Adding to the cost of board and lodging, transportation (railroad, stage, and wagon), and the delivery of paintings to his base in Chicago were fees paid to Indian sitters and, most frustratingly for Burbank, the commission charged by gallery owners who exhibited and sold his paintings. In July 1897 he anticipated earning $2,450 for the thirteen paintings he had completed since leaving Chicago six weeks before. In the meantime he reported being cash poor, having greatly depleted the mere $200 he had in reserve on departing Chicago.[62]

These details help explain why Burbank was so often on the lookout for commercial opportunities while in the field. He appears to have equivocated over his decision to have many oil paintings reproduced as chromolithographs. In September 1899 Burbank reported that the quality of these images was excellent and that they should appeal to a reliable mass market because they were inexpensively produced and cheap to purchase.[63] Four months later he admitted that the sales of original paintings might well have been negatively impacted by the widespread availability of chromolithographs. By July 1901 the situation had grown more serious. Burbank reported that Thurber was not selling Indian portraits anymore and then stated that if his images did not sell soon he would give up painting Native Americans. Bearing in mind these worries, it must have been a great relief when Burbank sold 106 unframed oil paintings to Joseph G. Butler in February 1902 for a total sum of $10,600.[64] He noted that Butler now owned 118 of his images, worked in the iron business, and was very much interested in Indians.[65]

Butler was a prominent leader in Ohio's iron and steel industries. In common with Ayer, he had progressed from humble beginnings in life to a position of considerable wealth and power in industry. Although he did not stand for political office, he regularly campaigned for the Republican Party and took great pride in having become personally acquainted with Republican presidents. Butler firmly believed in the gospel of progress and prosperity. In his autobiography, published in 1925, he wrote:

> Unquestionably the wonderful progress of this country has been due in part to our magnificent natural resources, without which it would have been impossible. But I believe that the principal factor in this progress has been the spirit of our free institutions, which have extended opportunity and rewarded effort as has never been done before in any part of the world.[66]

The natural resources Butler referred to were not landscapes such as the Grand Canyon, which he did visit in 1902, but the great coal and iron ore reserves that fueled the industrial development of the United States. Looking back at the period of his birth, in 1840, Butler viewed an environment in which there was no steel industry and "no railroads . . . no telegraphs, no telephones, no electric lights, no trolleys, no radio, no motion pictures, no automobiles."[67] While he remembered fondly "the quaint customs" of Niles, Ohio, where he grew up, Butler harbored no discernible nostalgia for an older agrarian way of life.[68] Instead, from his teenage years on, he sought success in the iron industry.

There was little room in Butler's mindset for those people and institutions, including striking workers and trade unions, that he considered obstacles to "progress and prosperity." Significantly the only reference Butler makes to Native Americans in his autobiography is in this vein and concerns a visit he made to Spokane, Washington, in 1905. At the time Butler and his wife, Harriet Vorhees Butler, were guests of the American Institute of Mining Engineers on an excursion trip to Alaska. Their party had taken "a very fine special train" from Chicago, and Spokane was the first stop on their rail journey to the Pacific Coast. Butler remarked that "the only unattractive thing we saw at Spokane was a surviving remnant of the Spokane Indian tribe, who were a miserable, dirty lot, even for Indians."[69]

Butler felt no need to justify his hostility toward the Spokane Indian he remembered seeing because he assumed that readers would share his viewpoint. His words dehumanize Spokanes in general and show no sympathy whatsoever for the circumstances in which they lived at this time. And yet the same man was prepared to spend thousands of dollars purchasing works of art in which the images of Native Americans were preserved through the medium of paint and Conté crayon. In addition to Burbank's portraits, Butler bought images by Eanger Irving Couse, Victor Higgins, Bert Geer Phillips, and Joseph Sharp that featured Indian subjects. These images, in turn, were donated to the Butler Institute of Art, which opened in October 1919. Taking the view that "every man of wealth owes something to the community in which he has lived, as well as to his country and society at large," Butler explained that the institute was his "free gift" to the people of Youngstown.[70] By collecting and displaying American works of art exclusively, Butler provided access for all the city's residents to art that he hoped would help develop their artistic and intellectual sensibilities and inspire a great sense of patriotism in all Americans. With aplomb he stated: "We lead the world in genius for invention, efficiency and utility. There is no reason why we cannot eventually do so in the genius for art and literature."[71]

How might Burbank have reacted to such words? One wonders if he shared Butler's grand vision of American supremacy in industry and world affairs. Did his experiences among Indians call into question Butler's confident vision of technological progress and national unity? It is unclear. Perhaps Burbank was simply grateful for Butler's patronage and saw no reason to doubt the cultural logic of social and economic advancement to which Butler and so many captains of industry subscribed. And yet one wonders again how Burbank reconciled himself to the rules of business and social conduct by which his two major patrons lived, for in their world there was little tolerance of Spokanes and other Indians who persisted in living without submitting to assimilation campaigns or who simply refused to fade away. Surely, one might ask, his experiences of travel among Indians would have allowed him to tell a story of endurance, cultural survival, and resistance to acculturation efforts? But, as we shall see in due course, when eventually Burbank did narrate his autobiography late in life, he demonstrated little if any awareness of the tensions and inconsistencies that lay at the heart of his ties with Indians and, in turn, his relationship with his patrons.

Burbank's bond with the trader J. L. Hubbell was quite different from his relation to either Ayer or Butler. Hubbell provided a long and supportive friendship and became a major sponsor of the artist's work. When Burbank first visited the trading post in November 1897, Hubbell refused to take money for board and lodging. Unlike Ayer and Butler, whose homes were hundreds of miles away from the Southwest, Hubbell's business and personal life were intertwined with the lives of Navajos and Hopis. Between the 1870s and his death in 1930, Hubbell built a local commercial empire that ultimately consisted of thirty-two trading posts and stores and many other business interests. As a competitive businessman doubtless he was paternalistic and even exploitative in his relations with Navajos and Hopis, but he was also a concerned patron who took seriously his obligations to the Native Americans on whose labors his wealth was founded. Hubbell pulled Burbank into his commercial world by purchasing and trading for twenty-six oil paintings and 180 drawings. These images account for a third of Hubbell's collection of art, which was displayed in his home. In common with other artists Hubbell dealt with, Burbank sold Navajo textiles and other arts and crafts on the trader's behalf. Burbank also worked for some time as a clerk in the trading post.[72] The letters sent between the two men indicate the warmth they felt toward one another, with Burbank often declaring his desire to return to Ganado soon. In one such letter, Burbank wrote: "I want to get out West soon as I can[.] I love the life[.] I can not stand civilization and I would rather live on a ranch like yours than live in New York city. Where you are[,] you are living like a King[.] [Y]ou don't know your good luck."[73]

Although Burbank made lucrative arrangements for the sale of his images to Ayer, Butler, and Hubbell, he appears not to have become wealthy from the income generated by his art. This is partly explained by the lack of business sense to which he referred in a number of letters to Ayer. Perhaps when Burbank first traveled West he overextended his finances by maintaining a household and studio in Chicago. Certainly there was no other bulk purchase of art to match the arrangement with Butler. As the years went by, Burbank appears to have struggled to maintain financial solvency. He continually searched for revenue by selling paintings, drawings, and chromolithographs to individual patrons, institutions, and the Santa Fe Railway. Unfortunately for Burbank he reached the point where he found it increasingly difficult to sustain a viable living from his art. In time these economic pressures, combined with the emotional toll of two failed marriages, proved too burdensome.

Burbank's Sorrow

When Burbank died in San Francisco at the age of ninety in 1949 there was no biographer to summarize his life. From the fragments of information that are available, a fascinating but melancholy story emerges of his later years. Burbank's letters to Ayer make many references to nervousness, exhaustion, and neuralgia while also expressing fastidiousness over accommodation, diet, and weight. Burbank suffered from manic depression and would go through periods of intense activity followed by comparative paralysis.[74] The breakup of his first marriage exacerbated this tendency. During his initial years of travel through the West, Burbank would spend a number of months each year at home in Chicago with his wife, Blanche Wheeler. This practice changed when he left Blanche after she had undergone her second abortion in early 1903. Five years later she was granted a divorce on the grounds of desertion. While Burbank wished to become a father, Blanche appears to have feared that her husband's mental instability would be passed on to their own children. Devastating as this experience must have been for each partner, there is added poignancy to the situation in the fact that while Burbank failed to communicate with Blanche, she continued to seek news of him through corresponding with Burbank's father, Abner, for many years after their divorce.[75]

The strain of these personal difficulties is expressed in a letter sent to Ayer from San Francisco in September 1903:

My trouble does not interfere with my work. I will not allow it. I am in hopes and expect to [be] free again soon. I *hope* so. I came West as I thought it best to and soon am going North of here for Indians. I want to remain West until matters are settled in the East. I have had enough sorrow to last me for the remainder of my life. It had changed me for years from what I was intended to be[—]cheerful and happy[—]but now I am all right again and will allow nothing to put me back.[76]

Burbank's words indicate how he took refuge from the consequences of abandoning his wife by traveling through the West and immersing himself in work. One senses that Blanche understood only too well the emotional frailty lying behind her estranged husband's actions and that she forgave him for them.[77] In the midst of drawing Pomos in Ukiah, California, at the end of 1903, Burbank stated that he wished to spend the rest of his life with Indians.[78] This comment indicates how Burbank experienced a sense of liberation and well-being in his interactions with Indians that he did not find elsewhere in American society. It certainly appears that the hours in which Burbank painted and drew Indians were for him the most meaningful hours of his life.

Around 1909 Burbank stopped traveling in search of Indian subjects, probably because he had married for a second time. His second wife was Nettie B. Taber, a twenty-two-year-old woman who was almost thirty years his junior. Without earning a regular income from Ayer for his Conté crayon drawings, Burbank struggled to make a living. He and Nettie first lived in Los Angeles and then moved to his hometown, Harvard, Illinois, where he tried to paint portraits and sell southwestern Indian arts and crafts that were supplied by Hubbell. When this venture proved unsuccessful, the couple returned to Los Angeles. Burbank opened a small studio and remained in the city for three years until 1916, the year that Nettie left him. Given the frailty of his mental health over the preceding years, it is not surprising that Burbank experienced another breakdown. He left Los Angeles for San Francisco, perhaps hoping that his condition would improve by moving to a fresh environment. This did not prove to be the case, and Burbank sought refuge in an institutional setting.[79]

On May 24, 1917, at the age of fifty-nine years, Burbank entered Napa State Hospital in California, where he remained a voluntary resident for the following two decades. He was diagnosed as suffering from manic depression, a condition that he had contended with throughout his adult life. In common with other people suffering from mental illness at this time, he spent many years in hospital. Burbank eventually left the hospital in April 1934 and was granted an official discharge two years later. A note written by Dr William A. Rogers, whose father, Dr J. B. Rogers, attended Burbank while working at Napa State Hospital, explains that Burbank had entered the hospital in a very confused state just after World War I. He was given a physical diagnosis of "severe pernicious anemia with mental changes." With the benefit of several years of treatment with raw liver and liver extract, together with "kind, gentle psychiatric help," Burbank was released from the hospital "very much improved." The elder Rogers considered Burbank to have recovered completely.[80]

Napa State Hospital provided a stable environment in which Burbank could recuperate and gather his energies. A hospital clerk noted that at the institution Burbank was free to move around at will and had been granted town privileges. She explained he had been happy in the hospital and that "in those days, patients stayed for years and years when they had a chronic mental illness."[81] Significantly, his years in the hospital were artistically productive. In June 1922, while Ayer was residing at the Hotel Maryland in nearby Pasadena, an agreement was finalized with the Huntington Library whereby Burbank would copy 445 Conté crayon drawings of California Indians housed in the Newberry Library's Ayer Collection. The images would be sent in lots of twenty-five or fifty every two to three months, and Burbank would be paid $7.50 for each drawing. George Watson Cole, the Huntington's librarian, wrote: "If you find that Mr. Burbank seems able to do this work we authorize you to pay his transportation to Chicago, where the work is to be done."[82] Two years later Ayer wrote to notify the Huntington that Burbank was making copies of the Conté crayon drawings at Napa State Hospital. It is not clear whether Burbank actually moved from California to Chicago to do the copying, had a relapse, and was returned to the hospital, or whether he was at the institution all along. But one thing is certain: Burbank was making copies quickly and efficiently at a rate of an image every other day. Ayer sent a letter to the Huntington Library in December 1924 confirming that Burbank had completed 394 drawings of California Indians so far and that he was contracted to copy a further 319 images of Indians from California, Arizona, and New Mexico.[83] Eventually the Huntington Library purchased 1,024 red chalk portraits, Burbank working on the assignment until 1930.

After leaving the hospital in 1934, Burbank moved to San Francisco, where he lived in the Manx Hotel until his death in 1949.[84] It must have been difficult for Burbank to emerge from the shadow of the hospital late in his life and during the Depression. Among the Burbank ephemera collected at the Huntington Library are indications of how the artist continued to revisit his images of Native Americans during the 1930s and 1940s. He proposed that the Huntington purchase copies at $7.50 apiece of a hundred glass-plate negatives he had had made of his oil paintings.[85] The librarian replied that no money was available for the purchase of either photographs or drawings of Indians.[86] In 1937 he created a postcard out of a sentimental pencil drawing of two Indian babies being licked by dogs, naming the scene *Helpless.* Another image, a copy of a Conté crayon drawing entitled *Red Rock, Ojibway,* indicates that Burbank sold copies of his Indian "heads" while living at the Manx Hotel. There is evidence to support this view in a note accompanying an article on Burbank's images of Native Americans in the *Pacific Rural Press* newspaper in 1934 that announced that his images were on sale at Wobbers Inc. of Market Street, San Francisco. Bearing in mind the weekly newspaper's focus on agriculture, the choice of Burbank's images of Native Americans—Geronimo, a small Hopi girl, and a Hopi woman—for three of its front covers seems incongruous. These images were reproductions in pencil of the older Conté crayon drawings. These sparse details suggest the manner in which Burbank improvised a living in the years after leaving hospital. He got by through the sale of a limited number of new and recycled images and through the help of friends.

Although the final decades of Burbank's life are characterized by hardship, through the efforts of careworkers he managed to live independently again. Somewhat against the odds, a book based on his experiences of painting Native Americans was finally published in 1944. Over forty years before, in December 1902, Burbank had told Ayer that his book was now ready for the publishers and that his wife was attending to the matter.[87] Such plans came to nil when Burbank left Blanche. It is hard to say exactly what form the original book manuscript might have taken, although there are some clues. When Burbank mentioned the book to Ayer, he noted that it was provisionally entitled *An Artist's Experience among the Indians,* would be dedicated to Ayer, and was to feature sixty full-page illustrations.[88] The key to the book's progress was clearly Blanche's participation in writing it. Burbank reported good progress on the project when she joined him in Seneca, Missouri, in March 1901. Within weeks of her arrival, she published articles on Native Americans in the *Chicago Post.*[89] But this momentum did not last and, in time, the book was abandoned. Four decades later, in 1944, Burbank narrated his story to Dr. Ernest Royce, a pharmacologist at Napa State Hospital, who worked with an editor, Frank Taylor, to complete *Burbank among the Indians*. The book was indeed dedicated to Ayer (and to the North American Indian) and copiously illustrated (with seventy-three images rather than a mere sixty). It featured chapters on Geronimo, Navajos, Pueblos, California tribes, Lakotas, Crows, Cheyennes, Chief Joseph, Comanches and Kiowas, Paiutes, Osages, and the Potowatami leader Simon Pokagon.

With its uncomplicated prose, sentimental tone, and personal interpretation of Native Americans, the narrative echoes Burbank's letters to Ayer. Despite its publication date, the book is more a document of the early 1900s than a narrative created during World War II. This would hardly constitute a surprise if indeed the book revised a manuscript that Burbank kept through the decades after the breakup of his first marriage. While the book does demonstrate some evidence of a culturally relativistic viewpoint, there can be no denying Burbank's ethnocentric paternalism when he states: "[T]he Indians I knew were grown-up children, tender-hearted, filled with superstitions, joyfully appreciative of the wonders of nature."[90] The impression that these words spring from an earlier age than the one in which the book was published is only enhanced when one reads: "It was my good fortune to know many tribes intimately before the white man's domination had completely destroyed the customs of the real Americans."[91] Viewing Burbank from one perspective, it is disheartening to read such statements if they are an accurate reflection of how little his way of seeing Native Americans changed over the course of a lifetime. And yet these words also indicate how throughout Burbank's lifetime from 1897 onward, his experiences of travel among Indians remained the focus of his memory and his continued existence.

Burbank died at the age of ninety in March 1949 after being struck by a cable car in San Francisco. He only accepted relief when in the final few weeks of his life he lay critically injured from the accident.[92] In the aftermath of Burbank's death, the public administrator examined his small room in the servant's quarters of the Manx Hotel. The administrator looked at walls splattered with paint, a battered chest of drawers containing a set of false teeth, old scrapbooks containing prints of Geronimo and the Lakotas No-Flesh and Stinking Bear, and an easel on which there was an unfinished drawing of a Native American girl. He then instructed the hotel manager to clear out the room, declaring its contents worthless.[93]

An Ambiguous Legacy

In the years after traveling to Fort Sill, Burbank believed a special tie had developed between Geronimo and himself. He claimed they had become "good friends" and that Geronimo had remarked: "I like Burbank better than any white man I have ever known. He has never lied to me and has always been kind to me and my family."[94] Recollecting his initial impression of Geronimo, Burbank admitted that he arrived in Fort Sill with stereotypical notions of Indian savagery: "Having heard of Geronimo only through the screaming headlines which exploited his daring raids and cruel massacres, I was prepared to meet a bloodthirsty savage. I gave thanks that I did not have to meet this crafty Apache at large, but instead could sketch him behind prison bars."[95] To his surprise, Burbank found Geronimo living in a cabin built by the government. He conveyed the impression that Geronimo had become subdued under white rule: "He is very domestic in his habits, and takes very kindly to civilization."[96] After observing Geronimo looking after his sick wife, doing the housework, and leaving milk for the cat, Burbank concluded that Geronimo was in fact "a kind old man."[97] Yes, Burbank suggested, Geronimo did have "peculiarities" that distinguished him from white men, but "he was certainly not as cruel as he had been pictured," and, more generally, he and the Apaches had been "misunderstood" by whites.[98]

Burbank's attitude was typical of the time. Although the demonized image of the "savage" Apache prevailed at the close of the nineteenth century, it was joined by the discourse of incorporation that claimed that Indians would be improved by virtue of their absorption into American society. Burbank's art thus shares ideological ground with middle-class reformers who called for the social and economic advancement of Native Americans at the beginning of the last century. When in 1897 Burbank claimed Geronimo was now domesticated and willing to cooperate with Anglos, he confirmed Ayer's progressive sympathies. Notably Ayer, in addition to his prominent roles with the Field Museum and the Newberry Library—not to mention his active membership in the Chicago Historical Association, the Art Institute of Chicago, the American Historical Association, and the American Anthropological Association—served on the Board of Indian Commissioners between 1912 and 1918. After Ayer's death in 1927, the board characterized him as a "practical idealist" in Indian affairs who "advocated justice for the Indians with vigorous and uncompromising speech and persuasive ardor" while telling "the Indians themselves that the way of their success must lie along the paths of good health, industrial education, obedience to the law, hard work, and good character."[99] These words indicate the degree to which Ayer considered Native Americans in the early twentieth century to be moving through a process of irrevocable change whereby they would lose their sense of tribal identity and become assimilated into American society.

There were profound limitations to this way of seeing Native Americans. Within Ayer's own lifetime the assimilation campaign he advocated was challenged, most notably by John Collier, who was later appointed Commissioner of Indian Affairs in Roosevelt's administration. As chief architect of the Indian Reorganization Act of 1934 in the decade after Ayer's death, Collier brought a new vision to the administration of federal Indian affairs. For Collier, the severe economic depression had rocked Americans' faith in capitalism and progress and left white society "psychically, religiously, socially and esthetically shattered."[100] In contrast, the cleaving against the odds of Native Americans to an integrated way of life in which spirituality, attachment to the land, and community prevailed above materialism, individualism, and social atomization was a phenomenon that Collier considered should be granted government support in its own right and that also offered an example of the values and practices that Americans at large must pursue if their nation were to have a future. The Indian Reorganization Act provided not only for far-reaching practical changes in tribal government and economic self-determination but also for the spiritual welfare of Native Americans. Collier considered the latter provision essential because federal Indian policy to that point had striven to undermine Native Americans' faith in the validity of their own cultures. "Indians have been robbed of initiative, their spirit has been broken, their health undermined, and their native pride ground into the dust," he stated.[101] The new legislation, he hoped, would help them overcome the psychological burden of dependency and assimilation campaigns.[102]

Looking back on Ayer's activities in the light of Collier's revised federal Indian policy, one may well be inclined to emphasize the differences in philosophy between each man. In actuality the outcome of Ayer's paternalism is not as clear-cut as it may at first seem, even if Ayer died believing that granting citizenship to Native Americans in 1924 effectively marked the end of "traditional" Indian cultures. By donating material to the Newberry Library and endowing his collection, Ayer provided the means for the serious study of Native American history without dictating the ways in which the collection should be used.[103] Thus in the twenty-first century the Ayer Collection is being used extensively by Anglo and Native American scholars to reevaluate the history of relations between Indians and Euro-Americans. More significantly, men like Ayer misunderstood the degree to which Native Americans would maintain their sense of cultural identity in spite of government programs to instill in them the value of property ownership, wage labor, Christian morality, and formal schooling. While Burbank shared his uncle's shortsightedness in this regard, his letters do contain observations (albeit often unwitting ones) that indicate the tactics Indians employed in order to resist his presence among them. Again it is instructive to turn to the figure of Geronimo.

We have seen how after their initial meeting in 1897 Burbank thought that Geronimo's character had been improved by virtue of his capture, imprisonment, and proximity to white culture.[104] Although Burbank later claimed to have entered into immediately friendly relations with Geronimo, a letter to Ayer from that time tells another story: "He is awfully greedy for money, he is not liked here on that account, every time I see him he has something to sell me."[105] Geronimo became well known for his financial opportunism and was savvy enough to demand a cut of any profit Burbank might make from painting his portrait, just as he made money from selling bows and arrows, his signature, and even the buttons on his coat.[106] This opens up the question more generally of Geronimo's engagement with white society in the decade before his death in 1909. During these years he willingly put himself on display at the Pan-American Exposition in Buffalo in 1901 and the St. Louis World's Fair in 1904, took part in President Theodore Roosevelt's inaugural parade, and collaborated with S. M. Barrett to write *Geronimo: His Own Story, The Autobiography of a Great Warrior Patriot,* a book that was dedicated to Roosevelt. In each case Geronimo used the opportunities made available to him to broaden his sphere of influence, earn money, and petition the president for the return of the Chiricahuas to their Arizona homeland. The revenue Geronimo gained through manipulating Euro-American fascination with his image helped provide for the welfare of his immediate family and other Chiricahuas. Bearing this in mind, we see that the behavior Burbank labeled "greed for money" was actually an example of the Chiricahua elder's resourcefulness and adroitness in adapting to the changed circumstances of his life in the aftermath of his surrender and incarceration.

To conclude, I refer again to *Burbank among the Indians,* the book published late in the artist's life. Over the course of two chapters Burbank discusses his interactions with the Hopis of Arizona and the Pueblo Indians of New Mexico. The juxtaposition of the two sentences in the following passage is telling: "Often their pueblos were reached only by ladders which could be drawn up when enemies threatened them. Because of this aloofness, I found portrait painting among the different Pueblo tribes an exciting adventure."[107] In addition to illustrating Burbank's assumed right of access to Indian cultures, the passage also demonstrates an obvious paradox at the heart of his activity. In being attracted to the most "authentic" tribes Burbank repeatedly failed to make the connection between denial of access and other forms of resistance to his presence and the preservation of the very traditions that made such tribes "authentic" in his own eyes. Reading Burbank's letters one does not gain the impression that any malice was involved as he took advantage of the asymmetrical power relations between Indians and whites to gain access to subjects. It is more accurate to say that he, along with so many Euro-Americans in the late nineteenth and early twentieth centuries, suffered from limited vision and insight into Indian cultures. This helps to explain what one might take to be the lack of innovation in his way of seeing Indians. Taken together, the Conté crayon drawings may impose an almost crushing weight of repetition on the viewer who today looks at the images at the Newberry or Huntington libraries. The fault, if it can be called that, is less in the content of the images—which given Burbank's eye for accurate representation constitute an invaluable record of the individuals and tribes he documented—than in the regularity of the pose of sitters and the framing of the portraits. In this regard, despite its studied attention to detail, Burbank's art might be understood as a record of misinterpretation and incomplete understanding. But it is also the case that Burbank shared with his Indian subjects a sense of marginalization from American society. The forces of marginalization were of course different for Native Americans than for Burbank. Whereas Indians had become marginalized from their older ways of life due to the processes of dislocation and enclavement that had pushed them onto reservations and into a modernizing economy, Burbank sought control and stability within his life by seeking out for months at a time the geographical and cultural periphery of his own country. For today's Native Americans, Burbank's images of the first and second generation of reservation dwellers represent both a troubling legacy of oppression and ironically, given the artist's belief that Indians' distinctive lifeways were fast disappearing, a record of cultural survival at a time when their population reached its nadir and pressures to change their lifeways through land allotment, educational programs, and religious oppression were at a height. At once a record of political oppression and cultural survival, Burbank's art leaves an ambiguous legacy.

CHAPTER SIX

"Indian Detours Off the Beaten Track": Cultural Tourism and the Southwest

ON SUNDAY, AUGUST 18, 1895, Adam Clark Vroman, a professional book-seller and keen amateur photographer, arrived at Walpi, a small village lying atop First Mesa, one of the three mesas inhabited by Hopi Indians in northern Arizona. He had taken the Santa Fe Railway from Los Angeles to Holbrook, Arizona, and from there proceeded by wagon to Walpi, camping out for two nights along the way. Viewing the Snake Dance transformed Vroman. In the late afternoon he watched with fascination as dancers took snakes, including a number of rattlesnakes, from the *kisi,* or sacred bower, and marched around the dance plaza with the snakes in their hands and hanging from their mouths. "Words cannot picture it all," he wrote. "The location[,] the surroundings[,] the costumes which are beautiful, the bodies of Dancers dyed a rich brown with the entire chin *white*, making faces look almost hideous. My first thought was after it was all over was to see it again & know more about it, why it was, and how it is planned. I felt I could spend a year right there, be one of them, and learn their ways and beliefs. It is a sacred rite with them and carried out to the letter as they believe it."[1]

Vroman noted that around sixty Euro-Americans watched the Walpi ceremony, including artists, sculptors, scientists, writers, and newspaper correspondents. He and twelve other "camarasts" jostled for best position to take photographs of the dancers. Three decades later the Indian agent Leo Crane recorded two thousand tourists in attendance for the same event.[2] They came in response to reading widely distributed newspaper and journal accounts, travelogues, and publicity material distributed by the Santa Fe Railway at a point when communications to the Southwest were being developed. Spurred on by corporate advertising and guidebooks to the distinctive sights of Arizona and New Mexico, travelers first used the railroad and local wagon drivers, and later automobiles, to reach the remote Hopi mesas.

In August 1924 the English author D. H. Lawrence traveled with his wife, Frieda, and Mabel Dodge Luhan to view the Snake Dance at Hotevilla in the western part of the Hopi Reservation. He guessed that three thousand people were in attendance and that the great majority of them had arrived in the eight hundred cars he saw parked a mile away from the village. In the first of two accounts he wrote about the experience, Lawrence reduced the Antelope and Snake priests to diminutive figures and enlarged the profile of the Euro-Americans onlookers. He surveyed the large crowd and satirized his fellow Euro-Americans: "And what had we come to see all of us? Men with snakes in their mouths, like a circus?" Concluding that the Snake Dance had been turned into an absurd spectacle, Lawrence ridiculed the way that the Southwest had been turned into a "natural circus ground":

> The southwest is the great playground of the White American. The desert isn't good for anything else. But it does make a fine national playground. And the Indian, with his long hair and bits of pottery and blankets and clumsy home-made trinkets, he's a wonderful live toy to play with. More fun than keeping rabbits, and just as harmless. Wonderful, really, hopping around with a snake in his mouth. Lots of fun! Oh, the wild west is lots of fun: The Land of Enchantment. Like being right inside the circusring! Lots of sand, and painted savages jabbering and snakes and all that. Come on boys! Lots of fun![3]

In response to fierce criticism from his host, Mabel Dodge Luhan—who accused him of displaying "no vision, no insight, no appreciation of any kind" in his account—Lawrence wrote more sympathetically about Hopi religious beliefs in a revised article.[4] Actually Lawrence had written with insight into the nature of the attraction that the Snake Dance held for Euro-American viewers in his original piece, although Luhan does not appear to have recognized herself in Lawrence's criticism. As we shall see later in the chapter, Luhan had her own reasons for valuing the Snake Dance and Indian ceremonialism more generally. Indeed she had lured Lawrence to New Mexico in order to take part in a new utopian community in which Euro-American and Native American cultural values and practices could be forged into a new syncretic whole. Lawrence's jaundiced view of the Hotevilla Snake Dance undermined such a vision by claiming that rather than wanting to understand Hopi culture, Euro-Americans really had turned ceremonial practices into cheap theater. Furthermore he suggested that there was neither real beauty nor great substance to the ceremony itself and that Euro-Americans were deceiving themselves when reading too much into the actions of dancers and the mythology behind their actions.

How do we make sense of the profound differences in perspective in the two accounts of the Snake Dance by Vroman and Lawrence? Why did the number of Euro-American visitors to this particular ceremony grow to such a large number between the 1890s and the 1920s? And how did Hopis respond to the interest generated in the Snake Dance? These questions lead to a broader consideration of the nature of travel and tourism in this period. When John Wesley Powell traveled to the Hopi mesas in the early 1870s, his visit came on the heels of his epic journey through the Grand Canyon. Writing about his experiences of travel in articles for *Scribner's Monthly,* Powell lent a palpable sense of discovery to his narrative account. Twenty years later, when Vroman visited Walpi, the language of discovery remained, but the means of access to the Hopis had changed. Although no railroad was built into Hopi country and Vroman had to travel there by wagon across seventy miles of rough roads from Holbrook, Arizona, nevertheless the construction of the Santa Fe Railway through New Mexico and Arizona during the 1880s had a profound impact on Hopis and other Pueblo Indians, especially the Laguna Indians who lived in close proximity to the line.

The development of the railroad provided the stimulus for the development of commercial tourism in the Southwest. The passenger department of the Santa Fe Railway played a fundamental role in creating a distinctive southwestern iconography through the reproduction of commissioned artwork in calendars and posters and through the publication of advertising brochures and guidebooks. Working in tandem with the Santa Fe, the Fred Harvey Company constructed a large and influential infrastructure of hotels, restaurants, and curio shops along the railroad in New Mexico, Arizona, and southern California. In 1926 the two companies combined resources to introduce "Indian Detours," specialized automobile tours of the Southwest through which privileged visitors could travel through "200,000 miles of matchless virgin territory."[5] As is suggested by the term "virgin," the language of discovery was still associated with southwestern travel in the 1920s, but by this time encounters with landscape, Native Americans, and Hispanos had become orchestrated by commercial interests. "Indian Detour" brochures promised clients access to Native Americans who would welcome tourists to their communities yet remain unchanged by participating in the new economy of tourism.

Organized tourism of the later years consolidated the process of social, economic, and political incorporation through which the natural resources and ethnically diverse human population of the Southwest had been colonized and drawn into the Union since the era of the U.S.-Mexican War. For the historian Hal R. Rothman, tourism in the American West is "the most colonial of colonial economies," whose "social structures and cultural ways are those of an extractive industry."[6] Rothman's crucial insight is that wealthy tourists who visited southwestern places, such as the Grand Canyon and Santa Fe, a hundred or so years ago inevitably transformed those locations in the process of visiting them. Belonging for the most part to the modernizing social and economic environment of the East, these travelers sought out places on the geographical and cultural periphery of the United States. Simultaneously the places they sought out became controlled by predominantly Euro-American private and corporate interests and, in time, the federal government (through, for example, the creation and administration of national parks). There is, then, a profound difference between the experiences of earlier travelers in the region, such as W. W. H. Davis, John Wesley Powell, and Charles Fletcher Lummis, and the experiences of wealthy tourists in the 1920s and 1930s moving through a series of staged encounters in which they "discovered" the wonders of the Southwest for themselves.[7]

Significantly, Euro-Americans were by no means unified in their enthusiasm for the development of commercial tourism in the Southwest. As the nature of travel changed between the 1880s and 1930s, so the question emerged as to what constituted a "true" experience of the region. It is important to bear in mind the contending viewpoints of D. H. Lawrence and Mabel Dodge Luhan as they argued over the meaning of the Snake Dance. A decade after she chastised Lawrence, Luhan published her autobiographical novel *Winter in Taos,* which she hoped "contain[ed] the slow readaptation to the essential form of life so many have lost."[8] Pueblo Indians, she thought, offered the key to the philosophy of life that Euro-Americans had forsaken in their rush into modernity and their embrace of ultimately destructive technology. Her positive outlook on the Pueblos' "primitivism" was shared by her fellow Euro-Americans Mary Austin and John Collier.

Their writings also mixed romance and politics as they campaigned for the preservation of Native Americans' lifeways. Austin combined a feminist outlook with a passionate conviction that all Americans must learn to celebrate the indigenous roots of their culture. She argued that the subjugation and forced assimilation of Indian cultures represented the nation's shame, while the efforts of her contemporary Indian rights activists had already affected "the thinking portion of the American people" sufficiently to warrant cautious optimism regarding the future of Native Americans.[9] After his appointment by President Franklin Delano Roosevelt as Commissioner of Indian Affairs in 1933, Collier would become chief architect of a radical change in federal Indian policy, the Indian Reorganization Act of 1934, through which the old assimilationist emphasis gave way to the goal of self-determination through tribal government.

When Euro-Americans first represented the Snake Dance in the 1880s, in all likelihood they would have found it hard to comprehend how such a change in Indian policy might come about fifty years later. As we shall see, travelogues and promotional writing from the 1890s played an important role in effecting such change. In time the Hopi Snake Dance, as a synecdoche for a romanticized vision of forms of knowledge and spirituality particular to Native Americans, became a site for Euro-Americans to imagine the possibilities of ways of living and comprehending the world that lay in counterdistinction to many aspects of modern American society. This phenomenon is most clearly seen in the writings and Indian rights activism of Luhan, Austin, and Collier, which will be discussed in greater detail later in the chapter. But arguably it can also be found several decades earlier. By taking a closer look at three men—Vroman, Frederick Monsen, and Sumner Matteson—who made repeat visits to northern Arizona to photograph the Hopi Snake Dance, we can discern more clearly the motivation for their travels and photographic activity. The motif of an "Indian Detour" is useful for comprehending the ways in which such individuals went out of their way to travel through and sojourn in the Southwest. Unlike early Euro-Americans commentators on the Snake Dance, such as John Gregory Bourke, who were repulsed by what they considered the pagan aspects of the ritual, these men became sympathetically disposed toward Hopi ceremonialism and spirituality. But inevitably their photography also contributed to the popularizing of the ritual among Euro-Americans. When the Santa Fe Railway implemented its "Indian Detours" in 1926, the commercial tourism in the Southwest gathered pace, with customers expecting unimpeded access to

Native Americans' communities. As we shall see, not only Native people but also some Euro-Americans came to resent the more intrusive forms of curiosity manifested by tourists.

"Let Them Fall Off":
Three Photographers of the Hopi Snake Dance

In August 1881 the army officer and ethnologist John Gregory Bourke visited Walpi to view the Hopi Snake Dance. He had heard "vague rumors" of the ceremony from mining prospectors "and others of the same genus, who delight in the marvelous," but after William Leonard, a trader at the Navajo Agency at Fort Defiance in Arizona, confirmed the rumors, Bourke endeavored to be the first white man "to carefully note this strange heathen rite during the moment of its celebration." Traveling among the Rio Grande Pueblo Indians and Navajos as well as the Hopis, Bourke set out to write "a modest description of a summer's ramble" rather than "a pretentious book of travel." Bourke journeyed west with the artist Peter Moran on the Atlantic and Pacific Railroad (precursor of the Atchison, Topeka, and Santa Fe Railway). Their train progressed at a mere four miles per hour along the last few miles of storm-damaged track into Wingate. After spending the night at Fort Wingate, Bourke, Moran, and the trader Thomas Keam set out for Fort Defiance, their next stop, before moving on the following day to the trader's quarters at Keams Canyon, fifteen miles to the east of the Hopi villages. From there a larger party set out for First Mesa, where the villages of Walpi, Sichomovi, and Hano are located on a mesa set six hundred feet above the surrounding desert. After establishing sleeping quarters in Sichumovi, Bourke and Moran walked the small distance to Walpi, where they promptly busied themselves climbing into kivas, or ceremonial chambers, where preparations were being made for the following day's public dance that would culminate the nine-day ceremony.[10]

In *The Snake Dance of the Moquis of Arizona,* his succeeding account of the trip, Bourke assured readers that "instead of being repelled" on entering a kiva in which he saw nineteen boys and men and a ceremonial altar and sand painting, he had "met with urbane treatment from the Indians within." He recorded shaking hands with several men, sharing a meal of piki (a thin, wafer-like corn bread), mutton stew, and chile colorado, and then looking around the room. Over two further visits to the kiva, Bourke identified objects, established the dimensions of the room, and described the men's costume and bodily adornment, quickly writing up his notes in the moonlight by the entrance. The next morning Bourke returned to the same kiva, looking for the snakes that were to be used in that afternoon's dance. He found, to his consternation, that the snakes had been taken out of the ollas in which they had been kept. Now they were free, watched over by respectful men who gently yet firmly prevented the snakes from moving away from their resting place. Bourke was horrified by "the dank vapours of this reptile dungeon," having to run up the ladder in order to breathe fresh air. Subsequently he wrote:

> Dante's Hell struck me as a weak, wishy-washy, gruelly concep-
> tion alongside of this horrible, grim reality.
>   I stuck a pin in my leg. Could this be the nineteenth century?
> Could this be the Christian land of America?[11]

Bourke was shocked by the recognition that yes, indeed, this was the nineteenth century and he was still located within the nominally "Christian" country of the United States. And yet, as we have seen with Vroman's account from the following decade, there was no single lens through which Anglos regarded the Snake Dance in the late nineteenth century. Bourke's dread would give way to Vroman's epiphany, which in turn would give way to a different kind of dismay in the case of Lawrence. The truth is, of course, that these reactions were by no means completely different from one another and that they shared common ground. Each reaction was premised on a fundamental sense of difference between "civilized" self and "primitive" other. Yet while viewing the Snake Dance appeared to confirm that sense of difference, it also called the opposition into question. This also is America, recognized Bourke. And this also is us, understood Lawrence, writing after the publication of Freud's studies of the unconscious.

How did Hopis respond to Bourke's presence in their kivas? Interestingly, his narrative provides direct evidence of how Hopis did not wish him to visit kivas but felt powerless to resist him overtly. Bourke acknowledged that while he was in kivas "some of the Indians then there evinced a desire to have me leave." The clearest sign of forceful opposition came from Nanahe, a Hopi man who had lived in the Zuni community for ten years but would return to Walpi to participate in the Snake Dance every two years. He explained that the ethnologist Frank Hamilton Cushing had prepared the way by informing the Hopis that they must cooperate with Bourke, who was viewing the ceremony on behalf of the Great Father. Nanahe informed Bourke that neither he nor any other Americans and Mexicans had the right to enter the kiva. This was also the case for uninitiated Hopis. Furthermore Bourke had broken one of their strictest rules: not to shake hands with strangers while conducting a ceremony. Nanahe continued:

> "We saw you writing down everything as you sat in the Estufa [kiva], and we knew that you had all that man could learn from his eyes. We didn't like to have you down there. No other man has ever shown so little regard for what we thought, but we knew that you had come there under orders, and that you were only doing what you thought you ought to do to learn all about our ceremonies. So we concluded to let you stay."[12]

Bourke was soon joined by many other Euro-Americans who gained access to Hopi culture and represented what they observed in words and images. They included ethnologists George Dorsey, Jesse Walter Fewkes, Walter Hough, Alexander Stephen, and the Reverend Heinrich R. Voth (a Mennonite missionary at Oraibi); travel writers George Wharton James, Charles Fletcher Lummis, and Charles Francis Saunders; photographers Kate Cory, Edward Curtis, Earle Forrest, Sumner Matteson, F. H. Maude, Frederick Monsen, Karl Moon, C. C. Pierce, George Rose, and Ben Wittick; and the artists Eanger Irving Couse, Elbridge Ayer Burbank, and Ferdinand H. Lundgren.[13] Although ethnologists wrote for specialized publications, such as the annual reports of the Bureau of American Ethnology, there was a crossover between their "scientific" work and popular travel writing. For example, ethnologist Walter Hough's *The Moki Snake Dance,* a slim volume that gave directions to the Hopi Snake Dance from several towns along the railroad in Arizona, was published by the passenger department of the Santa Fe Railway in 1900. Such texts were, in turn, illustrated with photographs by Vroman, Matteson, Maude, and others.[14]

Written and photographic representations of the Snake Dance contributed to the cultural incorporation of Hopis, and other southwestern Native Americans, by exoticizing their practices in the late nineteenth and early twentieth centuries. Myriad representations of the Snake Dance transported images of the Hopis to domestic and institutional settings throughout and beyond the United States. This was a period when considerable outside pressure came to bear on traditional life patterns of the

Hopis. Euro-American traders, missionaries, settlers, scholars, and tourists combined to impact dramatically a culture that had proved remarkably resilient to four hundred years of prior contact with Spanish, Mexican, and American populations in the Southwest. Between the 1880s and the 1920s Hopis were made the objects of unrelenting viewing by Euro-Americans as their ceremonies were observed, photographed, and transcribed by ethnologists, travel writers, and tourists. At the same time, powerful forces of assimilation worked to break down the cultural hegemony of "traditional" Hopi culture. Elders struggled to prevent the demoralization of their clans' sacred knowledge as young children were forced out of their homes to attend missionary and government-sponsored schools. And yet, contrary to forecasts of cultural decline, Hopis learned to combat the powerful forces of assimilation by resisting Euro-American efforts to acculturate them and, over time, by increasingly determining the grounds on which Euro-American outsiders should engage with Hopi culture. In the case of the Snake Dance this has come to mean the almost complete exclusion of non-Hopis from viewing the ceremony in more recent decades.[15]

Around 1900 the Snake Dance was performed biennially at five Hopi villages—Walpi at First Mesa; Mishongnovi, Shongopavi, and Shipaulovi at Second Mesa; and Oraibi at Third Mesa. It was conducted by two organizations, the Antelope and Snake societies, whose members had gone through a series of initiation rites in order to participate in the ceremony. As the anthropologist Arlette Frigout explains, "all Hopi life is based on the ceremonies, which assure vital equilibrium, both social and individual, and conciliate the supernatural powers in order to obtain rain, good harvests, good health, and peace."[16] The Snake Dance was an integral part of the Hopi ceremonial calendar and took place two-thirds of the way through August. Anthropologist Walter Hough explained in a popular account how the origin myth of the Walpi Snake society provided the rationale for the ritual observed in the Walpi Snake Dance:

> The legend relates that a youth, having the curiosity to know where the waters flowed, embarked in a hollow log, closed except for a small orifice, and went down the Great Colorado to its mouth, thus antedating the perilous feat of Major Powell by a long time! Here he found the Spider Woman, who prompted him in his dealings with the people living there. After many strange adventures, during which he was taught the rites now practiced by the Snake society, he won the daughter of a Snake chief and

brought her to this country. The first fruits of this union were snakes, who bit the Hopi and who were driven away on his account. Later, children were human, and with them originated the Snake clan, whose wanderings brought them at last to Walpi; and tradition affirms that they were among the first arrivals here.[17]

Hough went on to explain the stages of the nine-day ritual, conveying details about preparations in the kivas of the Antelope and Snake societies that Hopis did not wish to reach the public domain. He described events that took place in public: the gathering of snakes on four successive days, the dance of the Antelope priests on the eighth day, and the dancing with snakes, involving both Antelope and Snake priests, that occurred in the late afternoon of the ninth day. In addition to describing the ceremony, Hough interpreted its meaning. Stressing that the ceremony was not a form of snake worship and that it was mostly a prayer for rain, he pointed out that images on dancers' bodies were symbolic representations of lightning, that the cracking of bull whips evoked the sound of thunder, and that snakes were handled because they were seen as intermediaries between the underworld and the people on the surface of the world. He summarized the meaning of the Snake Dance:

> The ceremony of the Snake and Antelope priests, presumably like all other ceremonies, is a dramatization of a ritual which had its origin in myth, each recounting how, on some occasion in the distant past, various events happened in a certain way and certain definite and tangible results followed. As it is enacted to-day, the Antelope-Snake ceremony is an elaborate prayer for rain, the snakes carrying down to the underground world, where they are in direct communication with the great plumed water serpent, prayers to the god of the rain clouds that they will send copious rains as will save the Hopi from hunger, and possibly from starvation.[18]

Hough's narrative is typical of a number of popular accounts of the ritual published in the late nineteenth and early twentieth centuries. The account performs a pedagogical function by providing a detailed explanation of events and relaying to readers and potential visitors to the Southwest information about who the Hopis were and why ceremonial observances constituted such an important part of their lives. In an earlier text published by the passenger department of the Santa Fe Railway,

Hough claimed the experience of visiting the Hopi mesas would "amply repay a special journey across the continent" and that mind and body would be restored to health after visiting the Southwest. He continued: "Many a professional man (and woman), wearied in brain and enfeebled in body, having been solicited to make this or a similar outdoor excursion in Arizona has complied with misgiving and returned almost miraculously restored to health and vigor."[19] Using modern terminology that would not have been available to Hough, we can see that he was outlining a new form of cultural tourism, whereby predominantly wealthy Euro-American tourists traveled large distances to visit Native Americans in their home communities. While by no means the most important ceremony for Hopis, the Snake Dance became the ritual best known among whites, many of whom would have first learned about it through lurid and sensational newspaper accounts. When crowds of tourists jostled one another to view the public performance that culminated the ritual, inevitably its form and function were affected. Although Hopis were by no means defenseless in the face of fierce Euro-American curiosity and developed their own tactics for dealing with it, in the first third of the twentieth century, when audiences at some Snake Dances reached up to and perhaps beyond two thousand people, they must have been overwhelmed by public attention to their ritual.

The camera was a crucial instrument for documenting the Snake Dance, and photographic images by James, Monsen, and Vroman, among others, illustrated travel articles and ethnological reports on Hopi culture. When viewing these images today, it soon becomes apparent there were significant differences in how and why separate individuals photographed the Snake Dance. Vroman, for example, approached photography as a craft. His images were carefully balanced compositions that paid minute attention to the environmental setting of Hopi culture. He wrote relatively little about his repeated travels to the Hopi mesas, finding in photography the means to express his appreciation of Hopi culture. James's photography lacks Vroman's precision and subtlety. For him the camera was a vital aid in satisfying his relentless curiosity about Hopi culture, and he used photography to authenticate his accounts of the Snake Dance. In one account of the ritual, James declared at the outset his purpose to overturn false impressions of it as a "wild, chaotic, yelling, shouting, pagan dance" and instead to describe it as "the solemn dignified rite it is." Yet within two pages he proudly detailed his surreptitious image-taking in a kiva, or subterranean holy place:

It was with trepidation I dared to take my camera into the mystic depths of the Antelope kiva. I had guessed at focus for the altar, and when I placed the camera against the wall, pointed toward the sacred place, the Antelope priests bid me remove it immediately. I begged to have it remain so long as I stayed, but was compelled to promise I would not place my head under the black cloth and look at the altar. This I readily promised, but at the first opportunity when no one was between the lens and the altar, I quietly removed the cap from the lens, marched away and sat down with one of the priests, while the dim light performed its wonderful work on the sensitive plate. A fine photograph was the result.[20]

Thus we see at work the prying curiosity of the Anglo outsider, who apparently saw no contradiction in claiming the friendship of Hopis and then betraying their trust. If Hopis today should read this passage from James's travelogue *Indians of the Painted Desert* (1903), probably it would confirm their conviction that too often Anglo visitors in the past have pried where tribal protocol and plain good manners dictate they should not.

Vroman published little writing about his southwestern travels apart from a series of four brief articles for *Photo-Era* magazine, published between January and April 1901, which describe the approach to the Hopi homeland, the Hopi villages, the Snake Dance at Walpi, and a trip to the Petrified Forest. This small quantity of writing pales in comparison to the great number of photographs Vroman took of the Southwest. He was so enraptured by his first visit to the Hopis that he felt compelled to make return visits to see the Snake Dance. As Vroman explained in one of his articles, "few, if any see it once but wish to see it a second, or even four or five times, each time seeing and learning some new feature of it."[21] He came to realize that what he had witnessed at Walpi was but a small part of a holistic way of life and thus he photographed myriad aspects of Hopi culture. As Vroman made repeat visits to communities, so he became familiar with people he had photographed before and from whom he had purchased crafts.[22]

After the initial journey to Walpi, Vroman made a further eight trips to Arizona and New Mexico between 1897 and 1904. He traveled in the company of friends, southwestern enthusiasts, and professional ethnologists such as Dr. Frederick Webb Hodge. He photographed missions at the Rio Grande Pueblos in 1899 and two years later participated in the Museum-Gates Expedition, which conducted archaeological research on the Navajo

Reservation. While Vroman may have derived some extra income from commissions and the sale of images, he was a successful businessman with his own bookshop in Pasadena who did not travel with the intention of making a profit from his photography. Nevertheless Vroman probably welcomed some revenue from his images in order to offset the considerable costs involved in pursuing his chosen craft.[23] Most of his photographs were taken with a 6^{1}/2" x 8^{1}/2" large-format camera with which he exposed glass-plate negatives and a 4" x 5" view camera that could take either glass plates or celluloid film and that was primarily used to produce lantern slide images. Occasionally he used a more mobile hand-held camera. His photographs were featured in a number of publications, including ethnological reports, travelogues, and tourist brochures. After extensively photographing the locations featured in Helen Hunt Jackson's *Ramona,* an edition of the novel was published illustrated with his images.[24] He continued his interest in publicizing Indian rights issues by producing a pack of cards that also was illustrated with his photographs. Alongside these outlets, Vroman used his extensive collection of lantern slides for lectures on the Southwest. He also gave many photographs to the friends who accompanied him and to the Native Americans who were featured in his images.[25]

In 1895 Vroman made a set of nineteen prints with an accompanying narrative describing his journey from Pasadena to Walpi, which he presented to his traveling companion Horatio Nelson Rust.[26] His images also illustrated the account of the same trip that Rust published in Lummis's magazine *Land of Sunshine.*[27] Glued onto the back of the prints is a handwritten narrative that provides a fascinating insight into the photographer's impressions of his first visit to the Hopi mesas. The account begins by describing the drive from Holbrook to Walpi, a distance of about seventy miles. The party consisted of the aforementioned Rust ("a noted collector of Indian curios"), C. J. Crandall (a professional photographer and the man to whom Vroman went "when in trouble, photographically"), and Mrs. Lowe (who shared her husband Thaddeus's interest in Indian curios).[28] It had taken them twenty-four hours to reach Holbrook by train from southern California and it would take them a further twenty-seven hours of travel in a lumber wagon to get to Walpi. They camped out for two nights before moving on to Keams Canyon to eat and rest for several hours. The English trader Thomas Keam was away at the time but he had arranged accommodation for the party in Sichomovi, one of the three villages on First Mesa, and so on the eve of the Walpi Snake Dance they completed the remaining ten miles to their destination. Vroman slept little as dogs fought through the night, but the following morning he remained enthusiastic about his surroundings. He wrote: "We had no trouble in making our wants known but Moquis are slow at speaking English. They would pose for us when asked to do so, and would do anything we asked of them. And no objection made to our roaming about at will and walk into any house we wished without a word[,] look it over and go out."[29] These words indicate a self-assured right of access to Hopis and their homes that arguably lies at the heart of colonialist power relations. Thus while Vroman's account conveys the impression that Hopis cooperated with the party and did not protest outwardly about being photographed, what was said in private among Hopis is another matter. At the time Vroman visited, the Hopis were in deep crisis. Destitute because of prolonged drought and deeply divided over how to respond to the demands of government agents, missionaries, and now tourists, it was no surprise that factional conflict broke out among Hopis. Ongoing tension between so-called "friendlies" (to the U.S. government) and "hostiles" at Oraibi in the 1890s and early 1900s culminated in the departure of "hostiles" to the new community of Hotevilla in 1906.[30]

As we have seen, Vroman was enraptured by the Snake Dance. Quickly he moved from a position of partial knowledge about Hopis to a greater degree of understanding of their ceremonies and social mores. Through successive seasons of travel to the Southwest his camera work grew more surefooted and sensitive to the subtleties of Hopi culture. The historians of photography William Webb and Robert A. Weinstein argue that Vroman's portraits create an "atmosphere of relaxed confidence, possible *only* where mutual respect is operative" and that he "penetrated beneath the surface to present an image of the people's innermost selves."[31] They contend that by going beyond surface appearances and conveying the personalities of his subjects, Vroman became an advocate for Hopis at a point when they were under considerable threat from missionaries and educators to abandon their cultural traditions and assimilate to white ways.[32] Where other Anglos dismissed Hopis for lacking advanced technology and being in the thrall of nature—this was, after all, a time in which the gospel of large-scale irrigation was being preached in the West—Vroman understood that Hopi ceremonial life was intimately connected to the geographical setting of the Hopi mesas and the high desert aridity of northern Arizona.[33]

It would be foolhardy to claim that Vroman escaped or transcended his own society's prejudices regarding Native Americans; instead his great interest in southwestern Indians was typical of his time. Unlike Elbridge Burbank, who was painting Indians throughout the West during the years Vroman visited the Hopis and the Rio Grande Pueblos, Vroman does not appear to have been ill at ease in urban society. One senses that although he did not mind roughing it a little in order to reach the Hopi mesas, he welcomed a warm bath and clean sheets when they were available. The likely value of these creature comforts to him suggests that he was happy to remain in Arizona and New Mexico for relatively short amounts of time and that he did not wish to become a longstanding participant observer of Hopi culture in the way, for instance, of the anthropologist Alexander Stephen, who lived among the Hopis from 1880 or 1881 to his death in 1894.[34] This is not to say that Vroman's sense of transformation after having taken the Santa Fe Railway to northern Arizona was not genuine, but it does indicate his desire to return home after a limited amount of time away. He may have gone somewhat off the beaten track to reach Walpi in 1895, but the route he took was to become increasingly well traveled by Anglos over the ensuing three decades.

Frederick Monsen started photographing southern California and the Southwest several years earlier than Vroman. Although images by both him and Vroman were featured in Walter Hough's *The Moki Snake Dance* in 1900, they were substantially different sorts of photographer, not least by virtue of Monsen's being a professional and Vroman an amateur. Having been brought up in Salt Lake City from the age of three after his birth in Bergen, Norway, in 1865, to all intents and purposes Monsen was a Westerner. He began his professional career as a photographer working with the U.S. Geological Survey for five years from 1887 and later photographed for the Salton Sea Expedition and the Yosemite National Park Boundary Survey, while also making extensive journeys of his own through Death Valley and Baja California. Having first photographed Native Americans while working for the USGS, he carved out a career for himself as a lecturer-explorer who specialized in southwestern subject matter. By the 1920s he could boast of an extended repertoire of illustrated lectures—including "The Genesis of the American Indian," "My Friends the Indians," "Natural Wonders of American Deserts," and "On the Trail of the Spanish Pioneers"—that he had given to audiences at universities, museums, geographical societies, historical societies, and private clubs across the United States.[35] The lectures were illustrated with hand-colored glass lantern slides that Monsen contact-printed from his huge stock of negative film. While Monsen received praise for his speaking ability, it was his images that attracted the most extravagant praise. "In color, composition and perspective, they were wonderful," pronounced the *New York Times*.[36]

Throughout his lecturing career, Monsen maintained a passionate interest in southwestern Native Americans. The title of his article "The Destruction of Our Indians: What Civilization Is Doing to Extinguish an Ancient and Highly Intelligent Race by Taking Away Its Arts, Industries and Religion," published in 1907, conveyed the philosophy that guided his photography of Indians. He perceived Hopis and other Pueblo Indians as "the remnant of a fast-vanishing race, one of the many magnificent aboriginal races that have decayed so swiftly under the death-giving touch of the white man's civilization." Furthermore, their culture was at great risk of oblivion: "the chances now are that the paternal care of the Government will educate and civilize them to a swift and final doom."[37] Monsen's rhetoric suggests not only his critical stance toward federal Indian policy in the Southwest but also his endorsement of Hopi arts and crafts. He explained that if only Hopis were largely left to themselves then they would continue to live successfully in their homeland. If, however, missionaries, educators, and government officials persisted in promoting "a small smattering of the white man's stereotyped book learning in the place of [the Hopi's] own deeply significant and symbolic Nature lore," this would inevitably result in the destruction of Hopi arts and crafts. Not only would this constitute a tragedy for the Hopis, but the country would lose "a true and natural expression of art that our modern civilization can ill afford to spare."[38]

Similar to Burbank and the photographer Edward Curtis, Monsen dedicated himself to creating a document of Native American cultures he thought were vanishing in the face of multiple pressures to modernize their traditional lifeways. But unlike Burbank or Curtis, Monsen limited his photography of Indians to the Southwest and made no effort to produce a comprehensive account of Native Americans from across the United States. There were further differences in his approach to Indian subjects. Monsen specialized in candid photography of Pueblo communities, a form of imagery that he produced through using small Kodak cameras with fast shutter speeds that could be concealed around the person before being used quickly. Earlier in his career he had taken photographs with bulky large-format cameras that were not particularly mobile, were difficult to focus quickly, and required the subject to sit still for long exposures. In certain respects the photographic procedure for the earlier photographs was not dissimilar to Burbank's portraiture of Indians. According to artist Louis Akin, the crucial quality achieved in Monsen's collection of Indian images, which he considered "not only of great artistic value, but of absolutely unrivaled significance as historic and ethnological records," was the lack of self-consciousness on the part of his subjects. Akin detailed what he saw as the difference between these images and "the elaborately 'picturesque' photographs often seen" of Native Americans:

> This difference is the very obvious distinction between art and commercialism, the distinction that marks the work of the man who, because of years of tried friendship, is welcome in every pueblo, hogan or wickiup in all the Southwest, as entirely separate from that of the 'commercial traveler' who speeds through the country with camera in one hand and the ever-ready dollar in the other, apparently under contract to photograph every last living specimen of the American Indian, regardless of anything but quantity and popular selling quality.[39]

Since Akin had himself spent a year living among the Hopis while painting portraits, villages scenes, and landscapes, he considered himself qualified to make crucial distinctions in motive and achievement among the many Anglo artists and photographers who visited the Hopis in the early 1900s.[40]

Monsen's sense of mission went hand-in-hand with a strong streak of self-discipline. Because he was convinced the "Indian, as an Indian" was vanishing because of the impact of disease, white encroachment, and the adoption of white ways, it was essential to create "an ethnographic record of the Indians, photographing their life, manners and habitat, and thus preserving for future generations a picture-history which will show what these most interesting early Americans were like, before they were disturbed by the influences of the white man."[41] Given this premise, it is hardly surprising that Monsen was so admiring of Hopi culture for its lack of Spanish, Mexican, or American influence. The Hopis' successful resistance of Spanish colonization in the late seventeenth century meant that their rituals were remarkably free of Christian influence, while the efforts of American missionaries were sufficiently recent not to have had too adverse an effect on the supposed purity of Hopi religious expression. Monsen wrote of the Hopi: "We have here in the heart of the youngest and most progressive of modern countries a primitive race of men who have escaped the blight of civilization, and who are to us a perfect exposition of the way the prehistoric American lived and died, ages before the paleface came to bring destruction."⁴²

Today such rhetoric appears to be idealized and condescending, especially if one also takes into account the way that Monsen represented Hopi bodies. He referred to them as graceful and childlike and stated that although men were strong they lacked the muscular development of Caucasian males. Indeed, he claimed, the Hopis as a whole were both physically and mentally at an earlier stage of development than the white race, namely the Stone Age.⁴³ As for children, Monsen remarked on the natural state of "their beautiful, lithe little bodies, velvety bronze skin, ruddy with the underglow of healthy red blood, and absolute freedom of movement and poise."⁴⁴ Monsen celebrated what he saw as the unconstrained qualities of Hopi culture. For him, nudity among Indians conveyed to whites "the innocence, freedom and childlike joy of living that we like to think prevailed among all men in the morning of the world."⁴⁵ These words suggest that although Euro-Americans had expanded across America and triumphed technologically, they lacked spirituality, community, and perspective on their lives. And so Monsen idealized the spontaneity and lack of self-consciousness he perceived in Hopi children and by implication mourned the loss of innocence and the curse of corruption in his own culture.

Monsen's photography relied on the latest camera developments to take images. His magazine articles and lecture brochures, together with Eastman Kodak advertisements, extolled the virtues of the No. 3 Folding Pocket Kodak, which produced 3¹/₄" x 4¹/₄" negatives on celluloid film that he made into lantern slides through contact printing. He started using this camera, along with cartridge film and a small developing tank, around 1900, after laboring for years with large-format cameras. First he had used a mammoth-sized 18" x 22" camera and then moved through progressively smaller outfits—14" x 17", 11" x 14", 8" x 10"—before settling on a 5" x 7" camera. But for all that he saved in bulk and weight with the smaller apparatus, dry-plate photography still required careful preparation of materials and glass-plate negatives continued to break at an alarming rate when transported long distances across rough terrain. He found using the Kodak and celluloid film a revelation compared to large-format cameras with their slow shutter speeds: "The stiff, posed, time exposed attempt at dramatic effect I could not recognize as either truth or art but now there opened the new method, and I began to photograph the Indians *instantaneously*, without previous warning, posing, or preparation, securing the most charming pictures and actually getting the very spirit of their lives."[46]

The mobility and adaptability of the Kodak No. 3, with its wide range of apertures and shutter speeds, made it ideal for use at the Hopi Snake Dance, which usually took place in the late afternoon when the conditions were less than ideal for photography. Monsen's regard for the ritual echoed his enthusiasm for Hopi culture in general, and he considered photographing the Snake Dance and other events in the Hopi ceremonial calendar as an ethical responsibility. It was necessary to document these events if he were to produce images that possessed ethnological and historical value. Such photography, Monsen thought, relied upon an insider's knowledge of Hopi culture. He explained:

> [T]he customs and manners of a primitive people differ so widely from ours that the whole viewpoint of a civilized man has to be changed before he can come anywhere near to comprehending the nature of an Indian or realizing the way he looks at things. Before I could understand the Indian, I had to learn how to 'get behind his eyes,'—to think as he thought, to live as he lived, and to become, so far as was possible for a white man, an accepted member of his society.[47]

The degree to which Monsen did become integrated into southwestern Indian communities in the early twentieth century is debatable, as is his claim that he learned to think and live like an Indian.[48] Monsen suggested that if Euro-Americans wanted to understand Native Americans, they had to bridge a gulf that divided their separate cultures. The cynic might claim Monsen was endeavoring to bolster the audience for his well-known lectures through such statements, but the enthusiasm with which he photographed Hopis indicates that he was committed to educating Euro-Americans out of their narrow-minded prejudices about Native Americans. Such education, he intimated, would also lead to Euro-Americans' seeing "civilization" in a new light. Using today's language, we might say that Monsen called into question the ethnocentrism of American society through his photography of Hopis and other southwestern Indians. Hopis, according to Monsen, had survived by virtue of their isolation. But it would take a different sort of imagination to envisage a means by which southwestern Indians might be integrated into the United States without their cultural traditions being compromised in the process.

Sumner Matteson was a different sort of photographer from either Vroman or Monsen. So far I have discussed the work of a talented amateur and a committed professional who remained a photographer-lecturer for the duration of his working life. Matteson was an avid outdoorsman who ranged freely across the West at the turn of the last century and tried to make a living from the camera. He began photographing western scenes while working in Denver as an agent for the Overman Wheel Company, a manufacturer of bicycles. There he had sold Kodak cameras and photographic supplies in addition to bikes. In 1899, three years after his arrival in Denver, the Overman company abandoned its operation in the city, but Matteson stayed on, reinventing himself as a "traveling correspondent." In effect he became a freelance photographer at the age of thirty-one. In that capacity he spent the summer of 1899 exploring the ancient cliff dwellings of Mesa Verde in southwestern Colorado with the rancher Al Wetherill and Frederick Putnam, professor of anthropology at Harvard University, before moving on to explore Chaco Canyon in New Mexico. The following year he traveled to Taos to photograph Penitente rituals at Easter before returning to Mesa Verde. By August he was at the Hopi mesas, viewing the Snake Dance at Oraibi and the Flute Dance at Mishongnovi. His journey through the Southwest continued with a cycle ride to the Grand Canyon and visits to the pueblos of Acoma and Isleta. He returned to the Hopis mesas in the summer of 1901 as the backup photographer for the Field Columbian Museum's McCormick Hopi Expedition, led by George Dorsey, the institution's Curator of Anthropology, and the Reverend Heinrich R. Voth. Over the following summer he journeyed along wagon trails in Montana, taking photographs of frontier life just as the railroad was about to arrive. Later in 1903 he would pack up his home in Denver and journey first to Yellowstone National Park and then to Glacier National Park to climb the Mission Range of mountains.[49]

Matteson was a highly mobile and self-sufficient operator in the field. He carried compact and lightweight camera gear and often traveled by bicycle. Two cameras accompanied Matteson on his travels, a Kodak No. 5 and a No. 3. He sold individual images and photo essays to popular magazines such as *The Cosmopolitan, Leslie's Weekly, Housekeeper,* and *The Pacific Monthly.* In January 1903 Matteson presented a photographic album to Frank Klepetko, an investor in western mining operations.[50] Filled with 198 numbered prints and a small booklet containing an accompanying commentary for each image, the album provides a fascinating record of travel through the "Indian Country" of the Southwest. The images vary in size and shape and are often artfully fixed into the album at jaunty angles. Although a great number of private albums of journeys through the Southwest must have been created in abundance by tourist photographers, one doubts if many of them could rival Matteson's album for the range and abundance of imagery. A large proportion of the photographs was taken at the Hopi villages and includes many images of rituals.

Matteson's album opens with a small oval image of a bison and the brief comment: "'Junibo,' a Colorado Pioneer that died of a broken heart in the Denver City Park; April 1900." Given that Matteson was a dedicated conservationist, one imagines that by placing this image at the outset of the album he wished to make a parallel between the death of a captive bison and the marginalization of western Indians in the late nineteenth century, for a little later in the sequence there is a blurred image of Ute Indians leading horses loaded with jerked venison and hides. The accompanying note explains that Ouray Indians were in the midst of being driven out of the Colorado Game Fields toward their reservation in Utah. This is a scene that Matteson may well have come across while traveling from Denver to Mesa Verde or hunting deer and elk along the Colorado-Utah border in the summer and fall of 1899. Although the album includes photographs of the Colorado River, the cliff dwellings of Mesa Verde and Canyon de Chelly, and Hispano sheepherders, the great majority of the images represent some aspect of southwestern Indian life. Not surprisingly, given Matteson's role with the McCormick Hopi Expedition and Klepetko's probable interest in the best-known Hopi ceremonies, the album contains multiple images of the Snake Dance and Flute Dance. Overall the album provides a comprehensive view of Hopi life along with images of Navajos, Acomas, and other Pueblo Indians. Matteson was particularly attracted to people, and among other scenes he photographed a Navajo family camped near Pueblo Bonito; Pablo Albeita, the lieutenant governor of Isleta Pueblo; and Lololomi, the "friendly" chief of Oraibi, tending his field at Moenkopi. He photographed myriad aspects of everyday life in the Hopi villages: a train of burros near Hano that was loaded with melons, corn, and peaches; women shucking corn; and a family walking through a dry wash near Walpi after collecting agricultural produce from Moenkopi. Often Matteson's images convey the impression of having been taken on the fly, as though he had just come across a scene that struck him as interesting and had taken a photograph of what he saw.

Spontaneity and opportunism to a certain extent differentiate Matteson's photography from that of Vroman and Monsen. As we have seen, Vroman's southwestern images required careful preparation and typically were framed precisely. Despite his obvious empathy for the people he photographed, Vroman's images convey a clear sense of separation between himself and the objects of his gaze. This impression is only enhanced by viewing images Vroman took of himself while traveling in the Southwest, which convey a sense of his aesthetic sensibility and self-possession. Viewing Matteson's images of Indians, especially those containing a large number of people, one imagines that as the image was taken he was about to jump into the scene himself. There is a naive enthusiasm and vitality to many of Matteson's images that Vroman, one suspects, would have found inappropriate in his own photography. The directness of Matteson's street scenes, portraits, and group shots may take him closer to Monsen than to Vroman, but it is important to remember that Monsen gained his "instantaneous" images by hiding his camera until ready to take a photograph and thus often disguised his intention until the last moment.

Despite Matteson's enthusiasm for spontaneous imagery, he does not appear to have shared Monsen's preoccupation with concealed camera work and the subject's freedom from consciousness, which the latter considered a prerequisite for successful photography of Native Americans. Instead many of Matteson's images are distinguished by what appear to be friendly relations between himself and the people he photographed. Looking at such photographs, one senses tolerance, laughter, and mutual curiosity. Equally, however, there is evidence of wariness toward Matteson in his images of Hopis. For example, midway through the album three images in a row show Hopis resisting having their photographs taken. The first image shows a group of women on a rooftop watching the Mishongnovi Flute Ceremony with the accompanying note explaining that they were hiding their faces from the Kodak. The following photograph depicts a girl with a young boy on her back climbing up a ladder. In the light of Matteson's comment—"Beating a hasty retreat at Walpi on the unexpected appearance of a 'Ba-han-na' or white man at other than Snake Dance time"—the girl was clearly endeavoring to escape having her photograph taken. The third image is a view of a doorway in which a woman is dressing an adolescent girl's hair in the squash-blossom style distinctive to Hopi culture. The girl can hardly be seen because she is obscured by a burro in the foreground, but a small child is in clear view of the camera and she looks warily toward the lens. Although these images are all examples of intrusive photography, it seems that once Matteson became more familiar to children and bribed them with candy (which Vroman, Monsen, and George Wharton James also carried in abundance on visits to the Hopi villages), they were willing to cooperate with him. Like Monsen, Matteson took images of nude children.

The art historians Louis Casagrande and Phillips Bourne point out another quality that sets Matteson apart from his fellow photographers in the Southwest, namely his use of sequential imagery: "Like the modern photo essayist, Matteson moved with the action and managed to record the event before, during, and after. His photos were more than precise records of the single event; they are the photographs of the *mood* of the event—the preparations, processions, and people."[51] This statement certainly rings true on viewing the sequence of forty-eight images taken at snake dances performed at Mishongnovi, Oraibi, Shipaulovi, Shongopavi, and Walpi. These photographs take the viewer through the stages of the ceremony leading up to the public dance that culminates the ritual. Among them are flashlit images taken in both Antelope and Snake society kivas that show elements of preparation that members of those societies did not wish to be exposed to public view. Only a limited number of Euro-Americans gained access to kivas during ceremonies because of the strict protocol involved in the distribution of esoteric knowledge in Hopi society. One image shows the anthropologist George Dorsey in a kiva with the accompanying comment: "Dr. Dorsey of the Field Columbian Museum invited to smoke in the Mishong-no-vi snake circle after gaining their confidence and permission to write a book on the subject, promising to let no other Mokis see it."

Matteson's comment helps today's readers and viewers understand how Euro-American anthropologists and travel writers gained access to the normally hidden parts of Hopi culture. Esoteric knowledge that in the past had been restricted to members of the participating clans was put into the public domain through ethnological reports and travelogues. Indeed the renowned secrecy of Hopis spurred certain Euro-American inquirers into more vigorous efforts to reveal all aspects of Hopi ritual life. Euro-Americans' insatiable desire to *know* had the capacity to break down the distribution of knowledge and power within Hopi society. But as Hopis grew more aware of how Euro-American writing and visual imagery of rituals were being collected and distributed, they resisted further representations of this sort. Having shown considerable resistance to Bourke's curiosity about the Snake Dance in 1881, during the twentieth century Hopis would eventually determine the ground on which their ceremonies were represented, if at all, by not only banning photography at ceremonies but also precluding non-Hopis from attending the Snake Dance.[52]

Such control was still a long way off when in 1917 a representative of the Cliff Dwellers, a club for Southwest enthusiasts based in Chicago, considered the interaction of tourists with Hopis. Wishing members of the Cliff Dwellers to be differentiated from the mass of tourists, the anonymous author extolled the virtue of getting away to places beyond "the prying eyes of summer travelers."[53] This gesture was amplified in accounts of snake dances at Mishongnovi and Walpi. Whereas the experience at Walpi was spoiled by the presence of "hundreds of pale-faced rubberneckers," the Mishongnovi ritual was sparsely attended by whites and there the author's party found "the true Indian feeling for the thing."[54] The author urged government authorities to manage tourists better at Walpi because, despite being told to check their cameras with the Indian agent, many visitors "with characteristically American disregard for law" had smuggled their cameras in and taken photographs of the ritual. There had even been "a movie man there taking pictures for some institution."[55]

The Cliff Dwellers' visit to Walpi occurred around the time a complete ban was implemented on still photography and movie filming at the Hopi villages. Indian Agent Leo Crane recalled the disruption caused after Hopis agreed with his proposal to raise funds for the tribe by charging tourists a dollar each for the privilege of photographing the Snake Dance. Visitors tried evading the charge or protested it and gave up their cameras; rarely did they pay up willingly. After one man escaped with a movie he had not been authorized to film and it took an elaborate nighttime search to apprehend him, the Commissioner of Indian Affairs ordered that no photography of any sort should take place at Hopi. Crane considered this order "foolish" and difficult to regulate: "Nearly everyone was happy when he could bang away a roll of films for the family album and for a fee of one dollar. The tourist loses his chance to vie with Edward Curtis, and the Indians lose their feast money."[56] It is unclear how many Hopis preferred the system of payment Crane advocated, but it does appear that the crushing numbers of Anglo onlookers at the Walpi Snake Dance was a great irritant to local people. An exchange recorded by Crane between himself and a Hopi elder is instructive in this regard. They were debating measures to be taken to safeguard tourists who were gathered close to the edge of the small dance plaza at Walpi where it fell away precipitously:

"I see," said the old man, nodding; "these people are your friends, and you do not want them hurt."

Now I did not care to vouch for all those present and so corrected him.

"No, they are not my friends—not all of them; they are people who travel about the country and come to see your dance."

"Didn't you send them letters—write to them to come?"

"No."

"Well," he concluded, "I didn't send for them. They are no friends of mine. And you say they are not friends of yours. Why should we care about it? Let them fall off."[57]

The Hopi elder spoke these words around the time that D. H. Lawrence attended the Snake Dance at Hotevilla. His comments indicate a growing frustration among Hopis at the number of Euro-Americans present at their ceremonies. From this exchange, one certainly gains an insight into the contending views of different groups involved in the scene described by Crane. The Hopi elder clearly wished the Snake Dance to be performed according to historical precedent. Whatever Crane suggested about charging outsiders to take photographs, the elder is highly unlikely to have wanted to commercialize the ceremony. Probably he would have preferred that no photographs be taken at all. Crane, on the other hand, took a pragmatic approach to the desire of tourists to view the Snake Dance. He, after all, wanted to control both tourists and Hopi participants. But to a degree the ritual frustrated him, for he regarded its performance well into the twentieth century as an obstacle to the "civilization" of Hopi culture. As for Euro-American onlookers, regardless of their reasons for viewing the ceremony, their presence was almost bound to be disruptive. Arguably even the smallest number of Euro-American viewers could change the way in which a ceremony functioned within the Hopi community, even when those viewers were sympathetically disposed toward Hopis and wished themselves to be almost invisible at the scene. When the Cliff Dwellers attended the Snake Dance at Mishongnovi, they could not circumvent the influence of Euro-American spectatorship on Hopi culture. After all, their own travel and curiosity were necessarily part of the larger cultural apparatus whereby Hopis were being brought into the sphere of American society.

Indian Detour

In 1926 the Atchison, Topeka, and Santa Fe introduced a new travel service named "Indian Detour." Henceforth passengers on eastbound and westbound transcontinental trains would be able to experience "the lure of the real Southwest beyond the pinched horizons of [their] train window" by stopping over in New Mexico and taking "a glorious three-day motor outing through the storied heart of the Indo-Spanish Southwest." Promising to be "no ordinary sight-seeing tour," the Indian Detour would take travelers on the westbound Navajo and California Limited trains from Las Vegas to Santa Fe and on to Albuquerque, from where they would resume their journey to Los Angeles.[58] According to the Indian Detour brochure, between Las Vegas and Albuquerque "lie unforgettable days in a new-old land far from the beaten track—days of leisurely comfort spent in visiting the ancient Indian pueblos and prehistoric cliff-dwellings of the New Mexico Rockies, the old Spanish capital of Santa Fe, the inhabited Indian pueblos of Tesuque, Santa Clara, Santo Domingo, and other places in the great valley of the Rio Grande, as well as the huge ceremonial ruins of Puye—a cliff pueblo twenty centuries old."[59]

In addition to outlining schedules, accommodation, and prices, the brochure described two additional services. Motor drives entitled "Roads to Yesterday" took visitors in Packard "Eight" Harveycars to a variety of locations up to 185 miles away from either Santa Fe or Albuquerque. Travelers could visit Taos, famous for "its superb setting, splendid Indian types and changeless, picturesque life," or the ancient Indian dwellings of El Rito de los Frijoles in Bandelier National Monument, or Truchas and Cordova, "interesting, primitive types of the really remote Mexican towns."[60] Alternatively, "Motor Land Cruises" offered customized travel of around 100 miles a day through a "frontier empire" in which "the possibilities are unlimited for unusual motor cruises of any duration." The rate per day of these excursions covered the expense of running the car, the cost of meals and accommodation, and the services of a driver and private courier. The narrative continued: "There is, of course, no set schedule for these private Land Cruises. From an endless choice, you may have set your heart on the ruined cities of Pueblo Bonito, the Carlsbad Caverns or the Rainbow Bridge and Monument Valley country, or the Canyon de Chelly or Blue Canyon or Coal Canyon and the August Snake Dance in the Hopi villages; on Montezuma's Castle, or the Natural Dam or the trout streams of the White Mountains."[61]

Indian Detours were organized at a point when travel and accommodation along the Santa Fe Railway was most luxurious for wealthier passengers. Operated in tandem with the Fred Harvey Company, which ran hotels, restaurants, and shops along the railroad's main line, the detours consolidated a long process of economic and political incorporation through which the rich natural resources and ethnically diverse human population of the Southwest were colonized by the United States and drawn into the Union. The iconography used by the passenger department of the Santa Fe Railway to sell its services to travelers was dominated by portraits of Pueblo, Hopi, and Navajo Indians together with images of contemporary Indian villages and ancient Indian dwellings. Commissioned artwork by southwestern artists was displayed in Harvey hotels and railroad offices and reproduced in the Santa Fe's widely distributed annual calendar, while photographs were used in publicity materials, guidebooks, and popular lantern slide programs put on by touring publicity agents.[62]

The Santa Fe was not the first railroad to try to exploit southwestern themes in its advertising. Its great rival, the Denver and Rio Grande Railway, began publicizing tourist attractions in Arizona and New Mexico in the mid-1880s. The *Tourist's Handbook to Colorado, Utah and New Mexico* advertised attractions along the Denver and Rio Grande's extensive mileage of narrow-gauge track. The New Mexico extension terminated at Española, twenty-five miles north of Santa Fe, after twenty-one miles of "devious ways," "sharpest curves," and "steepest heights." The handbook featured Taos Pueblo as one tourist attraction and focused on the Feast Day of San Geronimo, held annually on September 30th, as an event that would prove of "great interest to either the ethnologist, ecclesiastic or tourist." In addition to providing details of the religious ceremony, running race, chicken pull, clowning, and pole climb that took place on the feast day, the handbook noted that travelers also might like to visit the pueblos of San Juan and Santa Clara: "The Pueblo Indians delight to adorn themselves in gay colours, and form very interesting and picturesque subjects for the artist, especially, when associated with their quaint surroundings."[63]

Despite the effort to promote the attractions of its line into northern New Mexico, the Denver and Rio Grande failed to profit from its operation. Instead it was the Santa Fe and the Fred Harvey Company that successfully capitalized on the touristic appeal of Arizona and New Mexico. As we learned in chapter 4, Charles Fletcher Lummis hiked along the tracks of the Santa Fe Railroad during his transcontinental walk in 1884–85. When Lummis returned to New Mexico to live later that decade and continued to travel through the Southwest in succeeding years, he received travel passes in exchange for the publicity he gave the railroad. Similarly, Elbridge Burbank exchanged art for free travel on the Santa Fe. It became common in the late nineteenth century for western railroads—the Denver and Rio Grande, Great Northern, Northern Pacific, and Southern Pacific as well as the Santa Fe—to arrange transportation and lodgings with artists who would repay the railroads with works of art that were often featured in publicity material in the form of chromolithographs.[64] From 1895, the year of its reorganization after near financial collapse and the year William H. Simpson headed its new advertising department, the Santa Fe Railway greatly expanded its use of commissioned artwork to sell the attractions of New Mexico and Arizona. For example, in 1903 the railroad sponsored the travel of Louis Akin, who had complimented Burbank on his work when it was displayed in Philadelphia in December 1901 and January 1902, to paint Hopi Indians. Akin's paintings from this trip were reproduced for publicity material and prints sold by the railroad. Subsequently Akin returned to the Grand Canyon, and Simpson made repeat purchases of his canvases.[65] The Santa Fe began collecting southwestern art in 1903, when it purchased Bertha Mengler Dressler's *Evening in the Arizona Desert,* and in 1907 alone Simpson acquired 108 paintings. Much of this work was completed by artists attached to the Taos and Santa Fe art colonies, both of which rose to prominence in the first two decades of the century. The Taos painters Oscar Berninghaus, Ernest Blumenschein, Gerald Cassidy, E. Irving Couse, William Herbert "Buck" Dunton, E. Martin Hennings, Victor Higgins, Bert Geer Phillips, Joseph Sharp, and Walter Ufer all sold art to the railroad featuring elements that were designed to raise the appeal of the Indian Southwest to potential customers throughout the country and abroad.[66]

When the Santa Fe Railway and the Fred Harvey Company joined forces to promote Indian Detours in the mid-1920s, their collaboration built on over four decades of cooperation. Formal arrangements between the railroad and Fred Harvey began in 1878 when it was agreed that trains would stop each day at his dining room in Florence, Kansas. Over the following decade Harvey expanded his operations to the point where a Harvey House was located every hundred miles along the main line. A second formal agreement made in 1889 guaranteed Harvey the exclusive right to operate dining rooms, lunch stands, and hotels along the Santa Fe's network west of the Missouri River.[67] After the railroad completed a branch line to the rim of the Grand Canyon in 1901, tourist facilities were constructed to accommodate the increasing numbers of visitors it hoped to attract to the area. The El Tovar hotel, a grand building that contained a hundred rooms for guests, was opened in 1905. Nearby Hopi House was constructed, a building modeled on structures at Oraibi, where Indian arts and crafts were for sale and where Native people demonstrated their jewelry and pottery-making techniques during the day and gave performances of songs and dances during the evenings. The Santa Fe and the Fred Harvey Company were instrumental in developing further facilities on the rim, such as Bright Angel Camp, Hermit's Rest, and, within the canyon, the Hermit Trail and Phantom Ranch. Although one suspects George Wharton James, the breathless enthusiast for all things southwestern, was repaying the Santa Fe Railway for free travel and accommodation when he heaped extravagant praise on Fred Harvey for being "synonymous in the minds of travelers with *super par excellence* in service," undoubtedly his admiration of the Santa Fe's engineering achievement was shared by many other travelers wealthy enough to take the trip to the Grand Canyon. He exclaimed: "One may take his seat—aye, the most delicate of transcontinental travelers may take her Pullman drawing-room, in Chicago, and ride direct to El Tovar, the perfect Fred Harvey hotel on the rim of the Canyon—and without a moment's weariness, ennui or deprivation of any accustomed luxury, gaze upon this wonderland of form, color and mystery."[68]

The Fred Harvey Company became the official concessioner when Grand Canyon National Park was established in 1919. That year 44,000 people visited the park. A decade later the figure was 200,000, and it rose a further 100,000 by the mid-1930s.[69] Indian Detours capitalized on the great increase in tourist travel during the 1920s. The nation's return to isolationism in the aftermath of World War I, combined with an economic boom that brought substantial wealth to a significant minority of the population, heightened the demand for travel within the United States. New Mexico, Arizona, and California had a clear advantage over other western locations in proximity to transcontinental railroads because access to the natural landscapes and Native people advertised in their publicity literature was guaranteed all year. When the Indian Detour brochure for 1928 was published, it boasted that none of the daily tours offered over the previous two years had been canceled.[70]

Excursions from the Santa Fe's main line were premised on the accessibility of valued locations, be they spectacular natural landscapes, ancient

Indian dwellings, or contemporary Native American and, to a lesser extent, Hispano communities. The Indian Detour brochure promised that tourists would encounter "splendid Indian types and changeless, picturesque life," as though Pueblo Indians could somehow live an unpolluted and authentic existence outside the modern world. In reality Native Americans' lives were anything but unchanged, as they responded to the pressures of modernization and acculturation.

Given the great popularity of the new tours, it is perhaps inevitable that there were protests over the presence of tourists in Pueblo communities. In fall 1927 the governor of Taos Pueblo declared that he wished to charge Indian Detour clients for admission to the village because the visits of tourists were more economically beneficial to other pueblos than to his own community, which at the time did not produce pottery or jewelry for the growing arts and crafts market. Tour organizer Major R. Hunter Clarkson, who thought payment for admission would risk commercializing the pueblo, proposed that henceforth tourists should be accompanied by drummers and a young boy dancing to whom they would make voluntary payments at the end of his performance.[71] At Santo Domingo Pueblo lookouts were posted to anticipate the arrival of tourists, who were then carefully watched to make sure they did not enter kivas.[72] On at least one occasion Santo Domingo men smashed tourists' cameras after they had been advised not to photograph a ceremony.[73] However such overt acts of resistance appear to have been rare. This was at least partly due to the influence of the couriers who liaised between tourists and Indians. Erna Fergusson, who first led tourists through New Mexico on her own Koshare Tours beginning in 1921 and was later employed by the Santa Fe Railway to train the young women who worked as couriers on Indian Detours, informed potential tourists about the protocol involved in visiting Indians. "The crude white tourist who looks upon Indians as animals in a zoo meets with very little attention," she warned. However courtesy, quietness, and a visit to the governor of Pueblo communities would earn respect. "Feathers for the governor, candy for the youngsters, or a brilliant white handkerchief for the governor's lady," she advised, "will show that you are a friend understanding the ways of courtesy."[74] To her credit, Fergusson did advocate terms for address between Euro-Americans and Native Americans that would satisfy both parties, even as her comment may strike readers today as rather condescending toward Indians.[75]

Surveying the popular representation of southwestern travel more broadly, there are crucial differences between the popular iconography of the Southwest during the 1920s and 1930s and much of the photography from only twenty or thirty years earlier, which illustrated ethnological reports and travelogues. Next to the more intrusive images from the earlier period, much of the photography featured in Indian Detour publicity material takes the form of obviously contrived images that indicate the places, events, and circumstances in which clients could expect to observe and meet Indian hosts. Such imagery is notably different from the candid photography pursued by James, Matteson, and Monsen. Although the later imagery derives from a situation in which Native American and Hispano communities held relatively little power in relation to Euro-Americans, it is important to note that the architects of promotional representations of the Southwest highlighted surface details of cultures and tended not to strive to discover their inner workings. The overtly commercial images and writings were part of a situation in which, increasingly, Indians had learned to stage ceremonies and craft displays for an audience of economically and socially privileged outsiders in ways that did not necessarily conflict with their "traditional" practices. Such acts in turn addressed the wider issue of how Native people, as individuals and communities, should make sense of the forces of modernization that had already brought great changes to their lives. This issue also became of great concern to a number of Euro-Americans who traveled and sojourned in the Southwest. They became advocates for Native American cultures and in the process could recoil against what they saw as the superficial and exploitative aspects of tourism. Simultaneously their own travel through the region, and of course their settlement in it, often led them to believe that they truly were experts on the cultures they championed.

Taos, New Mexico

"We came down the mesa at twilight. Where the river plunged to the iron-dark canyon, high-flung cottonwood trees were changing from gold to green. Cordova—the most perfect of the dozen old Mexican towns on the Taos plateau—seemed black against the sundown. From the west, walls and ruined homes were soft and luminous, a great loose-petaled rose drifting in windless air." So begins John Collier's influential essay "The Red Atlantis," which was written in order to raise greater public awareness about how the Bursum Bill and the pressures of "Americanization" threatened the integrity of Pueblo lives. Collier was a writer and social activist who endeavored not only to protect Pueblos from the alienation of their land in the 1920s, but also argued that the United States needed to become a more genuinely pluralistic nation in which Native Americans could secure their citizenship rights and partake of an equitable share of its economic and social benefits without having to renounce their traditional worldviews. To this end he suggested practical measures by which the U.S. government could work in cooperation with Taos Indians, the Hopis, Zunis, and other Pueblo communities in New Mexico to achieve this prospect, thus anticipating the reforms he would make after his appointment as Commissioner of Indian Affairs by President Franklin Delano Roosevelt in 1933. But as the opening of "The Red Atlantis" suggests, Collier combined this overt political message with romantic imagery that is familiar to us from both the discussion of writing by Wallace and Lummis in previous chapters and the discussion of travelogues and promotional literature earlier in this chapter.

Collier traveled to Taos in December 1920 at the invitation of the writer and patron of the arts Mabel Dodge, who herself had settled in the town after first visiting three years before.[76] Both Collier and Mabel were transformed by their initial visits to Taos. Undoubtedly Collier romanticized the "folk" cultures of both Pueblos and Hispanos, discerning in their long history in New Mexico and their enduring cultural traditions an antidote to the perceived woes of modern American culture. He shared this assumption with Mabel and the writer Mary Austin, much of whose life was spent living in and traveling through the Southwest. Austin wrote voluminously about the Southwest, from her sketches and stories of "the country of lost borders" in the desert to the east of the Sierra Nevada mountain range in her early books *The Land of Little Rain* (1903) and *Lost Borders* (1909) to her travelogue *Land of Journey's Ending* (1924), which concentrates on New Mexico and Arizona, and her intimate study *Taos Pueblo* (1930), a collaboration with the photographer Ansel Adams. For Mabel, who migrated to New Mexico from Manhattan in 1917, Taos became an idyllic location in which to reestablish a coherent sense of self and community in the face of ennui, spiritual pessimism, and the carnage of the First World War. There she entered into an adulterous relationship with Tony Lujan, a Pueblo man whom she married in 1923 after divorcing her third husband, the artist and sculptor Maurice Sterne. "The Pueblos," observes biographer Lois Rudnick, "offered Mabel what no advanced twentieth-century society was able to: an integration of personality that was achieved through an organic connection between the individual and community, work and living space, play and art."[77] Through writing her autobiographical novel *Winter in Taos,* published in 1935, Mabel strove to express a deeply rooted sense of place, self, and community.

How should we read the work of Collier, Austin, and Luhan in relation to the representations of southwestern landscapes, Native Americans, and Hispanos that have been discussed earlier in this chapter? Next to the promotional rhetoric of Indian Detours, their writing often appears informed, partisan, and impassioned, and yet to a large degree their writing and activism sprang from Indian detours of their own. All three individuals campaigned strenuously for the rights of Pueblo Indians in the early 1920s, when the Bursum Bill threatened to alienate Indian title to valuable land holdings. Whereas the language of tourist brochures could be glib in tone and presumptuous in attitude, Collier, Austin, and Luhan prided themselves on truly knowing Native Americans and on being sensitive to the needs of tribal cultures. Looking further back to the nineteenth-century representations of Gregg, Davis, and Wallace in which the demise of Pueblo Indian cultures was forecast and the elegiac tone employed, Collier, Austin, and Luhan celebrated the dignity and endurance of Pueblo Indian cultures and argued for the right of Native Americans to manage their own affairs, albeit with appropriate assistance from fair-minded representatives of the U.S. government. This cautious optimism also differentiates Collier, Austin, and Luhan from individuals such as Burbank and Monsen who were pessimistic about the capacity of southwestern Indians to participate in American society without their own cultures becoming, as Collier put it, "a veritable soon-to-be-lost Atlantis sinking beneath the waves."[78] And yet there were also limitations to the more modern way of seeing Indians as part of a pluralistic United States. Similar to their predecessors, Collier, Austin, and Luhan projected their own values onto Pueblo Indians. They too could be elitist and paternalistic in their attitudes toward Indians, although the nature of their elitism and paternalism clearly was different from that of an earlier generation of philanthropic figures, such as Edward E. Ayer, who sponsored efforts to document "traditional" Native American cultures before, as they saw it, Indians were absorbed into American society.

In order to assess the legacy of writing about Taos by Collier, Austin, and Luhan, it helps to pose several interrelated questions. How did experiences of travel help form their intellectual and moral attitudes toward Pueblo Indian communities? To what extent did their writing depart from, and even confirm, older visions of the Southwest that have been discussed in this and other chapters? And how did their writing anticipate the far-reaching changes in written and artistic representations of Native Americans and Mexican Americans that have occurred as a consequence of civil rights campaigning and cultural activism in the decades after World War II?

It also helps to consider recent criticism of their writings and political concerns. The anthropologist Sylvia Rodríguez has commented forcefully on what she regards as the colonialist mindset of many of the Anglo writers and artists who were drawn to Taos in the early twentieth century. She writes:

> This enclave of culturally disaffected spiritual refugees from urban, industrial America played an important role in the development of southwestern ethnic symbolism. Members of an alien, superordinate and colonizing society, they lived like expatriates and appropriated indigenous symbols as their own in a manner that relied on and yet belied a social system of stringent ethnic-racial stratification and segregation.[79]

Rodríguez's criticism alerts us to the problematic issue of how in the very process of articulating a utopian sense of place, community, and selfhood in the Taos locale, the presence of Collier, Austin, Luhan, and many other artists and writers contributed to social and economic inequalities in the area. Furthermore she argues that writers and artists in the 1920s and 1930s tended not to cast rural Hispanos in the same romanticized light as Indians. Although concerned Anglos sympathized with the plight of Pueblo Indians who were at risk of losing title to their lands in the early 1920s, for the most part they did not show similar support for rural Hispanos who were also subject to the pressures of modernization. Indeed, a certain amount of land claimed by the Hispano community was returned to the Pueblos or appropriated by the U.S. government for conservation purposes. Simultaneously Hispanos began to leave the land, searching for more viable livelihoods in cities or as migrant laborers. In time this migration would lead to rural depopulation and the growth of urban barrios in Santa Fe, Albuquerque, and cities further afield in the Southwest.[80]

Collier's essay "The Red Atlantis" was published in the progressive journal *Survey Graphic* in October 1922. It was a clarion cry for Americans to address the issue of Indian rights in general and the preservation of Pueblo Indians' cultural traditions in particular. The article was joined by

Stella M. Atwood's essay "The Case for the Indian." Atwood was chair-woman of the General Federation of Women's Clubs' Indian Welfare Committee, which worked cooperatively with Native Americans to bring civil and economic change to their communities. She employed Collier to research the conditions of life in New Mexico's Pueblo Indian communities and report his findings to the Indian Welfare Committee. At the conclusion of her essay, Atwood called for a new program of social welfare for Indians that would address issues of health, education, citizenship, and legislation. "The American people must realize that the Indian, instead of being a liability, is one of our national assets," she stated. "The ethnologist, the archaeologist, the artist, the dramatist, the musician, the economist are coming to a tardy realization of the wealth of material that lies untouched there."[81] Both articles were illustrated with reproductions of paintings by artists who lived or sojourned in Taos. Collier's piece was illustrated with reproductions of paintings by Victor Higgins, Joseph Sharp, and Walter Ufer, while a portfolio of eight portraits contained further images by Ufer, Ernest Blumenschein, Randall Davey, Robert Henri, Will Shuster, and Maurice Sterne, Mabel Dodge's estranged husband.[82] Mabel had approached the artists for contributions to the journal, while she provided her own photographs to illustrate Atwood's article. The work of Anglo artists was complemented by images of a deer and horses by Pueblo Indians John Coucha and Alfonso Roybal, respectively, along with several images of Pueblo ceremonies in the possession of the Smithsonian Institution's American Museum of Natural History.

These resources had been gathered in order to protest legislation that threatened Pueblo Indian land holdings. The Bursum Bill was introduced to the Senate in July 1922 in order to clarify the complicated issue of ownership of pueblo lands. The matter was confusing enough because the boundaries and ownership of land grants made in the successive Spanish, Mexican, and American eras were often not clear. But the main problem for Pueblos was that the bill upheld the multiple claims of non-Indians who had come to reside on their lands, either as squatters or as holders of title. At stake were around 60,000 out of a total of 340,000 acres of land held by twenty separate pueblos. A diverse group of Indian rights activists, writers, and artists mobilized their collective resources to mount unprecedented opposition to the bill.[83] Mary Austin's speech before the National Popular Government League in January 1923 is typical of the tenor of this opposition. First she made practical points about the need for welfare in Pueblo communities. Children were already suffering from malnutrition

and living in unsanitary conditions. She could also have noted the large
incidence of venereal disease and trachoma. Already the people of Tesuque
were without water for failing crops and were "quietly starving." Losing
up to one-sixth of their lands would compound their existing poverty.
Because Indians were "wards of the wealthiest nation," Austin considered
it "*our*" responsibility to provide support for them. Simultaneously Austin
exalted Pueblos for attaining "the highest pitch of culture attained by the
Indian within what is the now the United States." Furthermore, she
stated: "They possess a secret which our more complex civilization has
lost, a secret without which we shall never achieve the ideal democracy,
the secret of acting in a state of communal, or crowd mindeness *from a
higher plane* than that attainable by individual cerebration."[84] Shortly after
Austin gave her speech, opposition to the Bursum Bill triumphed,
although the vexed issues of land ownership and administration of Pueblo
Indian affairs continued to be debated.[85]

Similar to Austin's speech, politics and romance are combined in
Collier's "The Red Atlantis" to create a powerful argument upholding the
right of Pueblo Indians to garner the support necessary to maintain their
unique way of life in modern America. Much of the essay's effectiveness as
a critique of narrow-minded prejudice toward Pueblos, and by implication Native Americans in general, comes from the motif of travel. Collier
prefaced his arrival at Taos Pueblo by providing selective details of the
approach. Mentioning no mode of transportation—railroad, automobile,
wagon, horseback, or even foot—he instead provided an impressionistic
sense of travel. Cordova, some forty miles to the south of Taos, was old
and many of its houses decayed. Entering a church, Collier was struck by
the pious and humble scene of worship:

> Here was the living Cordova—four generations, and all blood-
> kin or marriage kin. Altar lamps and many candles glowed ruby
> and blue and soared in whiteness. The saints were gaily arrayed.
> The long prayer muttered, there was silence; the kneeling group
> breathed it back, an old woman resumed the lead, and again the
> congregation spoke long and low. There is no hurry in Mexican
> New Mexico; and at Cordova not one of the four generations
> spoke English.[86]

This passage is strikingly different from W. W. H. Davis's account of visiting a small adobe church in Las Vegas seventy years earlier in his book *El*

Gringo. Davis, we may recall from chapter 1, considered the church's adobe architecture crude and, as we also saw in his description of an Easter parade in Santa Fe, was not favorably disposed toward the display of religious icons—known as *santos* (saints). Even allowing for the fact that in Cordova Collier witnessed religious worship taking place whereas Davis walked through an empty church, nevertheless the difference in the two men's perspectives is profound. Davis, should he have somehow lived to view the scene in Cordova, might well have been appalled to find "Mexican" Catholicism remaining so influential in the everyday lives of Hispanos well into the twentieth century. Furthermore the maintenance of Spanish as the dominant language in the community probably would have frustrated him—a sure sign that Hispanos had not accepted the "Americanization" that he saw necessary for the growth and prosperity of New Mexico. For Collier, though, the church scene suggested an enduring and principled commitment to the values and practices that sustained Cordova's community. He was not troubled but reassured by the piety of worshipers and the lack of English being spoken. Leaving the chapel, he looked toward Taos Mountain, one of the highest peaks in the Sangre de Cristo Range: "To the Indians it is both an altar and a god, and in no fanciful but in an actual way, as things of the impassioned imagination are actual." Only then did he introduce readers to Taos itself, a place where Mexicans, Indians, and Anglo traders, sheep ranchers, and artists dwelled—a location, indeed, in which the "frontier still lingers by Kit Carson's grave in the Taos cemetery."[87]

For Collier, the Pueblo Indians as a whole comprised "the finest flower of the pre-history of the United States." Taos Pueblo was "alive, pregnant and potentially plastic," but alas it had been condemned, both tacitly and officially, "to die not by sudden execution but through proscription and slow killing." He continued:

These tiny communities of the red man, archaic, steeped in a non-rational world-view of magic and animism and occult romanticism—it seems a wild if a luring fantasy that they might live on, that they might use the devices of modern economic life, and pragmatically take over the concepts of modern science, and yet might keep that strange past of theirs, that psychic and social present as it truly is, so indolently industrious, so ecstatic while yet so laughing, so great with color, flooded with body-rhythm and song, so communal yet individually reckless, so human and so mystic.

These were eloquent and even extravagant words through which Collier argued not only that Pueblo Indians should be allowed to remain true to the practices that had sustained their culture for many hundreds of years but also that Americans as a whole should learn from them. The Pueblos' primitivism was not primordial, in his estimation, but an age-old repository of fundamental human values. They had "conserved the earliest statesmanship, the earliest pedagogy of the human race," and it was from both that the modern world needed to learn.[88] It would have been almost impossible for Collier to employ similar language and tropes to describe experiences of labor in most other parts of the United States at this time. After all, his idealization of the Pueblo community was premised on a Marxist critique of the alienation of labor in capitalist societies. Simultaneously his ecstatic reaction to visiting Taos Pueblo provided a new impetus to rethink the utopian possibilities of socialism.[89] Collier concluded that through cooperative enterprise Pueblo Indians would be able to adapt to modern life without forsaking their cultural traditions. However his optimism was tempered with caution: "Nothing but the white man's skepticism, nothing but departmental routines, archaic official ideals and jealous vested interests of white men, stand in the way. But they are a 'whole lot.'" Such rhetoric was radically different from the earlier representations of Pueblo Indians by Josiah Gregg, W. W. H. Davis, and even Susan Wallace that were discussed in the first chapter. Notably Collier thought that he shared common ground with Charles Fletcher Lummis, whom along with Adolph Bandelier he considered "the Southwest's most human scholarly interpreter."[90]

Mary Austin, as we have seen from her speech against the Bursum Bill, perceived southwestern Indians as exemplary souls from whom Anglos should learn if they were to be at ease with themselves in modernizing America. Learning from Indians would help Americans flee "from complexity to simplicity, from asphalt and machinery and wage earning to camp fire and open trail."[91] Pueblo society, she noted, lacked many of the ills of mainstream American society, among them prostitution, neglected widows, extremes of poverty and wealth, orphanages, and prisons. In all this Austin and Collier were of one mind. They also agreed that arts and crafts were integral to the cultures of southwestern Indians, both in forming a vital part of their holistic existence and in offering the distinct possibility of economic welfare. Noting that handicrafts had already been commercialized, Collier proposed that a "socially purposeful and businesslike crafts-effort would have amazing results in all the reservations of the Southwest. Output would increase, standards would rise and new creations begin; lapsed or degenerated arts and crafts would revive, as actually they have done in the cases of Navajo weaving and Hopi pottery."[92] Meanwhile Austin anticipated the day when tourists would pay admission to walk around the ruins of Taos Pueblo if aid for the continuation of their culture was not forthcoming. Conjuring this image, she foresaw the arrival of "Mainstreetism in its worst form." Much better, she reasoned, to have tourists visit a living and vital culture. Through visiting the pueblo, she reasoned, Americans would realize the value of Taos Indians "as a diversion, as a spectacle, as a form of entertainment, peculiarly our own, not too easily accessible to make them common, but just far enough removed to make seeing them one of the few remaining great American adventures."[93] This viewpoint almost seems to have anticipated the creation of Indian Detours several years later. Similar to the Indian Detour promotional texts, there is a class-based argument at work in Austin's writing. Here "common" has three meanings. Anglos could travel from far away and off the beaten track and come face-to-face with a place and people that were uncommonly different. In addition, by virtue of traveling to the Southwest they would show themselves a cut above ordinary folk. Finally, by coming into contact with an intelligent and discerning class of Americans, the Pueblos would not be rendered "common" by their interactions with Anglos.[94]

When Austin wrote in her book *Taos Pueblo* that "for those who have been admitted, ever so slightly, to the reality of Indian life, there is a profound and humble thankfulness," she was hardly alone in characterizing the community in such redemptive terms.[95] Mabel Dodge Luhan, her friend and fellow writer, may well have gone further in this direction by virtue of her marriage to Tony Lujan. That said, it is perhaps too easy to romanticize this relationship as clearly it became strained at certain points and to some extent marginalized both partners from their respective communities. Austin, who was well known for being outspoken on issues that she considered important, once criticized Mabel strongly for her treatment of Tony. She berated Mabel for allowing an atmosphere of "envy and malic [sic] and backbiting" in her social gatherings. The time had come for Mabel to know that she was guilty of treating Tony like "a simple minded old buck of Indian." Austin continued by illuminating what she considered home truths: "With the possible exception of Miss [Elizabeth Shepley] Sergeant, I am the only one of your friends who has ever treated Tony with entire respect. I have never mentioned this to you before, because I did respect your relations with him; but you make it necessary that I should explicitly tell you that not only is he a joke,—a good natured and occasional joke, but still a joke—to most of the people who come to your ribald house . . ." On the back of the letter is written: "Dear Mary— Snap out of it! ML."[96] While this retort suggests a meeting of two forceful and stubborn wills, one cannot help but wonder how Mabel coped with such a blunt observation from someone who knew her well. A decade later, in her autobiographical novel *Winter in Taos,* she wrote calmly and fondly of her seventeen years with Tony: "he seems like a rock; more than that, a mountain, that will support all the weight I can put on him."[97]

I mention this relationship in some detail because through it Mabel took to an extreme one of the fundamental desires in Western travel, the desire to become one with the "primitive" other. In a memorable image at the end of *Movers and Shakers,* her third volume of memoirs, Mabel described moving from a state of unconsciousness into one of "super-unconsciousness" while at home in Manhattan one night in 1916. She saw her husband Maurice Sterne's head and was afraid of it. "Then, as I gazed his began to fade and another face replaced it, with green leaves twinkling and glistening all around it—a dark face with wide-apart eyes that stared at me with a strong look, intense and calm. This was an Indian face and it affected me like a medicine after the one that had been before it." Soon a letter came from Maurice, who had traveled to Santa Fe to paint and sculpt. "Dearest Girl," he wrote. "Do you want an object in life? Save the Indians, their art-culture—reveal it to the world!"[98] Thus Mabel set about leaving for New Mexico and her prophesied meeting with Tony Lujan in 1917. And, as we have seen, she did indeed campaign zealously for the rights of Indians.

Eighteen years after arriving in New Mexico and by now fifty-six years old, Mabel published a quiet and meditative novel titled *Winter in Taos.* The epigraph is taken from Ralph Waldo Emerson—"The first farmer was the first man, and all historic nobility rests on possession and use of land"—and suggests the novel's preoccupation with the passing of the seasons, the agricultural cycle, and a deeply rooted sense of place. From the beginning, when the narrator awakes in her bedroom, *Winter in Taos* is a celebration of domesticity, small-scale agriculture, and the harmonious relationship between a husband and wife who also happen to be, respectively, Pueblo Indian and Anglo. In certain respects the book is the culmination of her search for a location in which Anglos could recover a holistic sense of self and community. Viewing the pueblo's hundred smoking chimneys from several miles away, she imagines "a tribe actuated with a single impulse," a collectivity in which "all move as one in a large rhythm of life." For her the Pueblos' integrated perspective and organic lifestyle contrasted with the Anglo ways of seeing and doing: "We watch things happen in Nature as though they were outside us and separate from us, but the Indians know they are that which they contemplate."[99] And so Mabel attempted to bridge the gap between the Pueblo and Anglo worlds through writing a novel that, as Lois Rudnick points out, was inspired in part by the Pueblos' observance of the ritual life cycle.[100]

Mabel structured the narrative over a single day, using the somewhat strained device of dramatizing her own growing anxiety as she anticipates Tony's return home from a ten-mile drive to trade oats for beans. Throughout the day Mabel characterizes not only the activities that sustain her household but also the actions necessary for a successful cycle of growth in the agricultural year. Hence she describes planting, irrigation, and the nurturing and harvesting of crops. She celebrates the household's near self-sufficiency. A steer and a sheep or lamb are bought each winter, butchered, and then kept frozen in a chamber outside the kitchen. Potatoes, pumpkins, squash, carrots, beets, onions, cabbages, turnips, cucumbers, cantaloupes, watermelons, and apples are all cultivated on land she owns. In a new age of burgeoning mass production, Mabel finds herself reverting to the ways of a previous generation: "Something left over in me from my grandmother has made me turn back to these earlier ways of living, made me to enjoy my storerooms full of the fruit of the earth, though it has meant so much hard work to stock these dark cellars and these storeroom shelves, and has, probably, cost more to fill them than to buy the efficient products of the shops."[101]

Ironically, at the moment Mabel found herself turning away from "mass productions" and looked for a house at the pueblo where she could buy home-ground whole wheat flour, she saw Taos Indians purchasing "bluish-white" bread from the stores that had "no taste and no virtue." Now Pueblo farmers used tractors and threshing machines to harvest grains and traded wheat and corn for canned foods. These observations led to a generalization: "The Indians are, by some kind of predilection, and by the destiny that has been determined for them by the influence of the Indian Bureau Schools, headed for Progress, a mechanical civilization and an undetermined racial stock, while some of us white people are said to be regressing to an earlier mode of life instead of conforming to our present-day environment." Mabel observed that the Depression had slowed the impact of modernization on the Pueblo people. Before the Wall Street crash in 1929, "one could see the influence of American money in the Pueblo. Several Indians opened curio shops out there and neglected to cultivate their fields. They let the earth lie fallow, and they began to make cheap little drums, bows and arrows, small, uninspired pots, and even oil paintings of the Pueblo, Indian horses, and men." Six years later the curio shops were disappearing, and in another year, she reckoned, all would be gone.[102]

How does Mabel's antipathy toward the commercial opportunism of vendors at Taos Pueblo square with her support for the revitalization of arts and crafts among southwestern Indians? This question takes us back to one of the key issues discussed in this book: the matter of experience and expertise in assessing the "worth" of Native Americans, Hispanos, and landscapes in the Southwest. The paternalistic assumption that Pueblo Indians had to be saved from their own innocence (or ignorance) as they were pulled more and more into the sphere of dominant society underlies Mabel's critique. According to her viewpoint, embracing technology and "progress" would have an inevitably corrosive effect on Native American communities. Reading Mabel today, the unanswered conundrum posed by her writing is the question of how Pueblos and other Indians were meant to sustain themselves if indeed they were not to participate fully in the modern economy. In the midst of the Depression and in her later middle age, Mabel appears to have thought it best for Pueblo Indians to be cushioned from commercialization and what she considered the less than worthy aspects of mass American culture. They would find a refuge in their geographical marginalization from centers of population and power in the United States. However, such isolation was threatened by the democratization of leisure travel, which allowed larger numbers of Euro-Americans to visit the Taos and Santa Fe locales. By the mid-1930s, Mabel was busy differentiating herself from the tourists who congregated in Taos during the summer. She noted that at the pueblo tourists asked "ten thousand foolish questions," while Indian guides answered patiently, "only their eyes betraying their amusement." These days, she commented, she avoided going into the town, only a quarter mile from her home, because doing so would only mean being "irritated by the slack, crowded atmosphere of the village, invaded as it is by the vacant-eyed tourist population." Her own home had become a refuge, a Taos Eden into which she retreated away from the prying eyes of tourists from Texas and Oklahoma. Outside the estate a sign had been posted: "Private Property. No Admittance. Tourists Unwelcome."[103] There is a certain poetic justice in Mabel's feeling it necessary to erect such a notice. One wonders if she ever realized that Hopis at the Hotevilla Snake Dance she visited with Lawrence in 1924 might well have been similarly inclined to keep out unwanted visitors to their sacred ceremony.

Reflections on Traveling through the Southwest

IN THE SUMMER OF 2001, I visited Taos Pueblo for the first time in five years. I found that since last visiting, guided tours of the pueblo have been instituted. A young man from the pueblo corralled fifteen visitors into a group and took us first to the Church of San Geronimo. The guide pointed out murals to the side of the altar that depict corn growing and explained that these symbols are a sign of how people within the community combine aspects of Catholicism with their native religion in a manner that they have done since Franciscan friars and Spanish colonial officials came into their midst in the seventeenth century. Ten minutes later we were standing beside the ruins of the old mission church, destroyed by the U.S. army in 1847 after local Hispanos and Pueblo Indians had rebelled against the new American administration of Taos, killing Governor Charles Bent in the process. Within the ruined building stand crosses for the 147 people who lost their lives after taking refuge within the church from the advancing force of Americans. Looking at the crumbling adobe, I thought that here is a dramatic metonymic device through which Pueblo Indians remember the impact of Spanish colonialism and the American conquest of the Southwest on their culture. For visiting Anglos, the ruined church makes uncomfortable viewing. In talking about the events that unfolded there, our guide clearly differentiated between his own culture and the colonizing Americans, as though that conflict is as present in the minds of Taos Indians today as it was over a hundred and fifty years ago.

We moved on to the five-floor North Pueblo building, which has been represented in myriad paintings, drawings, and photographs by Anglo visitors over the past two centuries. Before the brief tour concluded, our guide encouraged us to look at the jewelry, ceramics, drums, and other arts and crafts on sale in shops. And if we were merely hungry and thirsty, why not try the delicious fry bread and Indian tacos being sold at various stalls around the village. Talking with some of the visitors after the tour, I sensed that some people were disappointed by the sale of arts and crafts at the pueblo. They did not like the overt commercialism that had come into the tour and appeared to think it inappropriate that the guide had encouraged them to purchase goods. Perhaps, I thought, some visitors would feel more at ease walking through a kind of open-air museum with period displays and actors impersonating "authentic" Indians rather than observing the reality of present-day life. And yet it is not as if today's paying visitors have necessarily seen such "reality" by visiting the village. After all, very few people live in the old buildings on a year-round basis anymore. This is not just a matter of people preferring to live in homes with electricity, gas, and running water, none of which is supplied in the village, but also because tourism has impacted their desire to live in a place that curious outsiders frequent for much of the year.

Clearly organized tours have been introduced partly to curb the wandering tendencies of tourists and to bring a greater degree of control to the ways in which visitors engage with the pueblo. Where outside visitors once sought spontaneity and authenticity in pueblo life by seeking out its hidden corners, walking into homes unannounced, and climbing into kivas unbidden, today great efforts are made by Taos residents to counteract such desires. The greater degree of control extended over visitors stymies the tendency to venture into areas off-limits even as the pueblo capitalizes on their desire to capture the essence of local life by charging a $10 fee to photograph buildings. (A pueblo resident once told me that when he saw visitors trying to take photographs of him from a distance using a telephoto lens, he would pretend to hold a camera and snap them back.)

One of the striking aspects of taking a guided tour about the pueblo today is the degree to which the village is a kind of living theater in which contemporary Indians stage aspects of their lives for a tourist market while "real" life goes on elsewhere, beyond the immediate boundaries of the pueblo's old buildings. This situation changes in striking ways on feast days and ceremonial occasions and during the two months of the year when the pueblo is closed to tourists. The lack of a charge for admission and the denial of the right to photograph on ceremonial days is a sign of how pueblo residents view it necessary to downplay commercialism and deprive tourists of the right to represent tribal activities on the very days that they pursue more "traditional" aspects of their culture in view of the public.

Today, then, the tribal government has engaged with a certain degree of commercialism at the same time that outsiders' access to pueblo culture has been curbed. Taos Indians are thus in the midst of maintaining a difficult balancing act as they negotiate their participation in both pueblo life and the world beyond their reservation. The income derived from tourism has become an increasingly significant source of revenue for Indians throughout the Southwest. Over the past ten years certain pueblos have invested greatly in attracting vacationers to their casinos, hotels, and golf courses. When I first visited Taos Pueblo in 1990, there were no gaming facilities on the reservation. Today a profitable casino employs a number of pueblo residents and provides much-needed funds to the community at large. Driving north from Santa Fe, today's travelers cannot help but see the huge casino that is situated on Pojoaque Pueblo land. Writers such as W. W. H. Davis and Susan Wallace would have been astonished to see such a scene! There are clear signs of how today's pueblo tribes have capitalized on southwestern tourism and the special legal status that allows them to develop gaming in order to provide for the welfare of their communities. But we should remember that not all pueblo tribes have either the means or the will to develop resources in this way. Furthermore, Native Americans throughout the Southwest continue to experience poverty, ill health, and social discord.

The experience of Simon Ortiz is instructive in this regard. Ortiz hails from Acoma Pueblo, which itself has been running organized tours of its old "Sun City" pueblo for many years, and is the author of a number of well-regarded volumes of poetry. In the powerful introduction to *Woven Stone,* an omnibus collection of his poetry, Ortiz characterizes his thirteen-year-old self as "the silent, stoic child of a dysfunctional family, community, and nation." He describes the experience of growing up during the 1950s, when federal Indian policy took a conservative turn and called for the assimilation of Native Americans into mainstream society. As a boy he was cautious of Anglos, "wary of something that drove them willfully, aggressively, powerfully, and arrogantly." With the benefit of hindsight, he explains that this was "the same drive that had settled [Anglo] domain and rule over Native American lands and enforced an educational policy disguised as civilization."[1] For Ortiz alcoholism, with which he has struggled for many years, is a destructive force that undermines faith in one's own culture. Excessive drinking is often (although, of course, not exclusively) the sign of a divided sensibility and a person's inability to believe he or she belongs in the "Mericano" world while also feeling estranged from the "Indian" world.[2] These observations take us a long way from the iconography of tourism discussed in the last chapter.

Thankfully Ortiz also speaks more hopefully of the future. Against a haunting history of domination and disempowerment, he believes wholeheartedly in the "continuance" of the Acoma people. From his viewpoint, continuance is contingent on Acomas' truly knowing themselves and putting their own culture, together with the cultures of other Native Americans, at the center of the world. In all this, oral tradition is of vital importance. It is, for Ortiz, "the consciousness of the people." Put another way, "Oral tradition is inclusive; it is the actions, behavior, relationships, practices throughout the whole social, economic, and spiritual life process of people." Through prayers, songs, chants, stories, and even gossip, Acomas become connected to the land, create ties with their ancestors, and forge a strong sense of community. Ortiz is only too aware of how Native Americans' use of their own languages has been impacted by assimilation campaigns in the early twentieth century and after World War II. While celebrating the Acoma language, he assures his fellow Acomas, and by implication Native Americans in general, that "consciousness of our true selves [lies] at the core of whatever language we use, including English."[3]

During the 1850s W. W. H. Davis characterized New Mexico as a benighted land that was only coming into enlightenment in the aftermath of the American conquest of the Southwest. Almost 150 years after he wrote, we can say that the Southwest has not submitted to the cultural hegemony that Davis imagined. And how, after all, could it? In recent years writers, literary critics, and historians have explored the complex processes whereby the culturally and geographically peripheral areas of the Southwest were brought into the nation's expanded body from the second half of the nineteenth century onward. For example, the historian Ramón A. Gutiérrez and the anthropologist Sylvia Rodríguez have each argued that regional identities emerged out of the complex interplay between diverse groups of enclaved peoples, the physical environments they inhabited, and the particular relationships they forged with their allies and enemies. Gutiérrez points out the similarities between the American conquest of the Southwest in the 1840s and Spanish colonization three centuries earlier. The U.S.-Mexican War, he writes, initiated "an intense cycle of cultural conflict over the very same issues that had pitted the Spanish against the Pueblo Indians—religion, labor, land, and water."[4]

In her study "Land, Water, and Ethnicity in Taos," Rodríguez examines a local cultural conflict of the sort to which Gutiérrez alludes. She historicizes the situation of Hispanos in the Taos locale in the late twentieth century, where many of them strive to subsist on an ever-dwindling land base. Although Hispanos were able to hold onto their lands far more than Mexican Americans in other parts of the Southwest in the aftermath of the U.S.-Mexican War, over the past 150 years rural Hispanos have seen their land encroached upon by Euro-American settlers and expropriated by the federal government. Simultaneously economic pressures have forced Hispanos off the land in order to search for more viable livelihoods in cities or as migrant laborers. The result has been both rural depopulation and a concomitant growth in political activism: "the crystallization of land as a symbol of Hispano cultural survival and social self-determination."[5]

Rodríguez argues that through the influence of Anglo writers, such as Mary Austin and Mabel Dodge Luhan, and the painters of the Taos Art Colony, Hispano culture in northern New Mexico became "valued only for the quaint, 'relaxed,' Latin peasant ambience it lent the place, but not for any perceived intrinsic quality or beauty."[6] The Anglo activists who strove to uphold the rights of Pueblo Indians during the 1920s tended not to cast rural Hispanos in the same romantic light as Indians even though Hispanos also had a strong attachment to the land and a well-founded sense of place and community. According to Rodríguez, this dichotomy in the way Anglos have viewed Taos Indians and Hispanos has had profound repercussions. She ends her study of land, water, and ethnicity in Taos by stating both the local and wider significance of cultural conflicts between Native Americans, Mexican Americans, and Anglos in Taos today: "If New Mexico's and the Southwest's tourism industry has promoted the idea of cultural pluralism and flourished because of its existence, it has also gone hand-in-hand with a deeply entrenched, deeply mystified, system of structural inequality. One of the great challenges which today faces both modern and developing nations is whether and how ethnic and cultural pluralism can be reconciled with general social, economic, and cultural equality and self-determination."[7]

I have stated that it has often been the case that tourists visiting Taos have wondered what lies around the corner, be it a kiva at the pueblo or a penitente morada, and have wanted to investigate those places, if not actually then vicariously through representations of travel in both written and visual media. But what exactly have such visitors expected to see around such actual and metaphorical corners? To what extent do visitors to Taos Pueblo go there hoping for the renewal of essential life that Mary Austin wrote about in her eponymously titled book or as the voyeuristic rubbernecking tourists D. H. Lawrence was appalled by when he attended the Hopi Snake Dance in the early 1920s? More to the point, perhaps, both Simon Ortiz and Sylvia Rodríguez offer a profound challenge to all those wishing to comprehend the significance of the Southwest as a region and as part of the United States. Their writing is a sign of a widespread phenomenon whereby the formerly colonized populations of the region are affirming their right to contest the terms of incorporation imposed upon them between the 1840s and 1930s. As I hope to have demonstrated through the chapters of this book, Euro-American writers, artists, and photographers, while often themselves having been part of this process of incorporation, have also thrown doubt, both knowingly and only partly consciously, on the actions and language used to justify such conduct.

Notes

Introduction

1. Charles Fletcher Lummis, "In the Lion's Den," *Land of Sunshine* 4, no. 2 (January 1896): 89.
2. *Indian Detour* (New York: Rand McNally and Company, 1926), 5.
3. *Guide to Indian Country* (Los Angeles: Automobile Club of Southern California, 1994).
4. For studies of the contemporary tourist, see Dean MacCannell, *The Tourist: A New Theory of the Leisure Class* (New York: Schocken Books, 1976); and John Urry, *The Tourist Gaze: Leisure and Travel in Contemporary Societies* (London: Sage, 1990). For studies that either focus on tourism in the Southwest or examine it in relation to regional development, see Leah Dilworth, *Imagining Indians in the Southwest: Persistent Visions of a Primitive Past* (Washington, D.C.: Smithsonian Institution Press, 1996); Earl Pomeroy, *In Search of the Golden West: The Tourist in Western America* (1957; reprint, Lincoln: University of Nebraska Press, 1990); Hal K. Rothman, *Devil's Bargains: Tourism in the Twentieth-Century American West* (Lawrence: University Press of Kansas, 1999); and Chris Wilson, *The Myth of Santa Fe: Creating a Modern Regional Tradition* (Albuquerque: University of New Mexico Press, 1997).
5. See *Journal of the Southwest,* special issue, *Inventing the Southwest* 30, no. 4 (winter 1990), in particular Barbara Babcock, "By Way of Introduction" (383–99) and "'A New Mexico Rebecca': Imaging Pueblo Women" (400–437); Curtis M. Hinsley Jr., "Authoring Authenticity" (462–78); and Marta Weigle, "Southwest Lures: Innocents Detoured, Incensed Determined" (499–540); Marta Weigle and Barbara A. Babcock, eds., *The Great Southwest of the Fred Harvey Company* (Phoenix: The Heard Museum, 1996); and Dilworth, *Imagining Indians in the Southwest.*
6. Babcock, "By Way of Introduction," 385.
7. Dilworth, *Imagining Indians in the Southwest,* 2–3.
8. Mary Austin and Ansel Adams, *Taos Pueblo* (San Francisco: Grabhorn Press, 1930), n.p.
9. Thomas Hall, *Social Change in the Southwest, 1350–1880* (Lawrence: University Press of Kansas, 1990), 11.
10. Ibid., 11.
11. See, for example, Edward Said, *Orientalism* (New York: Random House, 1979); Stephen Greenblatt, *Marvelous Possessions: The Wonder of the New World* (Chicago: University of Chicago Press, 1991); Mary Louise Pratt, *Imperial Eyes: Travel Writing and Transculturation* (New York: Routledge, 1992); David Spurr, *The Rhetoric of Empire: Colonial Discourse in Journalism, Travel Writing, and Imperial Administration* (Durham,

N.C.: Duke University Press, 1993); and Robert J. C. Young, *Colonial Desire: Hybridity in Theory, Culture, and Race* (London: Routledge, 1995).

12. Pratt, *Imperial Eyes: Travel Writing and Transculturation*, 2.

13. Patricia Nelson Limerick, "What on Earth Is the New Western History," in *Trails: Toward a New Western History*, ed. Patricia Nelson Limerick, Clyde A. Milner II, and Charles A. Rankine (Lawrence: University of Kansas Press, 1991), 86.

14. Elliot West, "A Longer, Grimmer, but More Interesting Story," in *Trails: Toward a New Western History*, 105.

15. For revisionist historiography of the American West, see Patricia Nelson Limerick, *The Legacy of Conquest: The Unbroken History of the American West* (New York: W. W. Norton, 1987); Clyde A. Milner II, ed., *A New Significance: Re-Envisioning the History of the American West* (New York: Oxford University Press, 1996); Clyde A. Milner II, Carol A. O'Connor, and Martha A. Sandweiss, eds., *The Oxford History of the American West* (New York: Oxford University Press, 1994); Elliot West, *The Contested Plains: Indians, Goldseekers, and the Rush to Colorado* (Lawrence: University Press of Kansas, 1998); and Richard White, *"It's Your Own Misfortune and None of My Own": A History of the American West* (Norman: University of Oklahoma Press, 1991). For historical studies that concentrate on the Southwest and the Spanish or U.S.-Mexico borderlands, see Herbert E. Bolton, *The Spanish Borderlands: A Chronicle of Old Florida and the Southwest* (New Haven, Conn.: Yale University Press, 1921); D. W. Meinig, *Southwest: Three Peoples in Geographical Change, 1600–1970* (New York: Oxford University Press, 1971); David J. Weber, *Foreigners in Their Own Lands: Historical Roots of Mexican Americans* (Albuquerque: University of New Mexico Press, 1973); David J. Weber, *Myth and History of the Hispanic Southwest: Essays* (Albuquerque: University of New Mexico Press, 1988); David J. Weber, *The Spanish Frontier in North America* (New Haven: Yale University Press, 1992); John R. Chávez, *The Lost Land: The Chicano Image of the Southwest* (Albuquerque: University of New Mexico Press, 1984); Sarah Deutsch, *No Separate Refuge: Culture, Class, and Gender in an Anglo-Hispanic Frontier in the Southwest, 1880–1940* (New York: Oxford University Press, 1987); and Ramón A. Gutiérrez, *When Jesus Came the Corn Mothers Went Away: Marriage, Sexuality, and Power in New Mexico, 1500–1846* (Stanford, Calif.: Stanford University Press, 1991). For studies that focus on southwestern Indians, see Edward Spicer, *Cycles of Conquest: The Impact of Spain, Mexico, and the United States on the Indians of the Southwest, 1533–1960* (Tucson: University of Arizona Press, 1962); Alfonso Ortiz, *The Tewa World: Space, Time, Being, and Becoming in a Pueblo Society* (Chicago: University of Chicago Press, 1969); Richard White, *The Roots of Dependency: Subsistence, Environment, and Social Change among the Choctaws, Pawnees, and Navajos* (Lincoln: University of Nebraska Press, 1983). For additional literary and interdisciplinary approaches to the study of southwestern literature and culture, see Héctor Calderón and José Davíd Saldívar, eds., *Criticism in the Borderlands: Studies in Chicano Literature, Culture, and Ideology* (Durham, N.C.: Duke University Press, 1991); Richard Francaviglia, ed., *Essays on the Changing Images of the Southwest* (College Station: Texas A&M Press, 1994); Vera Norwood and Janice Monk, eds., *The Desert Is No Lady: Southwestern Landscapes in Women's Writing and Art* (Tucson: University of Arizona Press, 1997); José Davíd Saldívar, *Border Matters: Remapping American Cultural Studies* (Berkeley: University of California Press, 1997); Western Literature Association, *Updating the Literary West* (Fort Worth: Texas Christian University Press, 1997).

Chapter 1

1. John C. Fremont, *A Report of an Exploration of the Country Lying between the Missouri River and the Rocky Mountains on the Line of the Kansas and Great Platte Rivers* (1843).

Later, in conjunction with the text of Fremont's *Report of the Exploring Expedition to Oregon and North California in the Years 1843–44,* the 1843 report was made available to the general public. See editorial note, in Donald Jackson and Mary Lee Spence, eds., *The Expeditions of John Charles Fremont,* vol. 1, *Travels from 1838 to 1844* (Chicago: University of Illinois Press, 1970), 168–69.

2. Ibid., 270.

3. For discussion of Fremont's exploring expeditions and the activities of the Army Corps of Topographical Engineers in the West during the antebellum period, see William H. Goetzmann, *Army Exploration in the American West, 1803–1863* (New Haven, Conn.: Yale University Press, 1959).

4. For discussion of links between maps and the conduct of warfare, boundary making, the dissemination of official information, and the preservation of law and order, see J. B. Harley, "Maps, Knowledge, and Power," in *The Iconography of Landscape,* ed. Derek Cosgrove and Stephen Daniels (Cambridge, UK: Cambridge University Press, 1988), 277–312; and J. B. Harley, "Deconstructing the Map," *Cartographica* 26, no. 2 (summer 1989): 1–20.

5. "Map of an Exploring Expedition to the Rocky Mountains in the Year 1842, and to Oregon and North California in the Years 1843–44, by Brevet Capt. John C. Fremont of the Corps of Topographical Engineers, Under the orders of Col. J. J. Abert, Chief of the Topographical Bureau," accompanies Jackson and Spence, *The Expeditions of John Charles Fremont,* vol. 1, *Travels from 1838–1844.*

6. See, for example, Rodolfo Acuña, *Occupied America: A History of Chicanos,* 4th ed. (New York: Longman, 2000); John R. Chávez, *The Lost Land: The Chicano Image of the Southwest* (Albuquerque: University of New Mexico Press, 1984); Reginald Horsman, *Race and Manifest Destiny: The Origins of American Racial Anglo-Saxonism* (Cambridge, Mass.: Harvard University Press, 1981); Patricia Nelson Limerick, *The Legacy of Conquest: The Unbroken History of the American West* (New York: Norton, 1987); Eric J. Sundquist, "The Literature of Expansion and Race," in *The Cambridge History of American Literature,* vol. 2, *1820–1865,* ed. Sacvan Bercovitch (Cambridge, UK: Cambridge University Press, 1995), 125–328.

7. Limerick, *The Legacy of Conquest,* 27.

8. Richard Henry Dana, *Two Years Before the Mast* (1840; Harmondsworth, UK: Penguin, 1981), 237.

9. Ibid., 125.

10. Ibid., 128.

11. Ibid., 516.

12. Kevin Starr, *Americans and the California Dream, 1850–1915* (New York: Oxford University Press, 1973), 46.

13. Leonard Pitt, *The Decline of the Californios: A Social History of the Spanish-Speaking Californians* (Berkeley: University of California Press, 1966), 274.

14. Helen Hunt Jackson, "Echoes in the City of Angels," *Century* 27, no. 2 (December 1883): 199.

15. Helen Hunt Jackson, "Outdoor Industries in Southern California," in her *Glimpses of California and the Missions* (Boston: Little, Brown and Company, 1902), 257.

16. Charles Augustus Stoddard, *Beyond the Rockies: A Spring Journey in California* (London: Sampson Low, Marston, and Company, 1894), 69, 75.

17. Ibid., 85, 90.

18. Josiah Gregg, *Commerce of the Prairies, or the Journal of a Santa Fé Trader, During Eight Expeditions Across the Great Western Prairies, and a Residence of Nearly Nine Years in Northern Mexico,* 2d ed. (New York: J. and H. G. Langley, 1845), 1:vi.

19. For discussion of Gregg's career and *Commerce of the Prairies,* see Edward Halsey Foster, *Josiah Gregg and Lewis H. Garrard* (Boise, Idaho: Boise State University Press, 1977).

20. Howard R. Lamar, *The Far Southwest, 1846–1812: A Territorial History* (New Haven, Conn.: Yale University Press, 1966), 56.

21. Ibid., 63.

22. Gregg, *Commerce of the Prairies,* 1:226–27.

23. Ibid., 2:69.

24. Ibid., 1:156.

25. Ibid., 1:64–65.

26. Ibid., 2:157.

27. Ibid., 1:116–17.

28. Ibid., 1:197–98.

29. Ibid., 1:43.

30. Raymund Paredes, "The Mexican Image in American Travel Literature, 1831–1869," *New Mexico Historical Review* 52, no. 1 (1977): 24.

31. Gregg, *Commerce of the Prairies,* 1:201, 219.

32. Ibid., 1:158.

33. See, for example, Herman Melville's highly ironic dismantling of the "civilized" rhetoric justifying white enmity toward Indians in "The Metaphysics of Indian-Hating," a chapter in his novel *The Confidence Man* (1857). For studies of the representation of the frontier in American literature and culture, see Roy Harvey Pearce, *Savagism and Civilization: A Study of the Indian and the American Mind* (1953; Baltimore, Md.: Johns Hopkins University Press, 1971); Edwin Fussell, *Frontier: American Literature and the American West* (Princeton, N.J.: Princeton University Press, 1965); Richard Slotkin, *Regeneration through Violence: The Mythology of the American Frontier, 1600–1860* (Middleton, Conn.: Wesleyan University Press, 1973); Annette Kolodny, *The Lay of the Land: Metaphor as Experience and History in American Life and Letters* (Chapel Hill: University of North Carolina Press, 1975); Richard Drinnon, *Facing West: The Metaphysics of Indian-Hating and Empire-Building* (New York: New American Library, 1980); Lucy Maddox, *Removals: Nineteenth-Century American Literature and the Politics of Indian Affairs* (New York: Oxford University Press, 1991); and Sundquist, "The Literature of Expansion and Race."

34. Gregg, *Commerce of the Prairies,* 1:157–58.

35. Ibid., 1:46–47.

36. Max L. Moorhead, introduction to *Commerce of the Prairies,* by Josiah Gregg (Norman: University of Oklahoma Press, 1954), xvii–xxxviii.

37. James H. Simpson, *Journal of a Military Reconnaissance, from Santa Fe, New Mexico, to the Navajo Country, Made with the Troops under Command of Brevet Lieutenant John M. Washington, Chief of Ninth Military Department, and Governor of New Mexico, in 1849* (Philadelphia: Lippincott, Grambo and Co., 1852), 55, 56. This text is a popular press version of the original report, which was presented to Congress in 1850 under the same title (31st Cong., 1st sess., Senate Executive Document 64 (1850): 55–168). For discussion of Simpson's activities, see Goetzmann, *Army Exploration in the American West, 1803–1863,* 239–44.

38. Lamar, *The Far Southwest,* 81, 92.

39. Simpson, *Journal of a Military Reconnaissance,* 80.

40. Ibid., 46.

41. Ibid., 59. Simpson also praised the governor of Zuni Pueblo, who was "about six feet high, athletic in structure, uncommonly graceful and energetic in action, fluent in language, and intelligent." Indeed, added Simpson, "he actually charmed me with his elocution" (94).

42. Ibid., 66, 14, 17, 20.

43. Ibid., 76, 77, 81.

44. W. W. H. Davis, *El Gringo; Or, New Mexico and Her People* (New York: Harper and Brothers, 1857), 15–16. Information on Davis's career is drawn from "Description of the

Papers," W. W. H. Davis Papers, Yale Collection of Western Americana, Beinecke Rare Book and Manuscript Library, New Haven, Connecticut.

45. Davis, *El Gringo*, 300.

46. Major Horace Bell, who lived in Los Angeles for part of the 1850s and 1860s, wrote: "*Gringo,* in its literal signification, means *ignoramus.* For instance: an American who has not yet learned to eat chili peppers stewed in grease, throw the lasso, contemplate the beauties of nature from the sunny side of an adobe wall, make a first-class cigar out of a corn husk, wear open-legged pantaloons, with bell bottoms, dance on one leg, and live on one meal a week. Now the reader knows what a terrible thing it was in the early days to be a *gringo.*" Quoted in Franklin Walker, *A Literary History of the Southwest* (Berkeley: University of California Press, 1950), 55.

47. Davis, *El Gringo*, 57.

48. Ibid., 231.

49. Ibid., 388, 430.

50. Ibid., 231.

51. Ibid., 217.

52. Ibid., 234.

53. Ibid., 237.

54. Ibid., 52.

55. Ibid., 52, 365.

56. Ibid., 131, 129, 146.

57. Simpson, *Journal of a Military Reconnaissance,* 45. Notably Prescott followed the example of Spanish chroniclers and the German geographer Alexander Von Humboldt in proposing that the Aztecs had migrated from Aztlán, a homeland located in New Mexico. See William H. Prescott, *The Conquest of Mexico,* vol. 1, *The Complete Works of William Hickling Prescott,* vol. 3 of 12, ed. John Foster Kirk (London: Gibbings and Company, 1896), 16.

58. Gregg, *Commerce of the Prairies,* 1:272.

59. Davis, *El Gringo*, 154.

60. E. Conklin, *Picturesque Arizona: Being the Result of Travels and Observations in Arizona during the Fall and Winter of 1877* (New York: The Mining Record Printing Establishment, 1878), 280–81.

61. Susan Wallace, *The Land of the Pueblos* (New York: John B. Alden, 1888), 13, 14, 31–32.

62. Ibid., 45.

63. Susan Wallace wrote numerous articles for newspapers and magazines and published several books in addition to *The Land of the Pueblos.* These books are *The Storied Sea* (1884), *Ginevra, or the Old Oak Chest* (1887), and *The Repose in Egypt* (1888). Susan Arnold Elston was born in Crawfordsville, Indiana, on Christmas Day 1830 and there met Lew Wallace, her future husband. After a distinguished career in the Civil War, Lew Wallace resumed his old profession, the law, in Indiana before his posting to New Mexico. Between 1881 and 1885 he was U.S. minister to Turkey. Back in Indiana, he lectured a great deal and published *A Life of Benjamin Harrison* (1888) and *The Boyhood of Christ* (1888). Both Wallaces appear to have been greatly enthused by their travels through the Holy Land. See "Lew Wallace," *Appleton's Cyclopaedia of American Biography,* vol. 6, ed. James Grant Wilson and John Fiske (New York: D. Appleton and Co., 1889), 333–34.

64. Wallace, *Land of the Pueblos,* 14.

65. Ibid., 7.

66. Ibid., 15.

67. Ibid., 39–40, 60.

68. Ibid., 49.

69. Ibid., 108.

70. Ibid., 26–27.

71. Ibid., 52.
72. Ibid., 94.
73. Ibid., 96.
74. Chris Wilson, *The Myth of Santa Fe: Creating a Modern Regional Tradition* (Albuquerque: University of New Mexico Press, 1997), chaps. 2, 3, and 4.
75. Wallace, *The Land of the Pueblos*, 69. Interestingly Wallace qualified this statement by pointing out that although the tired women of the United States should learn from Mexican women how to rest, they must also realize how Mexican women lacked rights and access to the arts: "the weak-minded creature is not aware that men are great rascals, rob women of their rights, and bar the avenues to wealth and fame against them" (69).

Chapter 2

1. Originally entitled the Bureau of Ethnology, it was renamed the Bureau of American Ethnology in 1894. For the sake of consistency I have chosen to use the latter title.
2. For studies of Powell, see William Culp Darrah, *Powell of the Colorado* (Princeton, N.J.: Princeton University Press, 1951); Wallace Stegner, *Beyond the Hundredth Meridian: John Wesley Powell and the Second Opening of the West* (1954; Lincoln: University of Nebraska Press, 1982); and Donald Worster, *A River Running West: The Life of John Wesley Powell* (Oxford, UK: Oxford University Press, 2001).
3. For discussion of the formation of the USGS and Powell's role in the organization, see Stegner, *Beyond the Hundredth Meridian*, 243–93; Worster, *A River Running West*, 383–436; and William H. Goetzmann, *Exploration and Empire: The Explorer and the Scientist in the Winning of the American West* (1966; New York: Random House, 1972), 577–601.
4. For discussion of Powell's ethnological activities, see Curtis M. Hinsley Jr., *The Smithsonian and the American Indian: Making a Moral Anthropology in Victorian America* (Washington, D.C.: Smithsonian Institution Press, 1994), 125–89; and Worster, *A River Running West*, chaps. 7 and 10.
5. Darrah, *Powell of the Colorado*, 120–43; Goetzmann, *Exploration and Empire*, 530–76; Stegner, *Beyond the Hundredth Meridian*, 39–48; Worster, *A River Running West*, 155–202.
6. John Wesley Powell, *Report of the Exploration of the Colorado River and Its Tributaries. Explored in 1869, 1870, 1871, and 1872, Under the Direction of the Secretary of the Smithsonian Institution* (Washington D.C.: Government Printing Office, 1875), 10. Stegner notes that Sumner, Dunn, the two Howlands, and Hawkins were the only members of the team to receive wages; the remainder were volunteers. See Stegner, *Beyond the Hundredth Meridian*, 43–44.
7. For Powell's account of how the men died, see Powell, *Report of the Exploration of the Colorado River and Its Tributaries*, 130–31. Donald Worster, Powell's most recent and most exhaustive biographer, discusses several possibilities regarding the men's death, including the rumor that militant Mormons had killed them. The most likely explanation came when Powell met with the Shivwit band of Southern Paiutes the following year in 1870. They openly admitted killing the men in an act of retribution after concluding that Powell's men were the same as three miners who had caused the death of a Hualapai woman. As Worster points out, one must take into account the possibility of misunderstanding in the process of translation in encounters such as this. Nevertheless Powell appears to have been satisfied with the explanation. See Worster, *A River Running West*, 195–96, 213–15.
8. John Wesley Powell, "Green River, Wyoming Territory, May 24, [1869]," *Utah Historical Quarterly* 15 (1947): 72–73. The letter originally appeared in the *Chicago Tribune* on May 29, 1869.

9. "Letter from the Secretary of the Smithsonian Institution Transmitting Report preliminary for continuing the survey of the Colorado River of the West and its tributaries, by Professor Powell," House of Representatives, 42d Cong., 2d sess., Miscellaneous Documents no. 173. Copy in the Huntington Library, San Marino, California.

10. Powell, *Report of the Exploration of the Grand Canyon and Its Tributaries,* iii.

11. Ibid., iii.

12. "Major Powell's Journal," *Utah Historical Quarterly* 15 (1947): 130–31.

13. "Geological Notes and Sections by J. W. Powell," *Utah Historical Quarterly* 15 (1947): 139.

14. Powell, *Report of the Exploration of the Colorado River of the West and Its Tributaries,* 94–95.

15. David Wyatt, *The Fall into Eden: Landscape and Imagination in California* (Cambridge, UK: Cambridge University Press, 1986), 20, 30.

16. Powell, *Report of the Exploration of the Colorado River and Its Tributaries,* 38–39.

17. Ibid., 21.

18. Ibid., 9.

19. For details of the *Report on the Lands of the Arid Region of the United States* and its reception, see Worster, *A River Running West,* 354–60; Stegner, *Beyond the Hundredth Meridian,* 212–42; Henry Nash Smith, *Virgin Land: The American West as Symbol and Myth* (1950; Cambridge, Mass.: Harvard University Press, 1970), 196–200; and Marc Reisner, *Cadillac Desert: The American West and Its Disappearing Water* (Harmondsworth, UK: Penguin, 1987), 47–53.

20. For information on Powell's participation in the Washington, D.C.–based scientific community and his view of government science, see Stegner, *Beyond the Hundredth Meridian,* particularly 283–93, and Hinsley, *The Smithsonian and the American Indian,* 125–40. For discussion more generally of the growth of professionalism, see Thomas L. Haskell, *The Emergence of Professional Social Science: The American Social Science Association and the Nineteenth-Century Crisis of Authority* (Urbana: University of Illinois Press, 1977).

21. Hinsley, *The Smithsonian Institution and the American Indian,* 154.

22. John Wesley Powell, "The Ancient Province of Tusayan," *Scribner's Monthly* 11 (December 1875): 193–213.

23. Ibid., 196.

24. See Mark Twain, *Roughing It* (Oxford, UK: Oxford University Press, 1996), chap. 16.

25. Powell, "The Ancient Province of Tusayan," 199.

26. Ibid., 201.

27. Ibid., 202.

28. Ibid., 203.

29. See Stegner, *Beyond the Hundredth Meridian,* 134.

30. For examples of Powell's synthesizing essays, see John Wesley Powell, "From Savagery to Barbarism," *Transactions of the Anthropological Society of Washington* 3 (1885): 173–96; "From Barbarism to Civilization," *American Anthropologist* 1 (1888): 97–123; and "Are Our Indians Becoming Extinct," *Forum* 15 (1893): 343–54.

31. Powell, "The Ancient Province of Tusayan," 208.

32. Ibid., 208.

33. Ibid., 208.

34. James Clifford, "On Ethnographic Authority," in his *The Predicament of Culture: Twentieth-Century Ethnography, Literature, and Art* (Cambridge, Mass.: Harvard University Press, 1988), 31.

35. See Alexander Stephen, *Hopi Journal of Alexander M. Stephen,* ed. Elsie Clews Parsons (New York: Columbia University Press, 1936); and Jesse Walter Fewkes, "The Snake Ceremonials at Walpi," *Journal of American Ethnology and Archaeology* 4 (1894; reprint, Cambridge, Mass.: Riverside Press, 1977).

36. John Wesley Powell, *Canyons of the Colorado* (Meadville, Pa.: Flood and Vincent, 1895), 336.
37. Hinsley, *The Smithsonian Institution and the American Indian,* 180.
38. Ibid., 181.
39. Powell, "The Ancient Province of Tusayan," 212.
40. John Wesley Powell and George W. Ingalls, *Report of Special Commissioners J. W. Powell and G. W. Ingalls on the Condition of the Ute Indians of Utah; the Paiutes of Utah, northern Arizona, southern Nevada, and southeastern California; the Northwestern Shoshones of Nevada; and Report Concerning Claims of Settlers in the Mo-a-pa Valley, Southeastern Nevada* (1874). Reprinted in *Anthropology of the Numa: John Wesley Powell's Manuscripts on the Numic-Speaking Peoples of Western Northern America, 1868–1880,* ed. Don D. Fowler and Catherine S. Fowler, Smithsonian Contributions to Anthropology no. 14 (Washington, D.C.: Smithsonian Institution Press, 1971), 15. For discussion of Powell's commission and report, see Worster, *A River Running West,* 273–86.
41. Powell and Ingalls, *Report of Special Commissioners,* 99.
42. Ibid., 110. Clearly this language was exaggerated. It seems to have been employed by Powell to shock apathetic bureaucrats into action.
43. Ibid., 116.
44. Ibid., 118.
45. Ibid., 117.
46. Ibid., 119.
47. Ibid., 114.

Chapter 3

1. Chandler referred to the novel this way when interviewed by the author Ian Fleming on the radio during the 1950s. An excerpt from the interview was included in *The Detectives,* a series of three programs on detective and crime fiction written and presented by Nigel Williams that was broadcast on the BBC 2 television channel in Britain during May and June 1999. For critiques of Jackson's political conservatism in the context of broader discussions of southern California's cultural history, see Mike Davis's discussion "Sunshine or Noir" in his *City of Quartz: Excavating the Future of Los Angeles* (New York: Random House, 1992), 15–97; Carey McWilliams, *Southern California: An Island on the Land* (1946; reprint, Salt Lake City, Utah: Peregrine Smith, 1973), 70–83; and Kevin Starr, *Inventing the Dream: California through the Progressive Era* (New York: Oxford University Press, 1985), 55–62.
2. Davis, *City of Quartz,* 26.
3. Ibid., 20.
4. For historical studies of the impact of Spanish colonization on California Indians that undermine earlier accounts in which the actions of Franciscan missionaries were often celebrated, see Albert L. Hurtado, *Indian Survival on the California Frontier* (New Haven, Conn.: Yale University Press, 1988); Robert H. Jackson and Edward Castillo, *Indians, Franciscans, and Spanish Colonization: The Impact of the Mission System on California Indians* (Albuquerque: University of New Mexico Press, 1995); Florence Shipek, *Pushed into the Rocks: Southern California Indian Land Tenure, 1769–1986* (Lincoln: University of Nebraska Press, 1987); and David Hurst Thomas, "Harvesting Ramona's Garden: Life in California's Mythical Mission Past," *The Spanish Borderlands in Pan-American Perspective,* vol. 3 of *Columbian Consequences* (Washington, D.C.: Smithsonian Institution Press, 1991), 119–57.
5. George Wharton James, *Through Ramona's Country* (Boston: Little, Brown and Company, 1913), 7.

6. Ibid., xvii.
7. Helen Hunt Jackson, *Ramona* (1884; New York: Signet, 1988), 12.
8. McWilliams, *Southern California*, xxi.
9. Ibid., 83, 377, 373, 23.
10. Ibid., 76. McWilliams' "nothing much" includes the 1891 Act for the Relief of the Mission Indians and work conducted by Charles Fletcher Lummis and the Sequoyah League to find a new home for Indians evicted from their former lands on Warner's Ranch in San Diego County. For details of the act and events at Warner's Ranch, see Shipek, *Pushed into the Rocks*. For a discussion of Lummis's Indian rights activism, principally through the Sequoyah League, see Edward R. Bingham, *Charles F. Lummis: Editor of the Southwest* (San Marino, Calif.: Huntington Library Press, 1955), chap. 5.
11. McWilliams, *Southern California*, 76.
12. Jackson to Thomas Bailey Aldrich, 1 December 1884, quoted in Valerie Sherer Mathes, *Helen Hunt Jackson and Her Indian Reform Legacy* (Austin: University of Texas Press, 1990), 77.
13. For these and further biographical details, see Ruth Odell, *Helen Hunt Jackson* (New York: D. Appleton–Century Company, 1939).
14. For details, see Mathes, *Helen Hunt Jackson and Her Indian Reform Legacy*, 21–37.
15. Odell, *Helen Hunt Jackson*, 153.
16. Mathes, *Helen Hunt Jackson and Her Indian Reform Legacy*, 52–53.
17. Respectively, these groups had been attached to the missions San Diege de Alcala, San Gabriel Arcangel, San Juan Capistrano, and San Luis Rey Franca. For a clarifying note on the names of Indian groupings in southern California, see Mathes, *Helen Hunt Jackson and Her Indian Reform Legacy*, 178, n. 8.
18. Helen Hunt Jackson, "The Present Condition of the Mission Indians in Southern California" (1883), reprinted in Helen Hunt Jackson, *Glimpses of California and the Missions* (Boston: Little, Brown and Company, 1902), 159.
19. The population figures are drawn from Hurtado, *Indian Survival on the California Frontier*, 1.
20. Ibid., 1.
21. Robert F. Heizer and M. A. Whipple, "Number and Condition of California Indians Today," in *The California Indians: A Source Book*, 2d ed., ed. Robert F. Heizer and M. A. Whipple (Berkeley: University of California Press, 1971), 576.
22. The national census for 1890 recorded 248,253 Indians living in the United States, a population fall of over 150,000 from the figure for 1850. See Brian W. Dippie, *The Vanishing American: White Attitudes and U.S. Indian Policy* (1982; Lawrence: University Press of Kansas, 1991), 200.
23. Jackson to Thomas Bailey Aldrich, 1 December 1884, quoted in Mathes, *Helen Hunt Jackson and Her Indian Reform Legacy*, 77.
24. Jackson, *Ramona*, 11. Antoinette May contends that "documents such as newspapers and diaries indicate that [rape] was a frequent occurrence" in southern California during the second half of the nineteenth century. See Antoinette May, *The Annotated Ramona* (San Carlos, Calif.: Worldwide Publishing/Tetra, 1989), 197. For discussion of historical accounts that provide evidence of Anglo ethnocentrism and violence toward California Indians within a study that concentrates on the enclavement and political and cultural marginalization of the Californios during the second half of the nineteenth century, see Leonard Pitt, *The Decline of the Californios: A Social History of the Spanish-Speaking Californians, 1846–1890* (Berkeley: University of California Press, 1966).
25. Jackson, *Ramona*, 12.
26. "Twenty-Four Years After" was added to editions of *Two Years Before the Mast* after 1869.
27. Helen Hunt Jackson, "Echoes in the Cities of Angels" (1883), in her *Glimpses of California and the Missions*, 166–67.

28. Jackson, "Echoes in the Cities of Angels," 173–92.
29. Ibid., 192.
30. Ibid., 194.
31. Ibid.
32. Helen Hunt Jackson, "Outdoor Industries in Southern California" (1883), in Jackson, *Glimpses of California and the Missions,* 257.
33. Jackson, "Outdoor Industries in Southern California," 257.
34. See Renalto Rosaldo, "Imperialist Nostalgia," *Representations* 26 (1989): 107–22.
35. See Rosaura Sanchez, *Telling Identities: The Californio Testimonios* (Minneapolis: University of Minnesota Press, 1995), 167.
36. Ibid., 167.
37. Ibid., 165.
38. Sanchez argues that the Californio testimonials collected by Bancroft's agents amount to a counter-hegemonic form of historical representation through which Californios assumed a collective identity and "reposition[ed] and recenter[ed] themselves textually at a time when the physical and social spaces from which they could operate had become increasingly circumscribed." Sanchez, *Telling Identities,* x.
39. Gaudalupe Vallejo, "Ranch and Mission Days in Alta California," *Century* 41, no. 1 (November 1890): 191.
40. Ibid., 183.
41. Jackson, "Father Junipero and His Work," 8.
42. Quoted in Mathes, *Helen Hunt Jackson and Her Indian Reform Legacy,* 84.
43. Odell, *Helen Hunt Jackson,* 155.
44. Jane Tompkins, *Sensational Designs: The Cultural Work of American Fiction, 1790–1860* (New York: Oxford University Press, 1985), 126.
45. Ibid., 145.
46. Jackson, *Ramona,* 38.
47. Ibid., 48, 53, 224.
48. Helen Hunt Jackson and Abbot Kinney, "Report on the Condition and Needs of the Mission Indians of California, Made by Special Agents Helen Jackson and Abbot Kinney, to the Commissioner of Indian Affairs (1883)," in *A Century of Dishonor: A Sketch of the United States Government's Dealings with Some of the Indian Tribes,* by Helen Hunt Jackson (rev. ed., 1885; reprint, Minneapolis: Ross and Haines, 1964), 483.
49. Jackson and Kinney, "Report," 483.
50. Jackson, *Ramona,* 284, 286.
51. In a discussion of mythic discourses about the West that have both upheld and contested the cultural logic of Manifest Destiny and empire building, the literary critic Krista Comer argues that a number of women writers "looked at the vision of virile nationhood with chagrin and dread, for that kind of nation, they knew, is not generally compatible with secure, female pleasure." See Krista Comer, "Literature, Gender Studies, and the New Western History," in *The New Western History: The Territory Ahead,* ed. Forrest G. Robinson (Tucson: University of Arizona Press, 1998), 125. While there is evidence in *Ramona* to support this view, it is also important to bear in mind that at the end of the nineteenth century a significant number of male writers also called into question the legacy of frontier "heroism" and the imperial aggression of their own day. Significantly males such as George Wharton James and Charles Fletcher Lummis who advocated Indian reform in California praised *Ramona* for its appeal to sympathy. James, for example, likened the novel's reform initiative to that of abolitionists earlier in the century—"wonderful educators of the *emotions* of men in the right direction" (emphasis added). He also congratulated Jackson for "awaken[ing] public sentiment and public conscience on behalf of the Indians." See James, *Through Ramona's Country,* 10, xvii.
52. Jackson, *Ramona,* 286.

53. Michele Moylan, "Reading the Indians: The Ramona Myth in American Culture," *Prospects* 18 (1993): 155.
54. Jackson, *A Century of Dishonor*, 338.
55. Jackson, *Ramona*, 215.
56. Ibid., 348.
57. Francis Paul Prucha, *The Indians in American Society* (Berkeley: University of California Press, 1985), 53.
58. Prucha, *The Indians in American Society*, 53. Significantly, though, it was Indians' very resistance to modernizing forces that compelled the admiration of a growing number of Jackson's Euro-American contemporaries and later generations, particularly those drawn to the Southwest after World War I. Among others, Mary Austin, John Collier, and Mabel Dodge Luhan campaigned for Indian rights during the 1920s and 1930s while sojourning in New Mexico. See chapter 6 for further discussion of these key figures.
59. Jackson, *Ramona*, 169.
60. Jackson, "Father Junipero and His Work," 34.
61. George Harwood Phillips, *Chiefs and Challengers: Indian Resistance and Cooperation in Southern California* (Berkeley: University of California Press, 1975), 20–46. For an ethnohistorical account of the multiple ways in which the missions transformed the cultures of California Indians, see Jackson and Castillo, *Indian, Franciscans, and Spanish Colonization*.
62. James Rawls, *Indians of California: The Changing Image* (Norman: University of Oklahoma Press, 1984), 18.
63. Jackson and Kinney, "Report," 462.
64. For studies of Indian resistance to the American occupation of southern California, see George Harwood Phillips, *Chiefs and Challengers* and *The Enduring Struggle: Indians in California History* (San Francisco: Boyd and Fraser, 1981); for a detailed consideration of changing perceptions of California Indians, see Rawls, *Indians of California: The Changing Image*.
65. Frederick Hoxie notes that students from the Carlisle Indian School were featured on a float in the Philadelphia parade in order to "demonstrate the Indians' passage from the tepee to modern industrial life." See Hoxie "The Curious Story of Reformers and the American Indians," in *Indians in American Society*, ed. Frederick Hoxie (Arlington Heights, Ill.: Harlan Davidson, 1988), 209. For information on the Los Angeles Fiesta, see Christina Wielus Mead, "Las Fiestas de Los Angeles: A Survey of the Yearly Celebrations, 1894–1898," *Southern California Quarterly* 31, nos. 1 and 2 (1949): 61–113; and McWilliams, *Southern California*, 70–83. For a richly illustrated account of the world's fair that includes three chapters ("The Government and Administration Departments," "Anthropology and Ethnology," and "The Midway Plaisance") in which, respectively, Indian education, Native American "villages" and ethnological exhibits, and more carnivalesque presentations of Indians are described, see Hubert Howe Bancroft, *The Book of the Fair: An Historical and Descriptive Presentation of the World's Science, Art, and Industry, as Viewed through the Columbian Exposition at Chicago in 1893* (Chicago: The Bancroft Company, 1893). See also Robert Rydell, *All the World's a Fair: Visions of Empire at American International Expositions* (Chicago: University of Chicago Press, 1984), chaps. 1 and 2; and Robert A. Trennert, "Fairs, Expositions, and the Changing Images of Southwestern Indians, 1876–1904," *New Mexico Historical Review* 62 (1987): 127–50.
66. Margaret Allen, *Ramona's Homeland* (Chula Vista, Calif.: Denrich Press, 1914), n.p.
67. Charles Fletcher Lummis, *The Home of Ramona: Photographs of Camulos, the Fine Old Spanish Estate Described by Mrs. Helen Hunt Jackson, as the Home of Ramona* (Los Angeles: Chas. F. Lummis and Company, 1888); Edwin Clough, *Ramona's Marriage Place: The House of Estudillo* (Chula Vista, Calif.: Denrich Press, 1910); and George Wharton James, *Through Ramona's Country*.

68. George Wharton James describes turn-of-the-century stage adaptations of the novel in *Through Ramona's Country;* for more recent critiques of theatrical and screen presentations, see David Avalos and Deborah Small, "*Ramona:* Birth of a Miscegenation," *Discourse* 18, nos. 1 and 2 (1996): 23–31; and Moylan, "Reading the Indians: The Ramona Myth in American Culture."

69. James, *Through Ramona's Country,* 62.

70. Constance Goddard DuBois, *The Ramona Mission and the Mission Indians* (Publications of the Women's National Indian Association, May 1889), 18.

71. Ibid., 5, 6.

72. McWilliams, *Southern California,* 75.

73. This statement draws on James Clifford's discussion of salvage ethnography in the essay "On Ethnographic Authority," in his *The Predicament of Culture: Twentieth-Century Ethnography, Literature, and Art* (Cambridge, Mass.: Harvard University Press, 1988), 21–54. See also Rydell, *All the World's a Fair;* Dippie, *The Vanishing American;* and Curtis M. Hinsley, "The World as Marketplace: Commodification of the Exotic at the World's Columbian Exposition, Chicago, 1893," in *Exhibiting Cultures: The Poetics and Politics of Museum Display,* ed. Ivan Karp and Steven D. Lavine (Washington, D.C.: Smithsonian Institution Press, 1991), 344–65.

74. James, *Through Ramona's Country,* 384–85.

75. See Alan Trachtenberg, *The Incorporation of America: Culture and Society in the Gilded Age* (New York: Hill and Wang, 1982).

76. James, *Through Ramona's Country,* 373.

77. Ibid., xvii, 379.

78. The story of southern California land tenure is actually far more complicated that I have suggested here. For further information on the 1891 Act for the Relief of the Mission Indians, see Shipek, *Pushed into the Rocks,* chap. 3.

79. Shipek, *Pushed into the Rocks,* 153.

80. James, *Through Ramona's Country,* 265–66.

81. Ibid., 159, 161, 180, 161, 164, 172.

82. Ibid., 182, 185.

83. Lowell John Bean, preface to *Delfina Cuero: Her Autobiography, An Account of Her Last Years, and Her Ethnobotanic Contributions,* by Florence Connolly Shipek (Menlo Park, Calif.: Ballena Press, 1991), 2.

84. Shipek, *Delfina Cuero,* 23.

85. Ibid., 61.

86. Lowell John Bean states such interdependence is a key "aspect of California Indian cultures." See Bean, preface to *Delfina Cuero,* 3. Also see Robert F. Heizer and Albert B. Elsasser, *The Natural World of the California Indians* (Berkeley: University of California Press, 1980) for a study of California Indians' ecology, cosmology, and material culture.

87. Shipek, *Delfina Cuero,* 29, 41.

88. Shipek notes that in order for the autobiography to be written, a key custom—"one which was difficult and mentally painful to break"—had to be broken, "the taboo on the discussion of, and the naming of, deceased relatives and friends." See ibid., 12.

89. Ibid., 67.

90. Ibid., 15.

91. Ibid., 27.

92. Jeffredo-Warden prefers this word, a Luiseño term meaning "Westerner" that was used to describe coastal dwellers, rather than the terms "Gabrielino" and "Luiseño" to describe her ethnicity, because she wishes to stress a longer tribal history than is suggested by terms associated with the Spanish mission period. See Louise Jeffredo-Warden, "Expressing the Sacred: An Indigenous Southern Californian View," in *Over the Edge: Remapping the American West,* ed. Valerie J. Matsumoto and Blake

Allmendinger (Berkeley: University of California Press, 1999), 333–35, n. 1. The reference to "ceremonial couplings" is on p. 333 of her essay.

93. Ibid., 333.

94. Phillip Round, "'There Was More to It, but That Is All I Can Remember': The Persistence of History and the *Autobiography of Delfina Cuero*," *American Indian Quarterly* 21, no. 2 (1997): 187.

95. Shipek, *Pushed into the Rocks,* 153.

96. Matt S. Meier, "North from Mexico," in *North from Mexico: The Spanish-Speaking People of the United States,* by Carey McWilliams, new ed., updated by Matt. S. Meier (New York: Praeger, 1990), 320.

97. Jackson, *Ramona,* 359.

98. Carl Gutiérrez-Jones, *Rethinking the Borderlands: Between Chicano Culture and Legal Discourse* (Berkeley: University of California Press, 1995), 69.

99. For a historical study that analyzes how Theodore Roosevelt, Owen Wister, and Frederic Remington represented the West, respectively, in historical writing, fiction, and painting in ways that both explored and exacerbated such class, race, and gender anxieties, see G. Edward White, *The Eastern Establishment and the Western Experience: The West of Frederic Remington, Theodore Roosevelt, and Owen Wister* (New Haven, Conn.: Yale University Press, 1968). See also Gail Beiderman, *Manliness and Civilization: A Cultural History of Gender and Race in the United States, 1860–1917* (Chicago: University of Chicago Press, 1995).

100. *Dictionary of American Biography,* vol. 15, ed. Dumas Malone (New York: Scribner's, 1935–36), 412.

101. William Makepeace Thayer, *Marvels of the New West: A Vivid Portrayal of the Stupendous Marvels in the Vast Wonderland of the Missouri River* (Norwich, Conn.: Henry Bill Publishing Company, 1888), 715.

102. Thayer, *Marvels of the New West,* 715.

103. For historical accounts of the ways in which federal Indian policy changed between the Dawes Severalty Act of 1887 and the Indian New Deal of 1934, see Francis Paul Prucha, *The Great Father: The United States Government and the American Indians,* abridged ed. (Lincoln: University of Nebraska Press, 1986); Prucha, *The Indians in American Society;* Kenneth R. Philp, *John Collier's Crusade for Indian Reform, 1920–1954* (Tucson: University of Arizona Press, 1977); and Patricia Nelson Limerick, *The Legacy of Conquest: The Unbroken History of the American West* (New York: Norton, 1987), 180–221.

Chapter 4

1. For biographical information on Lummis, see Edwin R. Bingham, *Charles F. Lummis: Editor of the Southwest* (San Marino, Calif.: Huntington Library Press, 1955); and Turbese Lummis Fiske and Keith Lummis, *Charles F. Lummis: The Man and His West* (Norman: University of Oklahoma Press, 1975). Franklin Walker provides an overview of Lummis's literary and editing career in his study *A Literary History of Southern California* (Berkeley: University of California Press, 1950), 132–44. For more recent discussions of Lummis, see Sherry Smith, "Charles Fletcher Lummis and the Fight for the Multicultural Southwest," in her *Reimagining Indians: Native Americans through Anglo Eyes, 1880–1940* (New York: Oxford University Press, 2000), 119–44; and Audrey Goodman, "The Tasks of Southwestern Translation: Charles Lummis at Isleta Pueblo," *Journal of the Southwest* 43, no. 2 (2001): 343–78.

2. See, for example, Adolph Bandelier, *The Southwestern Journals of Adolph F. Bandelier,* vol. 1, *1880–82,* vol. 2, *1883–84,* vol. 3, *1885–88,* ed. Charles H. Lange, Carroll L. Riley, and Elizabeth M. Lange (Albuquerque: University of New Mexico Press, 1966–75); Frank Hamilton Cushing, "My Adventures at Zuñi," *Century* 25 (1882): 191–207,

500–511, and 26 (1883): 28–47, reprinted in *Zuñi: Selected Writings of Frank Hamilton Cushing,* ed. Jesse Green (Lincoln: University of Nebraska Press, 1979), 46–134; Jesse Walter Fewkes, "The Snake Ceremonials at Walpi," *A Journal of American Ethnology and Archaeology,* vol. 4 (1894; reprint, Cambridge, Mass.: Riverside Press, 1977); and Washington Matthews, *The Mountain Chant: A Navajo Ceremony,* Bureau of American Ethnology Annual Report 5 (Washington, D.C.: Government Printing Office, 1887) and *The Night Chant: A Navaho Ceremony,* American Museum of Natural History Memoirs 6 (Anthropology Series 5) (1902; reprint, Salt Lake City: University of Utah Press, 1995).

3. For details on the development of ethnological research in the southwestern field and the growth of professionalized anthropology in the United States, see Curtis M. Hinsley Jr., *The Smithsonian and the American Indian: Making a Moral Anthropology in Victorian America* (1981; Washington, D.C.: Smithsonian Press, 1994); and Don D. Fowler, *Creating a Laboratory of Anthropology, 1846–1930* (Albuquerque: University of New Mexico Press, 2000).

4. See *Journal of the Southwest,* special issue, *Inventing the Southwest* 30, no. 4 (winter 1990). The following essays are of particular relevance to the present discussion: Barbara Babcock, "By Way of Introduction" (383–99) and "'A New Mexico Rebecca': Imaging Pueblo Women" (400–37); Curtis M. Hinsley Jr., "Authoring Authenticity" (462–78); and Marta Weigle, "Southwest Lures: Innocents Detoured, Incensed Determined" (499–540).

5. My use of *production* deliberately echoes Edward Said, *Orientalism* (New York: Random House, 1979), passim. *Orientalism* has, in turn, been a key point of reference in the above-cited work of Babcock, Hinsley, and Weigle.

6. Curtis M. Hinsley Jr., "Authoring Authenticity," 462. See also T. Jackson Lears, *No Place of Grace: Antimodernism and the Transformation of American Culture, 1880–1920,* for a study of how and why middle-class figures such as Lummis sought out intense physical and spiritual experiences at the turn of the last century.

7. Ibid., 462.

8. Charles F. Lummis, *A Tramp Across the Continent* (1892; reprint, Lincoln: University of Nebraska Press, 1982), n.p.

9. Charles F. Lummis, *A New Mexico David* (New York: Scribner's, 1891), *A Tramp Across the Continent* (1892), *Some Strange Corners of Our Country* (New York: Century Company, 1892), *The Land of Poco Tiempo* (New York: Charles Scribner's Sons, 1893), *The Spanish Pioneers* (Chicago: A. C. McClurg and Company, 1893), *The Man Who Married the Moon and Other Pueblo Indian Folk-Stories* (New York: Century Company, 1894), and *The King of the Broncos and Other Stories of New Mexico* (New York: Charles Scribner's Sons, 1897).

10. For information on contributors to *Land of Sunshine/Out West* and visitors to El Alisal, see Fiske and Lummis, *Charles F. Lummis: The Man and His West,* passim; and Bingham, *Charles F. Lummis: Editor of the Southwest,* chaps. 6 and 7.

11. Charles [F.] Lummis, *Letters from the Southwest,* ed. James R. Byrkit (Tucson: University of Arizona Press, 1991), 90.

12. Ibid., 97.

13. Raymund Paredes notes that mid-nineteenth-century Euro-American travel writers tended to emphasize the bodily characteristics of Mexican Americans as the key to ethnic and cultural character. Following the example of earlier writers, Lummis caricatured facial appearances and bodily dispositions so as to bring together stereotypical images of the sly Indian and the sleepy Spaniard in the figure of the "Greaser." See Raymund A. Paredes, "The Mexican Image in American Travel Literature, 1831–1869," *New Mexico Historical Review* 52, no. 1 (January 1977): 5–29. Also see David J. Weber, "'Scarce More than Apes:' Historical Roots of Anglo American Stereotypes of Mexicans in the Border Region," in *New Spain's Far Northern Frontier: Essays on Spain in the American West,*

1540–1821, ed. David J. Weber (Albuquerque: University of New Mexico Press, 1979), 295–307.

14. Lummis, *A Tramp Across the Continent,* 97.

15. Ibid., 75.

16. Lummis, *Letters from the Southwest,* 186.

17. Ibid., 199.

18. Ibid., 199.

19. For a study of how by "playing Indian" Euro-American men have adopted the guise of Native Americans throughout American history, see Philip J. Deloria, *Playing Indian* (New Haven, Conn.: Yale University Press, 1998). In a statement that fits Lummis's case well, Deloria writes: "In the end, Indian play was perhaps not so much about a desire to become Indian—or even to become *American*—as it was a longing for the utopian experience of being in between, of living a paradoxical moment in which absolute liberty coexisted with the absolute" (185).

20. For studies of these Eastern figures and of changing ideas of masculinity in the late nineteenth and early twentieth centuries, see, respectively, G. Edward White, *The Eastern Establishment and the Western Experience: The West of Frederic Remington, Theodore Roosevelt, and Owen Wister* (New Haven, Conn.: Yale University Press, 1968); and Gail Bederman, *Manliness and Civilization: A Cultural History of Gender and Race in the United States, 1880–1917* (Chicago: University of Chicago Press, 1995).

21. White, *The Eastern Establishment and the Western Experience,* 184–85.

22. I have borrowed the articulation of the keywords *nature, youth, manhood,* and *the state* from Donna Haraway's essay "Teddy Bear Patriarch: Taxidermy in the Garden of Eden, New York City, 1908–36," in her *Primate Visions: Gender, Race, and Nature in the World of Modern Science* (New York: Routledge, 1989), 26–58.

23. Lummis, *Letters from the Southwest,* 127.

24. Haraway, "Teddy Bear Patriarchy," 55.

25. Ibid., 42.

26. Ibid., 26.

27. Before Lummis set out on the walk, he and Dorothea had already experienced a marital separation. They had secretly married in Boston in 1880, when Lummis was attending Harvard College. After failing to graduate, Lummis departed for the Scioto Valley in Ohio to manage his father-in-law's farm while Dorothea remained in Boston to finish her medical training. The decision to leave Ohio was made not long after the couple had resumed living together. Dorothea's letters to Lummis during the initial separation make poignant reading as she sought to rationalize her love for him and what appears to have been his neglect of her. For letters written by Dorothea to Lummis, see the Dorothea Rhodes Lummis Moore Collection, the Huntington Library, San Marino, California. For a discussion of Dorothea's struggle to balance her beliefs in romantic love and duty to the institution of marriage, see Karen Lystra, *Searching the Heart: Men and Romantic Love in Nineteenth-Century America* (New York: Oxford University Press, 1989), 207–10. The absence of comment from Lummis about Dorothea also disguises the extent to which Lummis was dependent on women throughout his life for emotional support. The other side of extreme physical exertion both on the walk and in Lummis's initial years in Los Angeles was profound anxiety about his constitution. This anxiety was expressed first through partial paralysis and later through temporary blindness. See Bingham, *Charles F. Lummis: Editor of the Southwest,* chap. 1; and Fiske and Lummis, *Charles F. Lummis: The Man and His West,* passim.

28. Lummis, *A Tramp Across the Continent,* 142.

29. Lummis, *Some Strange Corners of Our Country: The Wonderland of the Southwest,* 1–2.

30. Ibid., 28.

31. Ibid., 45–46.

32. Curtis M. Hinsley Jr., "The World as Marketplace: Commodification of the Exotic at the World's Columbian Exposition, Chicago, 1893," in *Exhibiting Cultures: The Poetics and Politics of Museum Display,* ed. Ivan Karp and Steven D. Lavine (Washington, D.C.: Smithsonian Press, 1991), 344–65. Hinsley notes that Frederick Ward Putnam, director and curator of the Peabody Museum at Harvard, was appointed as head of the Department of Ethnology and Archaeology at the Chicago World's Fair. Franz Boas, who later became one of the major proponents of professionalized anthropology in the United States, was Putnam's chief assistant.

33. Ibid., 356.

34. Lummis, *Some Strange Corners of Our Country,* 5.

35. See Edwin L. Wade, "The Ethnic Art Market in the American Southwest, 1880–1980," in *Objects and Others: Essays on Museums and Material Culture,* ed. George W. Stocking Jr. (Madison: University of Wisconsin Press, 1985), 167–91.

36. There is a growing amount of scholarship on tourism in the Southwest and its impact on southwestern Native American and Hispano cultures. See, for example, Leah Dilworth, *Imagining Indians in the Southwest: Persistent Visions of a Primitive Past* (Washington, D.C.: Smithsonian Institution Press, 1996), particularly chap. 2; Sylvia Rodríguez, "Art, Tourism, and Race Relations in Taos," in *Discovered Country: Tourism and Survival in the American West,* ed. Scott Norris (Albuquerque: Stone Ladder Press, 1994), 143–60; Hal R. Rothman, *Devil's Bargains: Tourism in the Twentieth-Century American West* (Lawrence: University Press of Kansas, 1999), 50–112; Marta Weigle and Barbara A. Babcock, eds., *The Great Southwest of the Fred Harvey Company* (Phoenix: The Heard Museum, 1996); and essays by Barbara Babcock, Curtis M. Hinsley Jr., and Marta Weigle that are collected in *Journal of the Southwest,* special issue, *Inventing the Southwest* 30, no. 4 (winter 1990) (full references are in note 4 above). See chapter 6 of the present study for further discussion of cultural tourism in the Southwest between the 1880s and 1930s.

37. Lummis, *Some Strange Corners of Our Country,* 165. Note that Pueblo Indians and, to a lesser extent, Navajos were in large measure valorized through their association with Spanish colonialism.

38. In this regard Lummis both drew on and contributed to the idea that the social standing of elite Hispanos rested in large part on their "pure" European blood. See David G. Gutiérrez, *Walls and Mirrors: Mexican Americans, Mexican Immigrants, and the Politics of Ethnicity* (Berkeley: University of California Press, 1995), 28–38, for a discussion of how ethnic awareness among Mexican Americans developed in the aftermath of the U.S.-Mexican War.

39. In a diary entry for the week of September 6–12, 1888, Lummis noted that "'The Penitentes'" article, seven thousand words long, was written in one day. In an entry for the following week he noted that *Century* had refused publication and that the article later came out in *The Cosmopolitan.* See "Diary Extracts," Charles Fletcher Lummis Collection, The Southwest Museum, Highland Park, Calif. These typed extracts from Lummis's much longer diary, which was handwritten in Spanish, were made late in his life as he prepared to write an autobiography (which he never finished).

40. Charles F. Lummis, *The Land of Poco Tiempo* (1892; reprint, Albuquerque: University of New Mexico Press, 1952), 56.

41. Information on the Fraternity is drawn from Marta Weigle, *Brothers of Light, Brothers of Blood: The Penitentes of the Southwest* (Albuquerque: University of New Mexico Press, 1976).

42. Ibid., xviii.

43. Ibid.

44. Ibid., xix.

45. Lummis, *The Land of Poco Tiempo,* 63.

46. Ibid., 77.
47. Ibid., 62.
48. Much the same tone is found in Lummis's diary writing. After sending his article on the Penitentes to *Century,* his fascination with the Brothers' practices continued. In an entry for September 12–18, 1888, Lummis wrote that he had photographed a morada and some Brothers. He added: "That night with a brave boy, burgle the Morada and steal the 2 only Penitente scourges ever acquired by museum or collector. We are detected and fired at with rifles 6 times as we bound over the rocky ridge behind the Morada. Luckily, they did not recognize us." See "Diary Extracts," Charles Fletcher Lummis Collection, Southwest Museum, Highland Park, Calif.
49. Lummis, *The Land of Poco Tiempo,* 62.
50. Ibid., 64.
51. Ibid., 66.
52. Ibid., 71.
53. Ibid., 75. The photograph may well be a fake. If indeed the crucifixion scene was contrived for the photograph, this only adds another level of invention to Lummis's "creation" of the Southwest.
54. The full sentence reads: "Romance is the chief riches of any people—though we begin to understand it only as romance fades from the world." Charles F. Lummis, *The Spanish Pioneers and the California Missions* (Chicago: A. C. McClurg and Co., 1930), 299.
55. See Fiske and Lummis, *Charles F. Lummis: The Man and His West,* 75.
56. Quoted in ibid., 82.
57. Villard funded half of the planned three-year expedition before his bankruptcy. While in Peru and Bolivia, Lummis conducted archaeological fieldwork, photographed, and collected fabrics, skulls, and other ethnological objects. Many of these objects found their way into Lummis's home, El Alisal, and the Southwest Museum. See Bingham, *Charles F. Lummis: Editor of the Southwest,* 14. For examples of Lummis's writing at this time, see, in addition to *The Gold Fish of Gran Chimu* (Boston: Lamson, Wolffe, and Co., 1896) and *The Enchanted Burro* (Chicago: Way and Williams, 1897), his celebratory articles on "Spanish American" subject matter, such as "The Spanish-American Face," *Land of Sunshine* 2, no. 2 (January 1895): 20–21, and "Something about Adobe," *Land of Sunshine* 2, no. 3 (February 1895): 48–50; and his highly romantic poems "The Spanish Lesson," *Land of Sunshine* 2, no. 2 (January 1895): 26, and "At the Old Hacienda," *Land of Sunshine* 2, no. 5 (April 1895): 77. Reporting the publication of *The Gold Fish of Gran Chimu,* Lummis commented dryly: "Those who like the author's other books will probably like this; those who don't, probably won't." See Charles F. Lummis, "That Which Is Written," *Land of Sunshine* 14, no. 4 (March 1896): 187. Late in 1895, he announced the beginning of a new campaign to preserve southern California's crumbling missions. "It is only in the Only Country in the World," he fumed, "that such precious things are despised and neglected and left to be looted by the storm and the tourist." See Charles F. Lummis, "In the Lion's Den," *Land of Sunshine* 4, no. 1 (December 1895): 43–44. Lummis went on to become one of the founding members of the Landmarks Club. For an overview of the foundation and work of the Landmarks Club, see Bingham, *Charles F. Lummis: Editor of the Southwest,* 103–11.
58. Fiske and Lummis, *Charles F. Lummis: The Man and His West,* 87.
59. See Kevin Starr, *Inventing the Dream: California through the Progressive Era* (New York: Oxford University Press, 1985), particularly chap. 3, "Art and Life in the Turn-of-the-Century Southland," 64–98.
60. "Editorial," *Land of Sunshine* 1, no. 1 (June 1894): 12.
61. Charles Dwight Willard, "The New Editor," *Land of Sunshine* 2, no. 1 (December 1894): 12.
62. Charles F. Lummis, "Editorial Column," *Land of Sunshine* 2, no. 2 (January 1895): 35.

63. For discussions of Lummis's editorship of *Land of Sunshine/Out West,* see Bingham, *Charles F. Lummis: Editor of the Southwest;* and Walker, *A Literary History of Southern California,* 137–44.

64. Charles F. Lummis, "In the Lion's Den," *Land of Sunshine* 4, no. 1 (December 1895): 43.

65. Lummis, "The Spanish-American Face," 21.

66. Lummis, "Editorial Column," 35.

67. Charles F. Lummis, *The Home of Ramona: Photographs of Camulos, the fine old Spanish Estate described by Mrs. Helen Hunt Jackson, as the Home of Ramona* (Los Angeles: Chas. F. Lummis and Company, 1888), n.p.

68. See Christina Wielus Mead, "Las Fiestas de Los Angeles: A Survey of the Yearly Celebrations, 1894–1898," *Southern California Quarterly* 31, nos. 1 and 2 (March and June 1949): 61–113; and Carey McWilliams, *Southern California: An Island on the Land* (Salt Lake City, Utah: Peregrine Smith, 1973), 70–83.

69. Anon., *The Spanish Fiesta,* n.d., n.p. A copy of this small pamphlet is in the Huntington Library, San Marino, Calif.

70. Charles F. Lummis, "Letter to E. S. Babcock," published in the *San Diego Union,* March 4, 1894, reprinted in *The Spanish Fiesta,* n.p.

71. Frank Van Vleck [probably pseudonym for Charles F. Lummis], "La Fiesta de Los Angeles, 1895," *Land of Sunshine* 2, no. 5 (April 1895), 83.

72. Ibid., 84.

73. See Theodore S. Jojola, "Charles F. Lummis and Isleta Pueblo," unpublished paper.

74. See ibid., 3–4, for details. During his residency at Isleta Pueblo between 1888 and 1892, Lummis had made strong ties with both the wealthy Abeita family, through whom he gained access to ceremonials and restricted tribal knowledge, and the non-Indian traders and missionaries who also lived in the pueblo locale. These ties suggest the degree to which Lummis associated with Pueblo "progressives."

75. For Mike Davis, the accruing of cultural capital for Los Angeles by Lummis and other agents who combined literary skills with promotional outlets involved the manipulation of both past and present "realities" in order to create a picture of a city that served as "the sunny refuge of White Protestant America in an age of labor upheaval and the mass immigration of the Catholic and Jewish poor from Eastern and Southern Europe." See Mike Davis, *City of Quartz: Excavating the Future in Los Angeles* (New York: Random House, 1992), 30.

76. Charles F. Lummis, "In the Lion's Den," *Land of Sunshine* 4, no. 2 (January 1896): 89.

77. Today the Southwest Museum in Highland Park, a few miles from downtown Los Angeles, is surrounded not by the Anglo population that Lummis envisioned, but by a predominantly Latino community. Thus the "Spanish" past resurfaces, albeit in quite changed form, in the multicultural present.

Chapter 5

1. Burbank to Ayer, 12 March 1897, Fort Sill, Oklahoma Territory, Ayer Collection, Newberry Library (henceforth cited as "AC, NL").

2. Burbank to Ayer, 28 April 1897, Fort Sill, Oklahoma Territory, AC, NL.

3. M. Melissa Wolfe, "'Out West Where I Belong': A Biography of Elbridge Ayer Burbank (1858–1949)" in *American Indian Portraits: Elbridge Ayer Burbank in the West (1897–1910),* by M. Melissa Wolfe (Youngstown, Ohio: Butler Institute of American Art, 2000), 14; and John R. Kiser, *Many Brushes: The Life of Elbridge Ayer Burbank,* unpublished manuscript, passim.

4. Burbank to Ayer, 2 July 1897, Crow Agency, Montana Territory, AC, NL.

5. Burbank to Ayer, 21 August 1897, Crow Agency, Montana Territory, AC, NL.

6. Ibid.
7. Elbridge Ayer Burbank, "Geronimo; Chief of the Apaches," *The Border* 1, no. 1 (November 1908): 1–5, 13.
8. See Frederick Hoxie, "Businessman, Bibliophile, and Patron: Edward E. Ayer and His Collection of American Indian Art," *Great Plains Quarterly* 9, no. 2 (spring 1989): 78–88; Alex Nemerov, "Doing the 'Old' America: The Image of the American West, 1880–1920," in *The West as America: Reinterpreting Images of the Frontier, 1820–1920,* ed. William H. Truettner (Washington, D.C.: Smithsonian Institution Press, 1991): 285–343; and Wolfe, *American Indian Portraits: Elbridge Ayer Burbank in the West (1897–1910).*
9. The Butler Institute of Art in Youngstown, Ohio, mounted *American Indian Portraits: Elbridge Ayer Burbank in the West (1897–1909),* a major exhibition of Burbank's art, between September and October 2000. Subsequently the exhibition traveled to the Montclair Art Museum in Montclair, New Jersey; the Panhandle-Plains Historical Museum in Canyon, Texas; and the Newberry Library in Chicago, Illinois. The accompanying catalogue is the aforementioned Wolfe, *American Indian Portraits: Elbridge Ayer Burbank in the West (1897–1910).*
10. Charles Francis Browne, "Elbridge Ayer Burbank: A Painter of Indian Portraits," *Brush and Pencil* 2 (1898): 19.
11. Charles Lummis, "Painting the First Americans: Burbank's Indian Portraits," *Land of Sunshine* 12, no. 6 (May 1900): 340.
12. Burbank to Ayer, 2 February 1904, Yuma, Arizona Territory, AC, NL.
13. For studies of changes in Euro-American ways of seeing Native people at the turn of the last century, see Robert F. Berkhofer Jr., *The White Man's Indian: Images of the American Indian from Columbus to the Present* (New York: Random House, 1979), parts 1 and 2; and Brian W. Dippie, *The Vanishing American: White Attitudes and U.S. Indian Policy* (Lawrence: University Press of Kansas, 1982).
14. M. Melissa Wolfe, "Elbridge Ayer Burbank," *American National Biography,* vol. 3, ed. John A Garraty and Mark C. Carnes (New York: Oxford University Press, 1999), 925–26.
15. Frank Lockwood, *The Life of Edward E. Ayer* (Chicago: A. C. McClurg and Company, 1929), 179.
16. Browne, "Elbridge Ayer Burbank: A Painter of Indian Portraits," 20.
17. Ibid., 16.
18. In one early letter to Ayer from Fort Sill, Burbank announced that he intended to paint images of African Americans before returning to Chicago. Burbank to Ayer, 18 April 1897, Fort Sill, Oklahoma Territory, AC, NL.
19. Burbank to Ayer, 16 January 1899, Darlington, Oklahoma Territory, AC, NL.
20. Burbank to Ayer, 21 March 1897, Fort Sill, Oklahoma Territory, AC, NL.
21. Ibid.
22. Burbank to Ayer, 25 March 1897, Fort Sill, Oklahoma Territory, AC, NL.
23. Many of the earlier oil paintings were only 6" x 8" in size, although Burbank came to prefer the 9" x 13" format. In December 1898, he reported to Ayer that he had decided to stick with the 9" x 13" format because while it took just as long to paint 6" x 8" images he earned $50 extra for the larger images. Burbank to Ayer, 21 December 1898, Darlington, Oklahoma Territory, AC, NL.
24. George Wharton James, "A Noted Painter of Indian Types," *The Craftsman* 7 (October 1904–March 1905): 280.
25. Brian Dippie, *The Vanishing American: White Attitudes and U.S. Indian Policy* (1982; reprint, Lawrence: University Press of Kansas, 1991), 25.
26. M. Melissa Wolfe, "Posed, Composed, and Imposed: Defining the Indian in the Portraits by E. A. Burbank" in *American Indian Portraits: Elbridge Ayer Burbank in the West (1897–1910),* 38. See also M. Melissa Wolfe, "The Influence of Ethnography on the

Indian Portraits of Elbridge Ayer Burbank" (Master's thesis, The Ohio State University, 1997), passim.

27. Everett Maxwell, "The Art of Elbridge A. Burbank," *Fine Arts Journal* 22, no. 1 (January 1910): 5.

28. Elbridge A. Burbank and Ernest Royce, *Burbank among the Indians* (Caldwell, Idaho: The Caxton Printers, 1944), 57; Burbank to Ayer, 23 December 1897, Keams Canyon, Arizona Territory, AC, NL.

29. Burbank to Ayer, 20 March 1898, Flagstaff, Arizona, AC, NL.

30. Ibid.

31. Ibid.

32. For discussions of how Hopis have viewed outside visitors in the late nineteenth and early twentieth centuries, see Peter Whiteley, *Rethinking Hopi Ethnography* (Washington, D.C.: Smithsonian Institution Press, 1998), chaps. 1 and 6.

33. Burbank to Ayer, 23 March 1898, Needles, California, AC, NL.

34. Burbank to Ayer, 14 June 1898, Ignacio, Colorado, AC, NL.

35. Burbank to Ayer, 8 May 1898, San Carlos, Arizona, AC, NL.

36. *Aztec Calendar, July to December 1899, Santa Fe Route.* This is a bound volume in the Ayer Collection, Newberry Library, which consists of a cover and a color plate accompanying each of the six months. The images are copyrighted "*Brush and Pencil,* Chicago, 1899."

37. Burbank to Ayer, 30 May 1898, Santa Monica, California, AC, NL.

38. Burbank to Ayer, 8 June 1898, Yuma, Arizona, AC, NL.

39. Burbank to Ayer, 2 September 1904, Polacca, Arizona, AC, NL.

40. Burbank to Ayer, 31 March 1904, Yuma, Arizona, AC, NL.

41. At the end of 1906 Burbank grew anxious that Ayer would no longer purchase the Conté crayon drawings. Burbank to Ayer, 29 December 1906, Fort Klamath, Oregon, AC, NL.

42. Burbank to Ayer, December 29, 1906, Fort Klamath, Oregon, AC, NL.

43. Burbank to Ayer, 14 January 1907, Los Angeles, AC, NL.

44. See Burbank Ephemera, Huntington Library, San Marino, California.

45. Burbank to Ayer, 8 September 1909, Ganado, Arizona, AC, NL; Martha Blue, *Indian Trader: The Life and Times of J. L. Hubbell* (Walnut, Calif.: Kiva Publishing, 2000), 210.

46. Burbank to Hubbell, 2 February 1911, Hubbell Papers, Special Collections Library, University of Arizona, Tucson, Arizona.

47. Lockwood, *The Life of Edward E. Ayer,* v–vi.

48. Ibid., 69.

49. Quoted in ibid., 49.

50. For details, see ibid., 44–59.

51. Ibid., 91.

52. Ibid., 78. It is worth noting that Lockwood uses terms such as "plunder" (79) and "ransacked" (83) to make digs at Ayer's "exuberant ardor" (79) for collecting. In what one hopes is a joke, he recounts a ghastly episode when Ayer placed the still-moist scalp of a murdered Indian in his wife's handbag while on business in Mexico (79).

53. Ibid., 78–79.

54. Ibid., 81.

55. Hoxie, "Businessman, Bibliophile, and Patron," 79.

56. Ibid., 82.

57. This disinclination helps explain why on two occasions—in 1909 and 1921—Ayer refused to purchase Edward Curtis's epic work *The North American Indian.* Given the significant standing of *The North American Indian* among today's buyers and critics, it is perhaps ironic that Ayer was prepared to bankroll work by his nephew that was not planned to result in a publishing project that matched the scope and ambition of Curtis's project. When Curtis's trustees approached Ayer the second time to purchase

his work, Ayer pointedly made reference to his own vast holdings in documents, books, art, and material culture: "it would take at least ten to fifteen of the best anthropologists in America twenty years to write the history of the North American Indian as it should be done and the work of a single individual in this line I considered would be valueless to the original work in my library." See Hoxie, "Businessman, Bibliophile, and Patron," 82; and Mick Gidley, *Edward S. Curtis and the North American Indian Incorporated* (Cambridge, UK: Cambridge University Press, 1998), 125–26, 137.

58. Burbank to Ayer, 6 May 1897, Fort Sill, Oklahoma Territory, AC, NL.
59. Hoxie, "Businessman, Bibliophile, and Patron," 85.
60. Press cutting in the Ayer Collection, Newberry Library. No further bibliographical information was available.
61. Burbank to Ayer, 5 May 1901, Darlington, Oklahoma Territory, AC, NL.
62. Burbank to Ayer, 29 July 1897, Crow Agency, Montana Territory, AC, NL.
63. Burbank to Ayer, 19 September 1899, Pine Ridge, South Dakota, AC, NL.
64. Burbank to Ayer, 4 February 1902, Philadelphia, AC, NL.
65. Burbank to Ayer, 22 February 1902, Philadelphia, AC, NL.
66. Joseph G. Butler Jr., *Recollections of Men and Events: An Autobiography* (New York: G. P. Putnam's Sons, 1925), 89.
67. Ibid., 9.
68. Ibid., 36.
69. Ibid., 171.
70. Ibid., 188.
71. Ibid., 101.
72. Blue, *Indian Trader: The Life and Times of J. L. Hubbell,* 207–11.
73. Burbank to Hubbell, 10 April 1902, Rockford, Illinois, Hubbell Papers, Special Collections Library, University of Arizona, Tucson, Arizona.
74. Hoxie, "Businessman, Bibliophile, and Patron," 85.
75. See Wolfe, "'Out West Where I Belong': A Biography of Elbridge Ayer Burbank (1858–1949)," 17.
76. Burbank to Ayer, 28 September 1903, San Francisco, California, AC, NL.
77. In 1950, a year after Burbank's death, Blanche wrote to thank the Butler Institute of Art for sending reviews of an exhibition of her former husband's work. She remembered with fondness a visit she had made to the museum almost fifty years before. Notably she signed herself "Blanche A. Burbank (Mrs E. A. Burbank)" even though she had been divorced over forty years and had long since remarried. See Blanche Burbank to the Butler Institute of Art, 31 March 1950, Elbridge Ayer Burbank Ephemera, Butler Institute of Art, Youngstown, Ohio. See also Wolfe, "'Out West Where I Belong': A Biography of Elbridge Ayer Burbank (1858–1949)," 20.
78. Burbank to Ayer, 10 December 1903, Ukiah, California, AC, NL.
79. See Wolfe, "'Out Where I Belong': A Biography of Elbridge Ayer Burbank (1858–1949)," 17–18; and Kiser, *Many Brushes,* passim.
80. This note is housed in Burbank Ephemera, Huntington Library, San Marino, California.
81. Anon., "The Napa State Hospital Mystery Painter," *The Napa Register* (no further details are available), Burbank Ephemera, Huntington Library, San Marino, California.
82. George Watson Cole to Edward E. Ayer, 5 June 1922, Huntington Library, San Marino, California. Burbank Ephemera, Huntington Library.
83. Edward E. Ayer to Huntington Library, 10 December 1924, Burbank Ephemera, Huntington Library, San Marino, California.
84. Wolfe, "'Out West Where I Belong': A Biography of Elbridge Ayer Burbank (1858–1949)," 18.
85. Burbank to Leslie Bliss, Huntington Library, 9 and 14 August 1934, San Francisco, California, Burbank Ephemera, Huntington Library, San Marino, California.

86. Leslie Bliss to Burbank, 17 August 1934, Huntington Library, San Marino, California. Burbank Ephemera, Huntington Library.
87. Burbank to Ayer, 22 December 1902, Rosebud, South Dakota, AC, NL.
88. Burbank to Ayer, 25 March 1901, Darlington, Oklahoma Territory, AC, NL.
89. Burbank to Ayer, 29 April 1901, Darlington, Oklahoma Territory, AC, NL.
90. Burbank and Royce, *Burbank among the Indians,* 201.
91. Ibid., 201.
92. Neil Hitt, "Forgotten Fame, Poverty, Death: This Is How E. A. Burbank, 90, Painter of Indians, Came to the End of His Trail," n.p. No further bibliographical information is available, but probably the article was published in the *San Francisco Chronicle* in May 1949 just after Burbank's death. Burbank Ephemera, Huntington Library, San Marino, California.
93. Ibid., n.p.
94. Burbank and Royce, *Burbank among the Indians,* 28, 38.
95. Ibid., 18.
96. Edward A. Burbank, "The Apache Indian," *Carter's Monthly* 15, no. 5 (June 1899): 463.
97. Burbank and Royce, *Burbank among the Indians,* 31.
98. Ibid., 31.
99. Quoted in Lockwood, *The Life of Edward E. Ayer,* 234.
100. Quoted in Dippie, *The Vanishing American,* 305.
101. Quoted in Francis Paul Prucha, *The Indians in American Society: From the Revolutionary War to the Present* (Berkeley: University of California Press, 1985), 67.
102. Philp, *John Collier's Crusade for Indian Reform,* chaps. 6 and 7.
103. Hoxie, "Businessman, Bibliophile, and Patron," 79.
104. Ironically the "civilized" virtues Burbank praised in Geronimo were typical of Chiricahua society. Geronimo's acts of kindness in the home were typical of Chiracahua men and should not be taken as a sign that he had come to accept white values he considered superior to those of his own society. See Angie Debo, *Geronimo* (Norman: University of Oklahoma Press, 1976), 382.
105. Burbank to Ayer, 28 March 1897, Fort Sill, Oklahoma Territory, AC, NL.
106. Debo, *Geronimo,* chaps. 20 and 21.
107. Burbank and Royce, *Burbank among the Indians,* 58.

Chapter 6

1. Adam Clark Vroman, "Photo-Diary of the Hopi Snake Dance" (1895). I have given this title to Vroman's untitled photo-diary. It is housed in the Photograph file at the Huntington Library, San Marino, California.
2. Leo Crane, *Indians of the Enchanted Desert* (Boston: Little, Brown and Company, 1925), 254.
3. D. H. Lawrence, "Just Back from the Snake-Dance—Tired Out," *Laughing Horse* (1924). Reprinted in Sharyn R. Udall, ed., *Spud Johnson and Laughing Horse* (Albuquerque: University of New Mexico Press, 1994), 359.
4. Quoted by Udall in her commentary on Lawrence's contributions to *Laughing Horse.* See ibid., 360.
5. *Indian Detours off the Beaten Track in the Great Southwest* (Chicago: Rand McNally and Company, 1936), 5.
6. Hal R. Rothman, *Devil's Bargains: Tourism in the Twentieth-Century American West* (Lawrence: University Press of Kansas, 1998), 11, 13.
7. For discussions of tourism in the Southwest, see Dilworth, *Imagining Indians in the Southwest,* 77–124; Earl Pomeroy, *In Search of the Golden West: The Tourist in Western America* (1957; reprint, Lincoln: University of Nebraska Press, 1990); Rothman, *Devil's*

Bargains, 50–112; Marta Weigle and Barbara A. Babcock, eds., *The Great Southwest of the Fred Harvey Company* (Phoenix, Ariz.: The Heard Museum, 1996); and the essays by Sylvia Rodríguez ("Art, Tourism, and Race Relations in Taos," 143–60), Dean MacCannell ("Tradition's Next Step," 161–79), Barbara Babcock, "Mudwomen and Whitemen," 180–95), Mark Neumann ("The Commercial Canyon," 196–209), and Marta Weigle ("Selling the Southwest," 210–24) in *Discovered Land: Tourism and Survival in the American West,* ed. Scott Norris (Albuquerque: Stone Ladder Press, 1994). The term "staged encounters" deliberately echoes Dean MacCannell's concept of "staged authenticity." MacCannell uses the latter term to describe the presentation of "traditional" aspects of tribal life for tourist consumers. Typically such presentations cater to the expectations and desires of tourists and necessarily reflect an uneven power relationship between "traditional" and "modern" cultures. See MacCannell, *The Tourist: A New Theory of the Leisure Class* (New York: Schocken Books, 1976), 91–107.

8. Mabel Dodge Luhan to Elizabeth Shepley Sergeant, 22 February [no year given, but probably 1935], Taos, New Mexico, Elizabeth Shepley Sergeant Papers, Beinecke Rare Book and Manuscript Library, Yale University, New Haven, Connecticut.

9. Austin, "Speech of Mary Austin before the National Popular Government League on the Burson [*sic*] Bill, Washington, D.C., Jan. 17, 1923," 20, Mary Austin Collection, Huntington Library, San Marino, California.

10. John Gregory Bourke, *The Snake-Dance of the Moquis of Arizona: Being a Narrative of a Journey from Santa Fe, New Mexico, to the Villages of the Moqui Indians of Arizona* (1884; reprint, Tucson: University of Arizona Press, 1984), 1, 56–57. See also Joseph C. Porter, *Paper Medicine Man: John Gregory Bourke and His American West* (Norman: University of Oklahoma Press, 1986), 100–07, for an account of Bourke's journey to Walpi.

11. Bourke, *The Snake-Dance of the Moquis of Arizona,* 105, 128.

12. Ibid., 182.

13. Ethnological and travel accounts of the Hopi Snake Dance from the late nineteenth and early twentieth centuries abound. They include George A. Dorsey, *Indians of the Southwest* (N.p.: Passenger Department, Atchison, Topeka, and Santa Fe Railway, 1903), 139–55; George A. Dorsey and H. R. Voth, "The Mishongnovi Ceremonies of the Antelope and Snake Fraternities," in *Publications of the Field Columbian Museum Anthropological Series* (1902; reprint, New York: Kraus, 1968), 159–262; Jesse Walter Fewkes, "The Snake Ceremonials at Walpi," in *A Journal of American Ethnology and Archaeology,* vol. 4 (1894; reprint, Cambridge, Mass.: Riverside Press, 1977); Walter Hough, *The Moki Snake Dance: A Popular Account of That Unparalleled Dramatic Pagan Ceremony of the Pueblo Indians of Tusayan, Arizona, with Incidental Mention of their Lives and Customs* (Chicago: Passenger Department, Santa Fe Route, 1900); Alexander Stephen, *Hopi Journal of Alexander M. Stephen,* ed. Elsie Clews Parsons (New York: Columbia University Press, 1936); George Wharton James, *The Indians of the Painted Desert Region: Hopis, Navahoes, Wallapais, Havasupais* (Boston: Little, Brown and Company, 1903), 102–23; Charles Fletcher Lummis, *Some Strange Corners of Our Country* (1892; reprint, Tucson: University of Arizona Press, 1989), 43–57; Charles Francis Saunders, *Finding the Worthwhile in the Southwest* (New York: Robert M. McBridge and Company, 1918), 116–29. For photographic images of the ritual, see Patricia Janis Broder, *Shadows on Glass: The Indian World of Ben Wittick* (Savage, Md.: Rowman and Littlefield, 1990); Kate Cory, *The Hopi Photographs, 1905–1912,* ed. Marnie Gaede (Albuquerque: University of New Mexico Press, 1988); Edward S. Curtis, *Indian Days of the Long Ago* (Yonkers, N.Y.: World Book Company, 1915), 114–28; Curtis, *The North American Indian,* vol. 12, *The Hopi* (Norwood, Mass: The Plimpton Press, 1922); Curtis, "Photographs of Hopi Indians," Beinecke Rare Book and Manuscript Library, Yale University, New Haven, Connecticut; Earle Forrest, "Hopi Photography (1906–08)," Photographic Archive, Huntington Library, San Marino, California, and *The Snake Dance of the Hopi Indians* (Los Angeles: Westernlore Press, 1961); Sumner

Matteson, *Cliff Dwellings, Pueblo Ruins, and Indian Life in the Southwest* (1903), Beinecke Rare Book and Manuscript Library, Yale University, New Haven, Connecticut; Louis B. Casagrande and Phillips Bourne, eds., *Side Trips: The Photography of Sumner W. Matteson, 1898–1908* (Milwaukee, Wisc.: Milwaukee Public Museum and the Science Museum of Minnesota, 1983); George L. Rose, *Photographic Album of a Trip to the Grand Canyon and Hopi Pueblos*, Beinecke Rare Book and Manuscript Library, Yale University, New Haven, Connecticut. A representative painting of the Snake Dance by E. Irving Couse appears in John F. Huckel, *American Indians: First Families of the Southwest* (Albuquerque, N.M.: Fred Harvey Indian Department, 1934). For recent academic discussions of representations of the Hopi Snake Dance, see Leah Dilworth, *Imagining Indians in the Southwest: Persistent Visions of a Primitive Past* (Washington, D.C.: Smithsonian Institution Press, 1996), 21–75; Lee Clark Mitchell, *Witnesses to a Vanishing America: The Nineteenth-Century Response* (Princeton, N.J.: Princeton University Press, 1981), 111–50; Sharyn R. Udall, "The Irresistible Other: Hopi Ritual Drama and Euro-American Audiences," in her *Contested Terrain: Myth and Meaning in Southwest Art* (Albuquerque: University of New Mexico Press, 1996), 31–42; Peter M. Whiteley, "The End of Anthropology (at Hopi)?" in his *Rethinking Hopi Ethnography* (Washington, D.C.: Smithsonian Institution Press, 1998), 163–87.

14. For information on photographers who traveled to the Hopi mesas from southern California, see Mitchell, *Witnesses to a Vanishing America*, 111–50; and Alan H. Jutzi, "Southern California Photographers and the Indians of the Southwest, 1888–1910," unpublished paper.

15. See Dilworth, Imagining Indians in the Southwest, 72.

16. Arlette Frigout, "Hopi Ceremonial Organization," in *Handbook of North American Indians*, vol. 9, *Southwest*, ed. Alfonso Ortiz, gen. ed. William Sturtevant (Washington, D.C.: Smithsonian Institution Press, 1979), 564.

17. Walter Hough, *The Hopi Indians* (Cedar Rapids, Iowa: The Torch Press, 1915), 156.

18. Ibid., 155.

19. Hough, *The Moki Snake Dance*, 54.

20. James, *The Indians of the Painted Desert Region*, 102, 104.

21. A. C. Vroman, "The Moki Snake Dance," *Photo-Era* 6, no. 4 (April 1901): 347–48.

22. See A. C. Vroman, "Photography in the Great South-West," *Photo-Era* 6, no. 1 (January 1901): 225–32.

23. For inventory of equipment and supplies in 1895, see William Webb and Robert A. Weinstein, *Dwellers at the Source: Southwestern Indian Photographs of A. C. Vroman, 1895–1904* (Albuquerque: University of New Mexico Press, 1987), 205–06.

24. Vroman's photographs are featured in an edition of Helen Hunt Jackson's *Ramona* that was published by Little, Brown and Company of Boston in 1913.

25. See Webb and Weinstein, *Dwellers at the Source*, 1–25, for details.

26. Jutzi notes the photographs were given to Rust by Vroman. See Jutzi, "Southern California Photographers and the Indians of the Southwest, 1888–1910," 25.

27. See Horacio Nelson Rust, "The Moqui Snake Dance," *Land of Sunshine* 4, no. 2 (January 1896): 70–76.

28. Vroman followed the pattern of his time in referring to Mrs Lowe in terms of her husband's interests. Professor Thaddeus Lowe was a noted scientist in Pasadena who did not accompany his wife on this journey.

29. Vroman, "Photo-Diary of the Hopi Snake Dance," n.p.

30. See Frederick J. Dockstader, "Hopi History, 1850–1940," in *Handbook of North American Indians*, vol. 9, *Southwest*, ed. Alfonso Ortiz, gen. ed. William Sturtevant (Washington, D.C.: Smithsonian Institution Press, 1979), 524–32.

31. Webb and Weinstein, *Dwellers at the Source*, 15.

32. See ibid., 24.

33. For discussions of water policy in the West, see Marc Reisner, *Cadillac Desert: The American West and Its Disappearing Water* (New York: Penguin, 1987); John Walton, *Western Times and Water Wars: State, Culture, and Rebellion in California* (Berkeley: University of California Press, 1992); and Donald Worster, *Rivers of Empire: Water, Aridity, and the Growth of the American West* (New York: Oxford University Press, 1985).

34. Dockstadter, "Hopi History, 1850–1940," 526.

35. This information is drawn from a brochure advertising the thirty-third season of Monsen lecturers. See Frederick I. Monsen, *The Frederick Monsen Lectures* (Rochester, N.Y.: Eastman Kodak Company, 1925). The remaining lectures advertised are "The Indians of the Enchanted Desert," "The Lure of the Desert," "The Lure of the Tropics," and "Pioneers of the Great West." In addition, the titles of a further twelve lectures that are not described in the brochure are given. These include talks on Egypt, Columbus, the Land of the Cliff Dwellers, Mission Trails in California, the Colorado River, and Norway.

36. While this quote is drawn from *The Frederick Monsen Lectures* brochure cited above, it does appear to be an accurate reflection of audience responses to Monsen's lectures.

37. Frederick Monsen, "The Destruction of Our Indians: What Civilization Is Doing to Extinguish an Ancient and Highly Intelligent Race by Taking Away Its Arts, Industries, and Religion," *The Craftsman* 11, no. 6 (March 1907): 683.

38. Ibid., 689–90.

39. Louis Akin, "Frederick Monsen of the Desert—The Man Who Began Eighteen Years Ago to Live and Record the Life of Hopiland," *The Craftsman* 11, no. 6 (March 1907): 681.

40. In a separate article Akin gladly confessed to not having completed many canvases during his year at Hopi because "[t]here was too much of living interest in this new world that I found myself a part of." He appears to have become too much of a participant in Hopi life to remain a mere observer of it. See Louis Akin, "Hopi Indians—Gentle Folk: A People without Need for Courts, Jails, or Asylums," *The Craftsman* 10, no. 3 (June 1906): 321.

41. Frederick I. Monsen, "Picturing Indians with the Camera," *Photo-Era* 25, no. 4 (October 1910): 165.

42. Frederick I. Monsen, "Pueblos of the Painted Desert: How the Hopi Build Their Community Dwellings on the Cliffs," *The Craftsman* 12, no. 1 (August 1907): 21.

43. Frederick I. Monsen, "The Primitive Folk of the Desert: Splendid Physical Development that yet Shows Many of the Characteristics of an Earlier Race than Our Own," *The Craftsman* 12, no. 2 (May 1907): 164, 175.

44. Ibid., 173.

45. Ibid.

46. Frederick I. Monsen, *With a Kodak in the Land of the Navajo* (Rochester, N.Y.: Eastman Kodak Company, 1909), 20. While Monsen's photography might well be taken as predatory, he was by no means the only photographer using a concealed camera around this time. Compare, for example, Paul Strand's photographs of people walking the streets of Manhattan in 1917. Strand's documentary work was influenced by the social welfare imagery created by the photographer Lewis Hine.

47. Monsen, "The Destruction of Our Indians," 684.

48. Anthropologist Jill Sweet, who during the 1970s and 1980s conducted research on the impact of contemporary tourism on Pueblo Indians in New Mexico, notes that even in the case of lifelong friendships "Anglo friends never become fully accepted or formally adopted members of a Pueblo community." Jill D. Sweet, "'Let 'em Loose': Pueblo Indian Management of Tourism," *American Indian Culture and Research Journal* 15, no. 4 (1991): 62.

49. This information on Matteson is drawn from Casagrande and Bourne, *Side Trips,* 4–64.

50. Sumner W. Matteson, *Cliff Dwellings, Pueblo Ruins, and Indian Life in the Southwest* (Denver, Colo.: privately published, 1903), Yale Collection of Western Americana, Beinecke Rare Book and Manuscript Library, New Haven, Connecticut. The caption to image #176 refers to the Klepetko claim, near Albright and the Northern Pacific Railway, suggesting that Klepetko had invested in mining in the area of Great Falls, Montana.

51. Casagrande and Bourne, *Side Trips,* 52.

52. See Whiteley, *Rethinking Hopi Ethnography,* 163–87.

53. Anon., *The Way of the Cliff Dwellers* (Chicago: privately printed, 1917), 24.

54. Ibid., 27.

55. Ibid., 48.

56. Crane, *The Indians of the Enchanted Desert,* 255.

57. Ibid., 250.

58. *Indian Detour* (New York: Rand McNally and Company, 1926), 5–6, 9.

59. Ibid., 4.

60. Ibid., 44, 49.

61. Ibid., 53, 54.

62. See Keith L. Bryant Jr., "The Atchison, Topeka, and Santa Fe Railway and the Development of the Taos and Santa Fe Art Colonies," *Western Historical Quarterly* 9, no. 4 (October 1978): 437–39.

63. *Tourist's Handbook to Colorado, Utah, and New Mexico* (Denver, Colo.: Passenger Department of Denver and Rio Grande Railway, 1885), 13, 17.

64. Bryant Jr., "The Atchison, Topeka, and Santa Fe Railway," 437–39.

65. Sandra D'Emilio and Suzan Campbell, *Visions and Visionaries: The Art and Artists of the Santa Fe Railway* (Layton, Utah: Gibbs-Smith, 1991), 19; Bryant Jr., "The Atchison, Topeka, and Santa Fe Railway," 441.

66. For examples of paintings sold to the Santa Fe Railway by these artists, see D'Emilio and Campbell, *Visions and Visionaries.*

67. Leslie Poling-Kempes, *The Harvey Girls: Women Who Opened the West* (New York: Paragon House, 1989), 35–37. Poling-Kempes notes that when Harvey's sons Ford and Byron took over the leadership of the Fred Harvey Company in the late 1890s, the company ran fifteen hotels, forty-seven lunch and dining rooms, and thirty dining cars on the Limited luxury trains (44).

68. George Wharton James, *Arizona the Wonderland* (Boston: Page Company, 1917), 102, 98.

69. Poling-Kempes, *The Harvey Girls,* 168–69.

70. Diane H. Thomas, *The Southwest Indian Detours: The Story of the Fred Harvey/Santa Fe Railway Experiment in "Detourism"* (Phoenix, Ariz.: Hunter Publishing Company, 1978), 189.

71. Ibid., 186–87.

72. Jill Sweet notes that kivas in Pueblo communities are invariably closed to today's tourists. Because sacred knowledge is believed to lose its power if divulged to the uninitiated, it is of paramount importance to maintain the integrity of such knowledge. The protection of kivas from tourists, then, is a strategy to control the terms of cultural exchange between hosts and guests. Sweet, "'Let 'em Loose': Pueblo Indian Management of Tourism," 59–74.

73. Thomas, *The Southwest Indian Detours,* 197–98.

74. Quoted in ibid., 192.

75. The guidance of an "expert" on the protocol involved when tourists visit tribal cultures was a relatively new phenomenon in the 1920s. Today such advice has become a vital part of many travel guides, especially those published under the Lonely Planet imprint.

76. To avoid confusion, I refer to Mabel Dodge Luhan by her first name in this part of the chapter. She was born Mabel Ganson and married three times. She kept the name of

her second husband, Edwin Dodge, for over a decade until her marriage to the painter Maurice Sterne in 1917. She married the Pueblo Indian Antonio Lujan in 1923, changing the spelling of the name to Luhan. See Lois Rudnick, *Mabel Dodge Luhan: New Woman, New Worlds* (Albuquerque: University of New Mexico Press, 1984).

77. Rudnick, *Mabel Dodge Luhan: New Woman, New Worlds,* 150.
78. Collier, "The Red Atlantis," *Survey Graphic* 49, no. 1 (October 1922): 63.
79. Sylvia Rodríguez, "Land, Water, and Ethnic Identity in Taos," in *Land, Water, and Culture: New Perspectives on Hispanic Land Grants,* ed. Charles L. Briggs and John R. Van Ness (Albuquerque: University of New Mexico Press, 1987), 344.
80. See Rodríguez, "Land, Water, and Ethnicity in Taos."
81. Stella M. Atwood, "The Case for the Indian," *Survey Graphic* 49, no. 1 (October 1922): 57.
82. Blumenschein, Higgins, Sharp, and Ufer were members of the influential Taos Society of Artists, while the Santa Fe-based Davey was an associate member. See *The Taos Society of Artists: Masters and Masterworks* (Santa Fe, N.M.: Gerald Peters Gallery, 1998).
83. See Brian W. Dippie, *The Vanishing American: White Attitudes and U.S. Indian Policy* (Lawrence: University Press of Kansas, 1982), 274–79; and Kenneth R. Philp, *John Collier's Crusade for Indian Reform, 1920–1954* (Tucson: University of Arizona Press, 1977), chap. 2.
84. Mary Austin, "Speech of Mary Austin before the National Popular Government League," manuscript, Mary Austin Collection, Huntington Library, San Marino, California.
85. For discussion of Austin's activism against the Bursum Bill, and a broader discussion of Anglo women reformers who became involved in the affairs of Taos Indians in the late nineteenth and early twentieth centuries, see Margaret Jacobs, *Engendered Encounters: Feminism and Pueblo Cultures, 1879–1934* (Lincoln: University of Nebraska Press, 1999), chap. 1.
86. Collier, "The Red Atlantis," 15.
87. Ibid.
88. Ibid., 16, 18.
89. Significantly Collier had served several years as the head of the People's Institute at Cooper Union in New York City prior to traveling to New Mexico. See Philp, *John Collier's Crusade for Indian Reform,* chap. 1; and Rudnick, *Mabel Dodge Luhan: New Woman, New Worlds,* chap. 3.
90. Collier, "The Red Atlantis," 66, 63.
91. Austin, "Speech of Mary Austin before the National Popular Government League," 15–16.
92. Collier, "The Red Atlantis," 18.
93. Austin, "Speech of Mary Austin before the National Popular Government League," 14.
94. Austin's comment anticipates the conferral of Taos Pueblo's special status as a World Heritage Site in 1992.
95. Mary Austin and Ansel Adams, *Taos Pueblo* (San Francisco: Grabhorn Press, 1930), n.p.
96. Mary Austin to Mabel Dodge Luhan, no date [probably 1925], New York City, Mabel Dodge Luhan Papers, Beinecke Rare Book and Manuscript Library, Yale University, New Haven, Connecticut.
97. Mabel Dodge Luhan, *Winter in Taos* (New York: Harcourt, Brace and Company, 1935), 42.
98. Mabel Dodge Luhan, *Movers and Shakers,* vol. 3 of *Intimate Memories* (1936; reprint, New York: Kraus Reprint Co., 1971), 534.
99. Luhan, *Winter in Taos,* 53, 196.
100. Rudnick, *Mabel Dodge Luhan: New Woman, New Worlds,* 271.
101. Luhan, *Winter in Taos,* 46.
102. Ibid., 48, 35, 48, 35.
103. Ibid., 152, 153, 157.

Conclusion

1. Simon Ortiz, *Woven Stone* (Tucson: University of Arizona Press, 1992), 14, 13, 14.
2. The Indian Health Service keeps statistics on alcoholism mortality rates. Among slightly more than a million Native people across the thirty-three states served by the Indian Health Service, the alcoholism mortality rate was 33.9 per 100,000 population in 1990, which was about 5.3 times the rate for the overall American population but 38 percent lower than the figure had been a decade earlier. See Jack Utter, *American Indians: Answers to Today's Questions* (Lake Ann, Mich.: National Woodlands Publishing Company, 1993), 190. Notably, two powerful Native American novels, N. Scott Momaday's *House Made of Dawn* (1968) and Leslie Marmon Silko's *Ceremony* (1977) feature Pueblo Indian protagonists whose excessive drinking is a sign of their alienation from what Ortiz calls the "Mericano" world.
3. Ortiz, *Woven Stone*, 7, 7, 27.
4. Ramón A. Gutiérrez, *When Jesus Came the Corn Mothers Went Away: Marriage, Sexuality, and Power in New Mexico, 1500–1846* (Stanford, Calif.: Stanford University Press, 1991), 340.
5. Sylvia Rodríguez, "Land, Water, and Ethnic Identity in Taos," in *Land, Water, and Culture: New Perspectives on Hispanic Land Grants,* ed. Charles L. Briggs and John R. Van Ness (Albuquerque: University of New Mexico Press, 1987), 314.
6. Ibid., 345.
7. Ibid., 388.

Index